Gist is a potent dose of advice from a pediatrician and a child psychologist, both of whom have witnessed the unfortunate results that come when parents try to protect, prevent, and control at every turn instead of preparing their kids for life. Combining the expertise of their respective professions with very practical tips, these authors offer a how-to manual for any parent who wants to prep~~ their kids to thrive as adults.

JULIE LYTHCOTT-HAIMS
Former dean of students, Stanfor~

I have been a colleague of . than thirty years and have f~ ~~vocatively insightful and practical. So it ~~ise that *Gist* is extraordinary. Michael is joinea by Dr. Tim Johanson, with his own stellar background as a pediatrician, and *Gist* is filled with their eye-opening, nontraditional insights. I would recommend *Gist* to anybody who has children or cares about them, whether parent, grandparent, teacher, or counselor. The writing is clear, profound, and immediately useful.

JEFF VANVONDEREN
Certified intervention professional

It has been many years since I have read a book that I recommend as strongly as *Gist.* I consider it a must-read for today's parents. I was absolutely riveted by how the authors wrote about self-esteem and shame in this book. Anderson and Johanson, a psychologist and a pediatrician, have written a grounded and remarkable book that will challenge parents to the core. It did me.

JANICE MCWILLIAMS
MDiv, licensed clinical professional counselor, and mom

GIST

GIST

THE ESSENCE OF
RAISING LIFE-READY KIDS

MICHAEL W. ANDERSON, LP, AND

TIMOTHY D. JOHANSON, MD

TYNDALE HOUSE PUBLISHERS, INC.
CAROL STREAM, ILLINOIS

FOCUS ON THE FAMILY®

Gist: The Essence of Raising Life-Ready Kids

© 2013, 2016, 2019 by Michael W. Anderson, L.P. and Timothy D. Johanson, M.D. All rights reserved.

A Focus on the Family book published by Tyndale House Publishers, Inc., Carol Stream, Illinois 60188

Focus on the Family and the accompanying logo and design are federally registered trademarks of Focus on the Family, 8605 Explorer Drive, Colorado Springs, CO 80920.

TYNDALE and Tyndale's quill logo are registered trademarks of Tyndale House Publishers, Inc.

The case examples presented in this book are altered stories or composites based on the authors' clinical experience with hundreds of clients through the years. People's names and certain details of their stories have been changed to protect the privacy of the individuals involved. However, the important factors of what happened and the underlying principles have been conveyed as accurately as possible.

The use of material from or references to various websites does not imply endorsement of those sites in their entirety. Availability of websites and pages is subject to change without notice.

Cover design by Paul Cooke

Cover photograph of kids ziplining copyright © Imgorthand/iStockphoto. All rights reserved.

For information about special discounts for bulk purchases, please contact Tyndale House Publishers at csresponse@tyndale.com, or call 1-800-323-9400.

Library of Congress Cataloging-in-Publication Data can be found at www.loc.gov.

ISBN 978-1-58997-586-6

Printed in the United States of America

25   24   23   22   21   20   19

7   6   5   4   3   2   1

Contents

To children everywhere who simply want to be raised in homes

where grace, love, firmness, and consistency are abundant.

To parents who strive to raise their children to be ready for life.

Introduction

THIS BOOK JUST WOULDN'T GO AWAY.

Both of us, in our own ways, tried to push it off for a decade or more. For the longest time we couldn't quite see how to write a book about "how to" parent when the "how to" advice nearly always started with, "That depends . . ." In both our respective offices, parents sat in the waiting room and hoped they would learn some way to "treat" the presenting problem, whatever that happened to be.

Frequently, the presenting problem was not the real problem. Bad grades, stress symptoms, frequent fussing, defiance, depression, self-destructive behavior, and conflict often brought families in for help. But the real issue was that the families were stuck, tired, angry, and confused about where their problem came from. They didn't know what to do and they wanted that behavior, fear, and pain to stop now.

We found ourselves helping parents think differently about a situation and were amazed at how quickly the problem improved or disappeared simply by seeing it in a new and accurate light. *We came to believe that the best hope in addressing parenting issues is to think differently about parenting issues.*

That belief is what motivated us to capture these thoughts and stories in a book. Thinking better won't solve every parenting challenge, as parenting is a difficult and formidable task. But better thinking is our best chance of making parenting successful, enjoyable, and hopeful.

We certainly don't intend to imply that healthy parenting is rare or nonexistent. However, too many parents are tired and lost these days. For parents who are drowning, this book could be a lifeboat. For parents who are doing well, this book will be a pleasant and validating read as they learn more about the wisdom of their own approach.

Long before we met, we were both troubled by how stressed out kids seem to be as they grow up, and we both chose careers that gave us the privilege to watch and learn. This book came out of our experience spending, collectively, more than fifty years listening to kids in our offices, then listening to their parents, then listening to kids again, and then their parents again. When we first met, we would spend hours discussing why we sounded like we were contradicting ourselves, when we knew we weren't. There isn't one right way to fall in love, to chase a dream, to have a career, or to grow spiritually—and there isn't one right way to parent.

A parent recently asked us at a workshop, "What should I do if my seventh-grade son leaves his homework on the kitchen counter when he leaves for school in the morning?"

"That depends on your son," we answered. "Tell us about your son. Overall, is he a fairly responsible seventh grader?"

"Oh yes, he's extremely responsible for his age."

"Then just jump in the car and run his book up to the school. And by the way, stick two dollars in his math book for a sports drink. You don't need to teach a responsible son to be responsible. He already knows that—he just forgot his homework. You have other things to teach him that are more relevant."

If the son had been perpetually irresponsible, we would have recommended a different approach. One-size-fits-all parenting would most likely recommend teaching him a lesson he didn't need to learn while adding needless strain to the whole process.

How to parent a situation will depend on in which areas your child is doing well and in which areas he or she is falling behind. We feel a good parenting book will show how and why one child should be parented differently from another child—or the neighbor's kids. Here's the thing: We don't know your children and where they come from. Are they biological or adopted? Are you a single parent or in a two-parent family? Do your children have reading disabilities or social limitations? Are they depressed or angry? All these factors will affect your parenting decisions.

Good parenting needs to be learned and practiced since it doesn't come naturally for most people. In fact, much of parenting is counterintuitive. The natural thing to do is often the wrong thing to do, so we need to learn new skills and practice them until they begin to feel natural. For example, too many reprimands—even those with best intentions— might actually hurt a situation without our awareness. Even the desire to be a "great parent" could hinder our ability to parent our child effectively and efficiently. It may sound like a good thing, but parents who are overly concerned with how well they are doing may lose perspective and become too emotionally involved in a situation to think clearly. Therefore, new skills are more effective than more effort.

We want parenting to be easier and more effective because wasted energy is a big problem for parents today. Many hours and much emotional energy are spent in parenting strategies where nothing positive is produced. We hope this book will be practical and helpful. Perhaps it will even be a breath of fresh common sense for an endeavor that has become far too complicated and laborious.

As professionals working with children and teenagers, we have both recognized that kids today need to be raised in a way that reduces stress, shame, and resentment. Too many kids struggle with discouragement, so we have taken an extensive look at why this is so. Perhaps the most pervasive struggle for older kids is their awareness that they are not ready for life. We have seldom come across any child older than ten who doesn't have some fear that adulthood will arrive before he or she is ready.

We have rarely met a child who didn't innately value and respect any adult exhibiting wisdom, kindness, strength, honesty, firmness, and humility. While kids act and talk as if they just want their own way, they really want adults in their lives they can lean on as they do the hard work of growing up, and do so without damaging the adults' feelings or their connection together.

We've chosen the title *Gist* as it means the bottom line, the truth, or the inner workings of something. We say "the gist of it" when we want someone to know the way something really works. This book is about preparing your kids for life, and doing that in an effective way. As we discuss what qualities a *life-ready* child would have, it seemed that it would be helpful to devote part of the book to a brief description of the nature of life as we see it. Therefore, the first part of the book is about love, learning, living, and joy. You may have a different opinion about these foundational characteristics of life, but at least you will know where we are coming from as we reflect on these crucial topics. We need to be life-ready adults if we are going to raise life-ready kids. We encourage you to read this first section as a way to gain valuable insight for parenting in a way that focuses on all of us being life-ready.

The second section of the book is about learning solid parenting thought processes and implementing proven strategies.

The third section takes a deeper look at the unintended consequences of ineffective parenting.

With all the stories, insights, and advice, we still know that the real power for change is learning how to think differently about parenting. We share this book as a labor of love and with excitement.

If you would like to discuss the ideas in this book with other parents as you read it, you can download a free study guide with additional Christian content at Tyndale.es/GIST.

PART I

Foundational
Principles
of Life

1

LOVE MUST EVOLVE

We are not the same persons this year as last;
nor are those we love. It is a happy chance if we, changing,
continue to love a changed person.

W. SOMERSET MAUGHAM

A FAMILY WAS OUT DRIVING and saw a dead adult female red fox lying in the road. In the weeds nearby they spied a baby fox. The little guy was clearly terrified and did not know whether to run or stay. About six weeks old, he was strong and agile, but without his mother he wouldn't be able to survive in the wild.

The family brought the fox home and built a wonderful and comfortable kennel for him. They named him Hank and fed him grain-free food from the pet store. He had a dozen toys in his kennel and enjoyed a wonderful life. Soon there was a mutual trust, and Hank became a much-loved pet. The family planned to raise the fox until he was fully grown. When he was ready to fend for himself, they would release him back into the wild near the spot where he was found.

Hank was a perfect specimen of a red fox. He was 10 percent bigger than most wild foxes, and his beautiful red coat glistened in the sunshine pouring through the living room window. This was the only sunshine Hank saw, with the exception of brief, leashed potty breaks. The family knew he would surely run away if unleashed, and he was in no way ready to survive on his own in the wild.

Soon the family celebrated Hank's fourth birthday. By then they had switched from their two-year plan to a four-year plan, fearing that Hank would more likely become prey than be able to find food on his own. For years, the family had told their friends they were raising Hank with the goal of setting him free. Now, four years into Hank's life, people were starting to ask why Hank was still lying on the couch and wasn't out in the woods. The family wanted to keep their commitment to release Hank, but they knew he had no skills for survival in the wild. Strong and beautiful as he was, after six hours in the woods Hank would have been looking for a bag that read "Science Diet." Hank's family reflected on how they got into this mess.

This family had brought Hank home four years earlier, intending to protect him and prepare him for life in the wild. They hadn't realized that love must evolve, and had failed to prepare Hank to live free and on his own.

A first child is born. Strong emotions fill us as the miracle of birth happens before our eyes. Impassioned, we reach down to touch tiny fingers and smell the unique newborn fragrance. We listen with wonder to cries, grunts, and cute infant squeaks. This child seemingly comes out of nowhere, yet contains our DNA. She holds our inheritance within her, along with a world of possibilities. We are captured and fall completely in love with this tiny, vulnerable child.

Along with this love, we face an endeavor of greater magnitude, potential, and pitfalls than any we've previously known. Instinctively jolted, at least temporarily, out of self-centeredness, we step into a new level of existence. With an acute sense of the task's importance, we realize that we have entered into legacy for the first time in our lives. This precious child before us is the enduring part of us that we will pass down.

When we break down the elements of this love, we are aware that this child:

- came from us
- needs our protection
- is our legacy
- has immense potential
- is a miracle
- is totally accepted
- is completely vulnerable and precious

The pure love we experience in that first week of life is so uncomplicated. Not easy, but certainly uncomplicated. Many parents find that first week to be perfection—a perfect child embraced in perfect love. Eventually this love will need to evolve into something different. In every relationship and aspect of life, love must evolve to survive.

Bringing this child home must evolve into sending that child into the world. Potential must evolve into limitation. Hope must evolve into disappointment. Perfection must evolve into reality and failure.

Because love always emerges as something other than what we hoped for and something different from how it started, it follows that our love as parents must evolve. It might even need to evolve from a "would never hurt" love into a "need to allow hurt" love. This little miracle may evolve into a bad dream.

When does the simple love during infancy need to start changing?

It Starts with a Will

The journey for parents to a new love is launched when a child exhibits a will. The caring and protecting mode changes into managing differences between the child's will and the parent's will. Bedtime is no longer driven by a primal need for sleep; now it is driven by a child's personal desire to stay up. We start on the road to adulthood with the onset of joys and disappointments, give and take, negotiation and compromise.

Both joys and disappointments are initiated when a child begins to have opinions. This exertion of demands or will is traditionally followed by wants, followed by opposing opinions, followed by conflict, leading to a relationship that is completely different from the one that began at the birthing center.

A new environment emerges from will and personal opinion. This environment includes such principles as authority, discipline, disappointment, relationship, and achievement. While this is not an exhaustive list, it captures a lot of the challenges facing parents. In its simplest terms, the essence of loving our children is about moving our vulnerable and beautiful child from infancy to adulthood. An understanding of authority, discipline, disappointment, relationship, and achievement will all be needed for the child to reach maturity. Any person without a significant understanding of these essentials has not developed and is not ready for adulthood.

This is why many parents reach out to get help. We hear, "My child has a problem with authority" or "My child has a problem with discipline" or "My child has a problem with relationships." Perhaps the most common is, "My child has a problem with disappointment."

Too many kids become adults who are underdeveloped or not developed at all in one or more of these areas. It is not surprising these children are underprepared for life. Their parents' love did not evolve over time and they did not learn the necessary lessons. This isn't to say the parents lacked love, only that it did not evolve.

Authority and hierarchy require a child to lay aside his or her will. This is a foundational truth for families and any society. Everyone has to answer to someone. All must comply with laws and authority that may differ from what they want or think is fair at that moment. Without a respect for this truth, one can't be adult. To correctly love our children we must teach them that this is the nature of life. It's not love if we're not preparing them for this reality. This is far more loving than giving presents, trophies, and encouragement.

Another aspect of this evolution involves oppositional bonding—practicing a love that stays constant or grows, despite differing opinions. In an unhealthy family, conflict or opposition can negatively affect relationships. Kids in these families can grow up to believe that harmony is an essential part of bonding. However, healthy families allow for oppositional positions; in these families, family members can disagree without having that conflict diminish the relationship. If this ability isn't developed, conflict can feel like abandonment.

Know Where You're Headed

We won't be afraid of or disillusioned by this parenting journey if we understand where the journey is to take us. It starts with a child who is adored and protected, but it must give way over the course of twenty years to a child who is free and equipped. That is our destination.

How does this evolution happen? The steps that lead to maturing transitions must be taken intentionally and skillfully. Except for the few truly "natural" parents who do this instinctively, most parents need to be deliberate about leading their child to a place of self-governance and being equipped for life. In our era and particularly in our Western culture, many parents have become sidetracked with performance and other urgencies, while the process of ensuring that their child becomes an equipped, independent, and responsible adult suffers due to lack of focus.

What if this process doesn't happen? The consequence will be a twenty-year-old with the maturity level of a fourteen-year-old. There's nothing wrong with a fourteen-year-old maturity level. It just looks awkward in someone who's twenty-something. If you wonder whether this is an exaggeration, just look around and see how many twenty-year-olds are living without direction, accountability, independence, and a sense of responsibility. Much of this can be traced back to a child who was deeply loved, but with a love that didn't evolve.

Age-Appropriate Development

Knowing when and how to transition to a different kind of love is a talent that parents need to develop. It is as problematic for a two-year-old to be given freedom and responsibility as it is for a twenty-year-old to be only adored and protected. In many families we can see both of these errors of focus. Some start too early in their zeal to be good parents, pushing their children to excel in their accomplishments beyond what's age-appropriate. This type of rushing is all too common and occasionally even reaches the news.

Several years ago a seven-year-old girl crashed a small plane in the western United States as she attempted to become the youngest person to fly across the country. She needed more protection and less self-sufficiency for this mission. In our opinion, her parents' love was not age-appropriate.

It is a wonderful thing for a child to develop in normal, healthy, and age-appropriate ways. Here are a few examples of expected tasks for a typical three-year-old:

- learning the language that allows the child to express ideas and thoughts related to his or her environment

- counting from three to five objects in a group to determine how many objects are in the group (rational counting)

- classifying objects into categories (size, shape, color, etc.), ordering objects and identifying shapes such as squares, circles, triangles, and rectangles

- recognizing characteristics of different seasons and weather

- beginning to observe, explore, and describe a wide variety of live animals and where they live

You get the idea. These are wonderful and amazing things for a three-year-old to learn. There is a corresponding list of wonderful and amazing things for an eighteen-year-old to learn. Expected skills for an eighteen-year-old include:

- listening to and evaluating the viewpoints of others

- delaying gratification (ability to put off what he or she wants to do now because there are more important things to do or because there is a better time to do it)

- accepting the fact that he or she can't always win, and learning from mistakes instead of being demoralized by the outcome

- differentiating between rational decision-making and emotional impulse

- separating true love from transitory infatuation

- taking ownership and responsibility for personal actions

These are just some of the developmental qualities a seventeen- or eighteen-year-old should be exhibiting.

Customizing Your Love

When you pay close attention to your child, it's not that difficult to know how your parental love needs to change next. A book—even ours—may not help with this process. Evolving love is a universal issue. Whether it's our relationship with an aging parent, an ex-spouse, a sibling, or a partner, if we're evolving, our love for the other must evolve too.

Without knowing you or your child, we can't tell you *how* this evolving love has to take place. But it *must* take place. We can't tell you how much to protect or push your eighth-grade child. Some children need to be held in and some need to be pushed out. Endeavoring to know this is what an evolving love is about.

The GIST of It

- It's very important for parents to recall the joy and pleasure they experienced at the birth or adoption of each of their children. Remember those precious times, full of hope and anticipation. When times get tough, it's easy to forget all the good—and great—times and focus on the negatives.

- If you love your child the same way for four years, your love is not evolving. Watch your child closely in daily life and you will figure out where and how your love needs to evolve.

- How we love our kids needs to change along the way. We cannot nurture them, compliment them, protect them, or adore them into becoming mature, life-ready young adults. It just won't happen that way. Our job is to train our children, prepare them, and in them leave a legacy. Training them for adulthood means freeing and equipping them. This is our primary role.

2

LEARNING AND
ANTI-LEARNING

The most dangerous untruths are truths slightly distorted.

GEORG C. LICHTENBERG

IT IS 1:00 A.M. in a city on a dark winter night. Two teenage boys see a car idling in front of a house. The owner of the car had stopped briefly to drop off or pick up something in the neighborhood and left the car running so it would stay warm. In two seconds, the boys make their decision and jump into the car. They drive straight to a garage that they heard will pay cash for late model SUVs, chop them up, and sell them for parts.

Over the next couple of days, these boys are going to learn one of two things: stealing a car pays off, or it is too costly to do again. Life is going to support one conclusion or the other. Over the course of their lifetimes, and if they live long enough, the boys will invariably learn that stealing cars is a bad idea. Most car thieves, drug dealers, and shoplifters eventually do learn this lesson, though it may take years. But if these boys conclude that stealing cars pays off, they have learned an untruth. Eventually, however, they will have to discard what they learned if they are ever going to become mature—or even survive.

Adults, kids, pets, livestock, and show animals all learn best when they get a good outcome from a good or desired decision and when they suffer a costly outcome from a bad or undesired decision. This is at the core of most learning. Perhaps no other principle is as essential to understand in parenting.

We are always learning, yet much of what we learn isn't true or helpful. Some of what we learn is well founded and true about life. But the things that are not true about life will need to be unlearned sometime in our future. There's a high cost to learning what is not true because any learning that we later need to unlearn takes us further from the truth and almost always arrests our development. It is what we will call "anti-learning." Here's how we best learn.

True Life Lessons or False Lessons

True life lessons are valuable and necessary. False lessons are highly overrated. Don't confuse the two. False lessons are setbacks, a waste of time, misleading, and unproductive. Contrary to what is often promoted by our culture, there is nothing to be gained by learning something that is false. True life lessons are often painful and laborious, but they are also good because they are essential for our growth.

We learn from our mistakes. Most of us who have walked life's path for a significant amount of time will agree. But we must separate our mistakes from learning false truths. We learn from our mistakes, but we learn nothing from false beliefs. The price for believing false truths is far too high to smugly accept it as a plank on the platform of learning life's lessons.

What good did it do for fourteenth-century Western Europe to believe for a decade that the Black Plague was the result of sin? Did anything beneficial come from that untruth? Goodness and spiritual growth did not occur because people of faith were confused by what they thought God was doing. Besides the plague's devastation, communities inflicted ruthless acts on suffering individuals because they presumed it to be a judgment instead of a disease epidemic. Their wrong guess about its source was not growth producing in any way.

This is a truth throughout human and personal history: The time we spend believing that something false is true can't be reclaimed. People use limited or false data to come to errant conclusions all the time. Sometimes we are taught wrong information that we believe to be true.

Stealing cars is a high-stake example of this dynamic. In a lower-stake example of the same premise, a three-year-old throws a huge fit at a store because she wants her parents to buy a plastic backyard swimming pool. If this child learns that throwing a tantrum will get her what she wants, she has just learned something she will have to unlearn later in life. If she learns that throwing a fit will not get her what she wants, she has learned a lesson that will serve her well over time.

Setbacks and Anti-Learning

Anything we learn interpersonally, developmentally, spiritually, or academically that we will eventually have to unlearn in order to grow is a setback or anti-learning. *Anti-learning is when we learn something that takes us further from the truth than just a neutral position.*

A second grader might learn that hitting another child is

the best way to be respected. A twenty-three-year-old might learn that if she drives slowly and carefully, she can drive home when she has had too much to drink.

The pattern is the same with the second grader and the twenty-three-year-old. A bad decision is followed by a short-term gain, which leads to learning a false lesson. False lessons must be unlearned before we can move ahead. Often false truths come from looking at an immediate outcome rather than the longer-range outcome of that decision.

Why spend time on this in a parenting book? Because we feel people of all ages are using maladaptive ways to get what they want. Every time we use maladaptive behavior to get what we want, it is a setback to growth. This has become an underlying issue in raising kids. Every time our kids learn something that will need to be unlearned, their progress has been slowed and postponed.

Alcoholics Anonymous and other substance abuse treatment programs say little or no growth happens during the years that addicts use anything to alter their moods. A twenty-eight-year-old who has been using drugs for twelve years will likely act in many ways like a fifteen- or sixteen-year-old. Little significant growth happened during those twelve years of drug abuse.

Part of the reason for this could be anti-learning. In many areas of their lives, drug abusers have come up with the wrong answers to life's right questions. They will need to unlearn these answers. Almost every person who has ever used cocaine, crack, or heroin ends up wishing he or she had never touched the stuff.

The lives of addicts may look completely different from each other, and the length of time spent abusing substances may vary by decades. But addicts all begin at the same place. They use a maladaptive behavior (drugs) to get what they want (acceptance, peace, or euphoria). Each time they repeat the behavior, their false learning is reinforced. They may believe this enhances their life and their fun. In the end, they all end in the same place—realizing that it has nearly cost them everything they hold dear.

For a parent of a four-year-old, this story will seem hard to relate to and irrelevant. But it isn't irrelevant. Replace the twenty-three-year-old woman with a four-year-old boy and her maladaptive use of drugs with his tantrum behaviors, and this principle is apparent. The longer we as adults—or our children—use unhealthy, maladaptive behaviors to get our needs and wants met, the further anti-learning will take us from healthy living.

Healthy and Unhealthy Learning

There is a fundamentally sound way to learn lasting lessons in life that result in maturity: When I make a good choice, something good happens. When I make a bad choice, something bad happens. Of course, there are numerous exceptions, but this is a primary way to learn. Unfortunately, distinguishing between good and bad is not always easy. We would learn much faster if it were.

LEARNING TABLE

	Good Outcome	Bad Outcome
Good Decision	Healthy Learning	Unhealthy Learning
Bad Decision	Unhealthy Learning	Healthy Learning

Even more disruptive to the process is that we often make poor decisions that end up with a positive outcome. This sounds really simple, but it isn't. Unfortunately, children of all ages consistently get what they want from a poor approach. It's important for parents to try to manage their parenting in a way that minimizes how often children derive a good outcome from a bad decision.

This dynamic is evident in the hundreds of conversations we've had with teenagers reflecting on their summer vacations. What they talk about as the "best night of the whole summer" is often the night they made the worst decisions of the entire summer. Perhaps they drank while underage, or used drugs, or took someone else's boat out without permission, or broke into a store or the local high school. But they didn't pay any cost for their bad decisions.

Every time a child makes a poor decision without a cost, it is a setback for growth. Here are some examples:

- An eighth grader copies quiz answers from the person next to him and gets his best score of the quarter.

- A tenth grader jumps in a lake with her cell phone in her pocket and her parents give her a new and better smartphone.

- A third grader screams that the family never goes anywhere fun. In response, the parents plan a trip to a theme park.

- An unpopular sixteen-year-old girl brings a bottle of vodka to a sleepover and is suddenly the center of attention.

- A fifteen-year-old girl badgers her mother mercilessly after she is told she can't go to a sleepover where no parents are at home. Out of sheer exhaustion, her mother gives in with these infamous words: "Just this once."

- A five-year-old who was supposed to be in bed at 9:00 p.m. cries and kicks and convinces her mom that she can't sleep and ends up in the master bedroom having stories read to her until 11:00 p.m.

- A bright and distracted fifteen-year-old who had played video games for a month straight now finds himself five assignments behind in math. He screams at his parents that he needs to move out of high math and be put in a lower class. He accuses his parents of not understanding him and repeats over and over that they never "listen." The parents sign a form, and the next Monday he has his first day in the lower math class.

- On his eighteenth birthday, a young man goes to a local casino and in forty minutes wins $1,800.

All of these are examples of anti-learning. This means that what the child just learned is eventually going to have to be unlearned. Unfortunately, unlearning can be a long and painful process.

When a Poor Decision Pays Off

Let's consider the final example listed above. Almost all boys in their late teens or early twenties who have serious gambling problems report that they were "fortunate" enough to have huge winnings the first or second time at the casino, betting with a bookie, or at the horse track.

Gambling at a casino as a financial strategy is a poor decision. In the end, the house wins. When a young man's poor decision to try to get a windfall at the slots results in huge winnings, it is a good outcome from a poor decision. Many young men are hooked quickly, and it may take years for them to realize that a casino is not a sound financial option. Even if a person wins during one of his first times at a casino and rarely wins after that, it can take decades for him to unlearn his first experience at the slots.

When kids break the law and police give them only a warning, some teens see this as a bad outcome. But more often than not, kids see it as just a close call without a bad outcome. Well-meaning and reasonable police officers will break up parties and tolerate minor consumption with an "I'll let it go this time" approach. This is not really being a friend to kids who don't learn a lesson from a close call. Instead of facing the consequences of underage drinking, including a possible court date, they are learning that the police aren't that serious about upholding this particular law.

It's important that parents learn to see when a poor decision is paying off for their child. Not for any great moral reason, but rather because growing up is a long enough process without the impact of anti-learning. Whenever kids learn things that they are going to have to unlearn, the journey to maturity becomes risky and needlessly prolonged.

When Good Decisions Don't Pay Off

Setbacks can also take place when a child makes a good decision and has a bad outcome. This dynamic is frequently found in alcoholic or dysfunctional homes, but it can be seen anywhere. A responsible teen in a dysfunctional home who shows how responsible he is may be given more and more of the burden of the home. It is less prevalent in society, but common enough to mention. An oldest child can carry enormous weight on his or her shoulders and pay a high price throughout childhood by taking on increasing responsibility. In this scenario, healthy learning is not occurring. These kids will often eventually rebel or act out when they see that being reliable is not gaining them anything they want in life.

Some of these kids hate conflict so much that they are willing to be over-responsible just to reduce tension in the home.

Parents seem to be confused about what is a good or a bad outcome. This confusion comes from a faulty way of seeing bad outcomes. They may see an outcome as bad because they themselves would interpret it as bad, but their child doesn't see it as bad. Some kids see conflict as a bad outcome and will alter their behavior to avoid conflict. Other kids love conflict and are energized by an argument. Even eye contact is a reward for young children. Looking at a child with a disapproving glare is not a bad outcome for some kids. It can actually be a reward.

Find out what is paying off for your child and what is costing him or her something. When you do that, you may need to redirect life to adjust the result.

GPS and Perfect Learning

To illustrate nearly perfect and productive learning, we are going to use a fictional example for a couple of reasons. First, there just aren't very many perfect examples in real life because real life has a way of altering perfection. Second, we learn *so quickly* from productive learning that we hardly even realize we have learned a lesson.

Imagine that a new law for teenage drivers requires a GPS device to be installed in their vehicles that would send real-time data to a law enforcement computer. This device would keep track of where a car is at all times as well as the speed limit where the vehicle is being driven. A computer would know the car's speed in relation to the speed limit, and that data would be analyzed and stored. This system would allow a moment or two of speeding for passing or on a downhill stretch of road.

But if the teen were speeding more than a minute or two, the computer would notify a chip in the car that too much time had been spent over the speed limit, and the teen would then be charged a penalty.

The GPS would know when the car was at home in the driveway, and the chip would wait as long as needed for the car to get home and be shut off. Once the car was turned off, the chip in the car would send a message that the car would not start for twenty-four hours because the driver had been speeding. After twenty-four hours, the car would return to normal operation.

This system (apart from the problems and exceptions inherent with any fictional example) would stop nearly all teenage speeding in a matter of days. It would work so efficiently that, within a month, teenage speeding would be a thing of the past. Here's why this lesson would be learned so thoroughly and rapidly.

- There is a positive outcome (driving) from a positive decision and a negative outcome (car won't start for twenty-four hours) from a negative decision.

- The law (i.e., parents) did not bring extraneous factors into the situation like grades or a messy room.

- There is no dialogue between the parents and teen. All the parent needs to say is, "Oh, that is too bad; you can try it again tomorrow."

- The cost of speeding is significant but not punitive. Kids learn best from brief consequences that aren't excessive.

- The rules apply to everyone, so a teen who is penalized doesn't feel singled out.

- There are no setbacks to learning since there is no one else to blame, no one with whom the teen can plead his case, and no excuses.

This type of productive learning, though seldom available to us in real life, illustrates how efficiently and completely a lesson is learned without anti-learning and the static interference that delays most learning situations.

Healthy and productive learning takes good choices even further. It adds the concept of delayed gratification. With delayed gratification, we learn that repeatedly making good choices usually or eventually pays off. Good choices don't always pay off and might not immediately, but they are our best bet. Day after day, choosing to do homework, coming home on time, eating healthy, and saving money will usually and eventually pay off.

The GIST of It

The most efficient way to learn is to have a good outcome from a good choice, and a bad outcome from a bad choice.

This is efficient learning because it avoids anti-learning; we avoid learning things we will need to unlearn at some time in the future.

- As a parent, be mindful of how your child learns. Try to help him or her learn the inevitable lessons of life as early as possible.

- Minimize the number of good outcomes your children have from poor decisions, and try to make sure that their best decisions result in something positive.

- Make sure your child is not having bad outcomes for performing well.

- A household that resembles the way life really works is one where it is taught that there is not always a good outcome from a good decision, but over time making good decisions is our best bet.

3

THE NATURE OF LIFE

Life is not a spectacle or a feast; it is a predicament.

GEORGE SANTAYANA

CHANCES ARE that extension cord you buy for your Christmas lights will be a foot short when you get home. Life is the teacher best qualified to prepare us for living. But if we aren't paying attention, it's easy to block life's lessons from our kids and ourselves. If we miss these lessons of life, we will prevent our children from being life-ready.

It's hard to know how life-ready someone may be, but it's easy to see when he is not.

A twenty-something young adult who can't manage his money, apply himself in college, or get himself out of bed in the morning is not life-ready. This may be due to his family's lack of focus on the nature of life. Sometimes there are learning disabilities and other reasons for this delay, but usually it is because the family system does not think in terms of kids being life-ready.

Innumerable things go right in this world—thank goodness. These are not things we need to prepare for, so they don't require much attention. But there are things that can go wrong in life, and there are skills needed to handle those things when they go wrong. Our kids need to be preparing for the times when life kicks back.

When experienced campers spend weeks preparing for a trip into the wilderness, most of their prep time is for the moments where something could go wrong. There isn't a lot of prep needed for a warm, sunny day with a light breeze out of the southwest. Veteran campers are preparing for the circumstances that can go wrong on a journey. The better prepared they are for difficult situations, the better the trip will go.

We have collected what we believe to be the six most necessary perspectives for living a well-functioning life. Though there are thousands of lessons to learn, usually these six will keep young adults from imminent danger in those early years of adulthood. These six life lessons are:

1. accepting that life is difficult,
2. developing self-discipline,
3. being resilient,
4. acquiring age-appropriate relationship skills,
5. experiencing personal achievement, and
6. understanding that both hope and pain are necessary parts of growing.

The backbone of our parenting philosophy is that the parents' job is to prepare their kids for life. Not counting years one through three, we have about seventeen years to give our kids some kind of view of how life works and enough practice runs for them to develop life skills. We suspect there is not a lot of disagreement about this goal. If that's true, then why are a huge percentage of kids not life-ready when they turn twenty?

1. Life Is Difficult

A random group of men met one weekend at a men's conference in Colorado. Nothing in particular brought them together other than the fact that they were all men. By national standards, these men could easily have been seen as having good lives because most were employed, healthy, educated, and successful.

The talks and events of the weekend were designed only to get the men to open up and talk about things they typically didn't talk about. The agenda steered the men toward being real and nothing more—just talking about what life had been like for them.

As the men started to talk, a hushed silence fell over the group. Smartphones were put away and no one was daydreaming or distracted. As each man took a turn awkwardly sharing the narrative of his life, the others seemed riveted by the stories being told.

After half of the men had revealed their perhaps previously untold stories, a man sitting near one of the leaders leaned over and asked, "Were these men all handpicked or screened ahead of time? How is it that you gathered so many men together who all had so much pain and disappointment in their lives?" The leader pondered this question, knowing there had been no screening. All of these men had taken a shot at living life—that was all.

Many people seem to have misperceived the nature of living. The true nature of life has always been that it is difficult. Many in our culture may not believe this truth, and many children are not being taught this reality. People who have not internalized this are not hard to identify. These are the ones who complain when normal obstacles and disappointments converge on their lives. They feel as if life is unfair and proclaim this injustice repeatedly. From the outside looking in, people who don't accept that life is difficult seem to be tormented by normalcy.

Our kids need to know the truth. In an easy life, tires still go flat, cars don't start, zippers break, gift cards are lost, connections are missed, and phones go dead. In a normal life you can expect to lose a job, be unable to pay your bills, have a serious illness in your family, experience a divorce, have parents with dementia, or lose property in a storm.

Young people may be shocked at the inequity of it all if their lives are not going smoothly. If you own a house on a flood plain, you should not feel outraged when the water occasionally rises too high. Don't be bewildered by debt if you take out six years of school loans. Expect to ruin your transmission if you repeatedly squeal your tires. The tragedy in these examples is not the flooded basement, the debt, or the transmission. The tragedy is when people lose hope because they didn't think life would be this difficult. This is a lesson they needed to learn earlier.

> I have never in my life envied a human being who
> led an easy life; I have envied a great many people
> who led difficult lives and led them well.
> —THEODORE ROOSEVELT

Relatively few people get by with an easy life. Even people who say they have an easy life often mean it could be worse than it is. Music superstars, famous actors, great athletes, even kings and queens often have tremendous difficulties in life.

"Life is difficult," M. Scott Peck wrote in his ground-breaking bestseller, *The Road Less Traveled*. Peck argued that the problems many people face come from the failure to accept that truth. He said, "This is a great truth, one of the greatest truths. It is a great truth because once we truly see this truth, we transcend it. Once we truly know that life is difficult—once we truly understand and accept it—then life is no longer difficult. Because once it is accepted, the fact that life is difficult no longer matters."[1]

A glance back at the previous thirty generations shows us that much of life consisted of problems, and much of living was solving those problems. This has never changed, and it never will change. There was the occasional dance, holiday, birthday party, afternoon at a swimming hole, or harvest celebration. But for the most part, life was a struggle to solve one problem after another just to stay alive.

A few hundred years ago, a young woman would be aware that if she were going to have two children survive to adult-hood, she would likely need to bear three or four children. That was a given and, in a way, was accepted. Those were difficult times and, in some ways, terrible times. But life was made easier because very few people dreamed of having it easy.

When we don't accept the truth that life is difficult, we wonder what we or someone else did wrong for life not to go smoothly. We blame ourselves, others, or God, or we engage in denial to try to justify why things are going wrong in a life where things are *supposed* to go right.

Try hosting Thanksgiving at your house intending for the day to turn out perfectly. Compare that approach with hosting Thanksgiving recognizing that difficulty is inevitable. Flaws don't matter that much when we accept that everything can't go perfectly. There is less stress, less blaming of self and others, and less denial.

Feeding a family is difficult. Going to school is difficult. Playing a sport is difficult. Relationships are difficult. Injuries are difficult. Dating can be difficult. Even owning a dog can be difficult. The more we fail to accept that difficulty is inherent in life, the more we will struggle, blame, medicate, and feel depressed and overwhelmed. Anger and frustration are often indicators that we believe our lives should go smoothly. An angry person is often someone who has not accepted that life is difficult.

While life will always be difficult, it's not always constantly a struggle. There are periods of time, sometimes years and sometimes decades, in which we are spared serious adversity. Whether anticipated or not, some hardship touches most people eventually. No amount of wealth, faith, education, or health can keep us immune from these trials.

Those who have not yet faced some type of tragedy in their lives, or perhaps haven't had one in decades, may start to believe that they are exempt from the struggles that others face. They might believe that they know how to build a start-up company, how to avoid a heart attack, or how to even raise perfect kids. They may feel that they have solved life's problems or they are being spared these hardships. Something humbling is often in their future. These are the people who say, "Three years ago I never dreamed I would be in this situation." When tragedy comes, they experience a collision between their hopes and their reality.

While some lives may look blessed for a time, very few people avoid feeling lost, confounded, or strained. We need to tell kids that this universal truth is the nature of life. It will not serve children well to grow up believing that a problem-free life is the goal—or even an option. To enjoy life in the long term, our best hope is to learn to enjoy problem-solving.

If you've been living for a while and are engaged in life, chances are you have been exposed to more pain or sadness than you anticipated. It's a myth that we all deserve relatively problem-free lives. As a culture, we are quickly moving toward a mind-set that little or nothing should go wrong in life. We are led to believe that after retirement or a divorce we should be able to maintain the lifestyle to which we have grown accustomed. We start out believing that our children will grow up healthy. Autism will be something the neighbor in the green house has to deal with. Our kids won't struggle with sexual identity or deal drugs or carry some potentially terminal illness.

It is astounding to see the extent to which we believe we should not have to struggle. We hear, "I never thought that this (fill in the blank) would happen to me." We seem to believe we shouldn't get fired, lose a season ticket lottery, have hypertension, miss our flight connections, get food poisoning, or be shorted in an estate settlement. Our kids should be at least above average, and they shouldn't be inadequate or ungifted in any way.

In one collision after another, life reminds us how false these myths are. Life is more difficult than we are led to expect. Through painful life events we learn that a trouble-free life is rare at best. Few have suffered like the fictional character Fantine in *Les Miserables*. But when she sings "now life has killed the dream I dreamed," tears flood faces in the audience. People relate to this universal theme: Life is harder than they expected.

To raise life-ready kids, teach them the lesson that life is difficult. This is not bad news. It is just the nature of life, and we need to accept it.

2. Developing Self-Discipline

Once we have accepted that life will always present problems, the next skill is to solve those problems. Solving problems requires facing problems. The most effective way to face problems is by using self-discipline.

Nothing can truly take the place of discipline in life, although our culture has tried to find a replacement. Some people hope that grace can replace discipline. They try to solve their problems by letting themselves off the hook or finding someone else to solve them. Perhaps they hope that, without the weight of guilt or the burden of failure, they will just naturally face life's challenges better. While appealing, this approach is simply not reality. We all need moments of grace from time to time; however, if grace is too often dispensed it slows the process of developing self-discipline.

Discipline is as different from self-discipline as "others' esteem" is from self-esteem. Both are needed in life, but they are not the same. Sometimes discipline evolves into self-discipline and sometimes it doesn't. This is important for parents to remember. The primary purpose of instilling discipline in our kids is that it will, hopefully, evolve into self-discipline.

Let's distinguish between discipline and the self-discipline we hope our kids will have learned by age twenty-one. Discipline can be thought of as external motivations we use to make good choices, usually from an authority figure. The hope is that necessary motivations will be internalized into self-discipline. Discipline that never makes this transformation to self-discipline is good, but it has limited value. Not all parenting approaches are conducive to facilitating this transition. In fact, some parenting strategies are far more likely to develop self-discipline in our kids. These kinds of interventions should be used predominantly.

The degree and frequency of college freshmen struggling and failing in their first year away from home indicates that too often the transition to self-discipline isn't happening. Discipline may motivate an eighteen-year-old girl to keep her room straight and get a reasonable night's sleep when she is home. But if her primary motivation in doing so is "others centered"—e.g., "I don't want to make Mom mad" or "I don't want to have my parents ground me"—the parent's discipline hasn't evolved into self-discipline. In that case, the girl's dorm room will likely be a disaster and she might be staying up half the night. In this situation, the transition has not yet occurred.

The evolution from discipline to self-discipline is not automatic. It is something that needs to occur in all of us, even into adulthood. Self-discipline often involves conforming to an internal motivation, while discipline usually involves complying with an external motivation. This, in part, explains why the development of self-discipline needs to evolve. We start learning a truth or principle with the benefit of an outside influence and finish learning it when we have made it our own.

A traveler may pack lightly for a trip or two because of a luggage limit set by a tour company. Then a few years later, she may pack lightly because she has learned the burden of hauling too many belongings around on a trip.

The road to self-discipline may be a relatively direct route, but it can also be painfully circuitous. How we parent and how we talk will influence how long this journey is, but it will never eliminate the journey completely. Parents who are aware of this progression will watch and value this shift when they see it. Creativity is needed to assist kids as they transform discipline to self-discipline.

Scolding children for leaving belongings in the family room might get them to put their things away (though it is doubtful). But this approach will rarely result in self-discipline. In contrast, quietly dumping a child's belongings in a large designated box in the garage without a word is more likely to promote self-discipline. The issue will become personal for our kids when they are inconvenienced enough by digging through three bushels of junk to find an item they left out. The child's thinking process will develop from *I pick up after myself so Dad won't be mad* to *I pick up after myself because I don't want to dig through the box again.* Letting consequences teach the child is more likely to result in the development of self-discipline.

Self-discipline is our friend. It plays a more important role in our lives and in our role as parents than obedience. Without it, we will be lost and ill-equipped for life. While all discipline can help prepare us for life, it is self-discipline that provides the greatest tools for handling life's difficulties.

3. Resilience and Grit

You had better be ready for failure if you hope to be ready for life. Failure is a part of life. Resilience is what separates failure from defeat. When we fall, we need to get back up. To be ready to face life we need an ample supply of resilience.

We all need the ability to handle disappointment. Thousands of entrepreneurs do not succeed until their fourth or fifth idea. Many physicians did not get into the medical school they wanted, but they got in somewhere. Great athletes blow out their knees. Perhaps most painful, some people have the love of their life reject them and walk away unconcerned with the pain they have left behind. Preparing our children for life is preparing them to pick themselves up, dust themselves off, and try again—the next time with greater humility and determination.

Many kids today have an easy life and they don't even know it. Some think losing a smartphone for a couple of days is hardship. Unless children have experienced an event that puts their struggles in perspective, they may lose their balance over life's minor inconveniences.

Unfortunately, many parents do not want their kids to have a rough time in life. They want their kids to have fun, fit in, and not have to struggle. Overly accommodating a son or daughter might make for a pleasant-appearing childhood, but it runs a huge risk of leaving that child unprepared for adulthood. We have never seen adolescents thrive when they are living life their way. Left to their own devices, kids care little if they are solving a problem, delaying a problem, dumping a problem on someone else, or medicating a problem.

They need the struggle. They need disappointment. They need limits. They need something to push against to become strong, and the struggle must be against life and not against us as parents.

Resilience is essential to life. When the annual NCAA basketball tournament called March Madness starts, it is a given that sixty-three of the sixty-four best basketball teams in the country will end their season with a loss. We experience lost papers, lost love, lost freedom, lost purpose, lost health, lost pets, and lost reputations.

So much of resilience is perception. Your child may need help assessing not only the magnitude of the difficulty he or she experiences, but also the appropriate degree of emotional response. Consistent and accurate feedback as to how much an event should or should not disappoint him or her will help a child have a mature grid by which to develop resilience.

Children of all ages need help in assessing the magnitude of a difficulty. Small children do not know inherently how afraid they should be of a tornado. When they hear that a funnel cloud is in the area they may look into their father's eyes and listen to his tone of voice and his words, and from that, determine the magnitude of the risk. Without knowing it, the dad is developing the child's spectrum of risk. Likewise, we need to help our children develop a spectrum of difficulty. Consistent and accurate feedback on how big a disappointment is will help a child develop an assessment grid for disappointments and struggles.

"Isn't that overcontrolling your kids' emotions? Shouldn't they feel free to feel whatever they want?" Our answer is "No." A child's feelings are not just his or her own. They affect the whole family and are often not rational. Feelings are just the intersection of beliefs and reality. You cannot control what your child feels, but you can and should comment on reactions resulting from a distorted belief.

If a ten-year-old boy cries, screams about an injustice, and no longer wants his friends over because his video game controller broke, he needs some help putting this disappointment into perspective. He needs help recalibrating the event. Perhaps he needs to be told that this is a mild disappointment as disappointments go in life. Over time, this will immensely help his resilience.

Kids who are not well adjusted to disappointment will not be resilient. Don't protect your children from disappointments. Let them face them at age-appropriate levels as they grow. More importantly, dispel the myth that everything should go well. That way your children will at least not be surprised when they are confronted with challenges later in life.

Steve and Anne had two young daughters who particularly loved helium balloons and their capricious ability to defy gravity. If the girls asked for balloons at a fair or a carnival, sometimes Steve would buy them and sometimes he wouldn't. When he did buy them, he'd always remind the girls before the purchase, "Now remember, every balloon has a sad ending. If we buy you balloons we want you to remember that the balloons don't tend to end well." Steve was right. Balloons don't end well. They pop, shrivel, or accidentally float off into the clouds. On the disappointment scale, the loss of a balloon is miniscule. Steve and Anne were aware that the girls would soon and invariably lose what they received. They wanted the girls to be aware of that truth too.

When I heard this story, I was impressed by the acceptance

and resolve with which both the daughters handled the untimely demise of their balloons. Yet, I wasn't surprised. Just knowing that some form of disappointment would follow the purchase seemed to equip the girls better for the inevitable. Like all of us, they were better able to emotionally handle the loss by knowing the risks going in.

Kids should be told that the family's cocker spaniel has a typical life span of twelve years and that Shaggy is already seven years old now. The teenage boy should be told that the pickup truck he wants to buy may need a new transmission fairly soon. Parents should tell their daughter that her new basketball coach tends to belittle his players, so she shouldn't be surprised if he embarrasses her in front of the team.

These are simple ways of teaching and reminding kids that they can expect life to be tough, but that you believe they are just as tough and will be able to handle most anything thrown their way.

If we recognize that life is difficult and unfair, we—and our kids—will be better able to face problems when they arise. We'll also enjoy life more during the good or easy times. How many times have we all heard someone with a serious illness say, "I will never take my health for granted again"? When we expect and enjoy an easy life or a healthy life, we take it for granted. We don't savor the joys of life as much.

Steve and Anne taught their girls a resilient way of looking at life:

- They knew balloons burst.
- They were better prepared to handle disappointment.
- They appreciated the balloons more as they didn't take them for granted.

As you teach your children to be resilient, you'll also be paving the way for them to develop grit. Children and adults who exhibit grittiness tend to be resilient, self-motivated, and focused, qualities they have learned or been taught along the way through life experiences or older mentors. Grit is a product of self-motivation and resilience. It's more than self-motivation—it's really something that describes a bigger concept.

Grit has many things that cumulatively lead up to its development, puzzle pieces that are all important to the end result of forming grit in a child. Understanding what grit is allows parents to focus their parenting on cultivating grit in their child. In psychological terms, grit is defined as "a positive, non-cognitive trait based on an individual's perseverance of effort combined with the passion for a particular long-term goal or end state (a powerful motivation to achieve an objective)."[2]

Grit must have a focus that originates from a passion *the child has*. This is why it's so important for parents to expose their children to a wide variety of experiences musically, athletically, socially, and academically. A child's passion must come from within; it must be his or her own. It is not the parent's passion. This may sound logical, yet for many parents it is not. Overinvolved parents frequently have passions that differ from their child's passion. This can strain relationships and cause unneeded stress in kids.

The long-term goal that grit realizes comes from a passion-motivated work ethic that becomes part of that child's handling of setbacks and success. *Long-term* means developed over many years; excellence and meaningful achievement seldom come quickly or easily, regardless of a person's degree of talent, intelligence, or resources. The child is so passionate and involved in attaining the goal, he or she becomes hard to stop. The deep meaning a child gets from an achievement that was self-earned becomes the fuel for ongoing perseverance and motivation to attain and strive for their next level of excellence. Grit feeds itself, over and over.

So really, grit is a process by which children discover their passion and, through *personal* dedication and *self*-discipline, practice their talent to such an extent that they reach a potential that was thought to be beyond them. From a parenting perspective, grit is taught, grit is modeled, and grit is reinforced.

Parents can practice doing several things to foster a gritty child:

- Allow your children to find their own passion in life. This means that a parent's job is to bring a variety of opportunities into their children's lives for them to "taste."

- Encourage your children to live in a place of frustration as they learn to practice and develop their passion. Impress on your child that frustration is a crucial part of becoming an expert at anything.

- Focus on effort and skill development more than accomplishments. The research is clear; effort is far more important than intelligence, genetics, or natural ability. Effort is a good indicator of having a successful life.

- Allow your child to fail. Failure does not define you, but quitting can.

• Finally, when your children find something they are passionate about, push them to go beyond what's comfortable. Comfort and immediate gratification have become driving forces in the decisions of our culture today, and it takes a constant awareness that these goals are overvalued and contrary to the development of grit. The army pushes soldiers to go well beyond what is comfortable in order to develop grit in their troops. Soldiers repeatedly report that they didn't know what they were capable of until they were pushed harder than they wanted to be. There's a good lesson here for parents.

4. Relationship Skills

Relationships are essential to every aspect of life and are a huge part of what makes life meaningful. Kids need to develop as many skills as they can for the myriad of relationship situations life will throw at them. Family, school, job, and sports all involve relationships. None of us would want to do adulthood without relationships. And none of us can do relationships without some highly developed skills. To be good at relationships, certain skills are essential: forgiveness; the ability to receive and give a gift; loving, caring for, listening to, and trusting others; and honesty.

How do we help our kids develop these relationship skills? Demanding of a child, "Say you're sorry to your brother," will not develop a child who is sorry he hit his brother. No, there is a more difficult lesson to be learned than that. A child must learn to be able to put himself or herself in another person's position and pause a moment to imagine what life would feel like if the situation or event were happening to him or her.

Until age eight, it is normal and appropriate for a child to be egocentric. The child views everything in relation to himself or herself, is self-centered, and feels the effect that an event has on him or her. After eight, a child needs to develop the skill of seeing things from someone else's point of view. It is a lesson to be learned in the second half of childhood. To feel empathy for someone else's sorrow or struggle is the essence of compassion. Kids are not all born with this capacity; it needs to be developed. Compassion is actually a skill that can be cultivated and strengthened.

If your child is ten or older and still can't see aspects of life from another person's perspective, you need to give this some attention. Ask your son to tell you what he imagines the neighbor boy feels like now that his parents are getting a divorce or after his dog has died. You can talk with your son and ask him to imagine this before he goes over to his friend's house for the day. Throughout his lifetime he will use this ability to keep healthy relationships.

The digital age and social media have added new challenges in developing relationship skills for adults, but especially for kids. The digital shorthand we are all exposed to is convenient and quick, but there are aspects of socialization and interpersonal skills that are clearly being bypassed. Unfortunately, social media is a uniquely Touchpoint type of communication. It doesn't foster relationships with all the nuances and complexities that they require.

Texts and Twitter and Facebook posts, as well as email, tend to be short conveyances of data. They resemble the past communication style of leaving sticky notes all over an apartment to communicate with a friend or roommate. This form of contact connects but doesn't really relate. In essence, young people are connecting more frequently than ever before and relating less.

There is a difference between a boy texting his boss that he is going to be ten minutes late for work and a boy calling his boss to tell her that he is running late or, before cell phones, arriving late and explaining face-to-face why he was late. Texting and voicemails are emotional shortcuts. Emailing the neighbor to say you can't mow his lawn this week is different from telling the neighbor the same thing in person. All of these examples are insignificant on their own. However, when these Touchpoint communications are pervasive and there is no human interaction, some important skills and reality are bypassed.

Consider the same dynamic in emotionally charged situations. We have all heard stories of kids starting a dating relationship with a text and then breaking up with another text. This is connection without texture. Birthday wishes, sympathy expressions and condolences after a death, congratulations for a graduation, and get-well wishes are now often done in Touchpoints. These connections are more prevalent than ever. While Facebook users typically receive more birthday wishes now than they ever have, there is also less depth and nuance to these wishes.

To have successful relationships, dozens of unique skills are needed. All need to be at least partially developed during childhood.

5. Experiencing Achievement and Creativity

Achievement and creativity are often underplayed as an important part of personal development. It is from achievement that hope evolves into self-esteem. Without achievement, hope never evolves past being a wish. Kids who try to like themselves without achievement find it a hollow and hopeless journey. But to achieve or create, a price must be paid. If we want to run a marathon, write a paper or a song, earn a degree, or hunt a deer, an effort must be invested for that achievement. Adulthood involves accepting this truth and paying the price.

People do everything from camping to cross-country skiing to Sudoku and crossword puzzles for recreation. Some people will spend years fixing up an old Camaro or building deck furniture. Others enjoy golf, which is essentially one problem after another. People enjoy doing hobbies because they have found a focus where achievement is fun.

In our respective practices we have heard kids list their latest achievements as hanging out at the mall and getting a tattoo. Getting to level six on a video game or exceeding five hundred Facebook friends are sometimes called achievements. These are *not* achievements. The video game is virtual; it's not real. Having five hundred Facebook friends means that a teen has added hundreds of people she doesn't necessarily know to her account. Parents should remind their children that these things are games, events, purchases, or pleasures. An achievement is something totally different.

To turn the corner into adulthood, young people need real achievement for a real world. Without real achievement, growth tends to dissipate and the hope and competence longed for is not produced.

When parents or social workers try to help kids who have lost their way, one of the hardest hurdles is to find that first significant achievement on which the child can build. It may sound easy, but it isn't. Parents frequently discover themselves in this predicament. If a child spends years never following through on anything, he will gradually find he has no tangible achievements. If a teenager spends years smoking pot, playing video games, breaking friendships, losing assignments, and having poorly developed social skills, he will end up with nothing that qualifies as a legitimate accomplishment. This is a problem.

Nicole's Story

When Nicole was placed in a foster home, she had achieved virtually nothing that could be called an accomplishment in years. With her truancy record she hadn't even accomplished going to school or turning in any assignments, let alone passing a grade. She had no real friends, no identifiable skills, and a limited ability to relate to people.

As she reluctantly got in her new foster family's van, Nicole complained. Going anywhere in the van with this family was a bona fide nightmare to her. Even worse, the family was going to "the cabin." To her, the cabin was nothing more than a small, crowded shack in the middle of nowhere. She hated everything about it.

On her third day there, out of boredom, Nicole agreed to go out in a fishing boat. An hour later, with her negative attitude, no patience, and an awful cast, she somehow hooked an eight-pound northern pike. Even more unlikely, she was able to land the fish safely.

As the boat pulled up to the dock, the family immediately ran for their cameras, shocked to see the transformation of Nicole's body language and the appearance of her smile. She wouldn't hold her own fish, but she was happy to stand near while cameras and smartphones clicked away. Nicole whispered quietly but clearly, "I'm so proud of myself." When she saw everyone seemed comfortable with this shy utterance, she said it again and again—louder and louder.

Four hours later, the fish had been cleaned and prepared and was more than enough to feed the family and a guest with leftovers. By this time, Nicole had left her frown and her timidity behind and was nearly yelling, "I'm so proud of myself" over and over again. She had finally stumbled onto an achievement on which she could start building.

Achievement is often the first step in any child's journey to heal or build self-esteem.

6. Hope and Pain

Kids learn and grow when they have a combination of hope and pain in their lives. They usually need both. This means that an adolescent who has no pain will likely not mature. Likewise, a teen with no hope will not grow. Kids like Nicole have enough pain to grow, but their hope has dissipated along the way and they have nothing left on which to build successes.

Hope and pain are the nature of life. Call it struggle, difficulty, or challenge, but for ground to be fertile for growth, hope and pain usually need to be present. Life can't be too easy or too dark. Growth in a child slows down if pain and hope are not balanced. To jump-start growth, keep an eye on what part of this balance needs to be adjusted.

This is important for parents and youth professionals to keep in mind. Many youth camps today have a ropes course, a zip line, or some other apparatus that creates this combination. A twenty-five-foot-high rope to cross provides the fear or pain to face, and peers cheering on the rope-crossers provide the hope.

How this happens is not always clear—it is not a science. For Nicole, catching a big fish was clearly hope. It wasn't planned to work out that way; the family just went fishing. After that, Nicole had an achievement and several photos for her Facebook page to build on. There was a chance for her next activity to also become an achievement.

Exposure to struggle and hope is not easily arranged or contrived. Often life presents challenges and anticipation in its own natural way. Some children will have this natural balance in their lives. A young child who falls off a skateboard or horse without serious injury will instinctively balance the fall with the adding of a new skill. An older teen might find this balance by trying out for a school play or waiting tables at a restaurant.

More than anything, this is just a helpful way of thinking about your child's experience. If you're not seeing growth in your child, it may mean there's not enough pain in his life (he has gotten too comfortable), or there's not enough hope in his life (he has despair). For example, if your son is living with you and lacking hope, lending him a car to go to a job interview would be a good option. Telling him you are going to start charging him rent would be a good option if he doesn't have enough pain. This quick assessment will help parents know whether their children need help and encouragement, or whether they need to sit with a difficulty on their own or have more expected from them.

The GIST of It

- If our kids are going to be ready for adulthood by age twenty, they will need to accept that life is difficult.

- The more we accept that life will be a struggle, the less difficult it becomes.

- The healthiest approach for solving problems in life is self-discipline.

- Creativity, self-control, and a disciplined life are the best tools to solve most of life's inherent problems.

- Resilience allows us to try several times to correct a problem and provides the strength to get up when we have been knocked down.

- Resilience can only be strengthened through practice.

- We cannot go through life alone, so it is imperative that we learn relationship skills.

- Everyone proficient at life can get along with others.

- Compassion is essential to being a good friend and family member.

- Growth will not likely take place without a sense of achievement.

4

THE DIFFERENCE
BETWEEN FUN AND JOY

Joy is to fun what the deep sea is to a puddle.

TERRY PRATCHETT

YOU CAN LITERALLY FEEL THE DIFFERENCE. You notice it when your daughter tells you that her volleyball team's four-game winning streak is more awesome than the party with her classmates, when your teenage son explains that training for a triathlon feels so unlike playing *Call of Duty*, or when your child invites an unpopular classmate to a movie outing with friends and you see a different kind of smile. When a person does the right thing, the hard thing, the kind thing, the self-care thing or the "others care" thing, the smile on his or her face is different from the smile that comes from just having fun. This is joy!

The line between fun and joy has become carelessly blurred in our culture, as fun has become a more prominent goal.

"I didn't have any fun today" is a complaint we've heard from the children and teens we see in our practices. The comment seems simple enough and yet, on closer examination, it grows complex. Whether spoken indignantly or with contempt, a child saying this reveals implications and assumptions about his or her cultural bias and worldview.

First, this simple statement implies that the child believes fun is something that *should* be part of his or her experience every day. It doesn't matter if the child had fun yesterday. The issue is the irrefutable fact that he or she had no fun today.

Second, the complaint "I didn't have any fun today," spoken in the tone that conveys that this *should not have happened*, reveals a deep-seated belief that a child has a fundamental right to daily fun. The baseline has shifted on this in recent years, and some kids have come to assume that fun is an inherent entitlement, every day.

Third, the comment "I didn't have any fun today" implies it was *someone else's duty* to make this happen. While kids are aware that the lack of fun is not a form of neglect, they can see it as an injustice. It is as though they are saying: "Now look what you've done! You've blown it! You have contributed to a day of my life in which fun did not exist. It isn't fair that you did that to me!"

Perhaps more alarming is the number of times a parent takes on the weight of these assumptions. Usually this happens subconsciously. But if a mother hears, "I didn't have any fun today," and feels guilty or feels like she failed, she has unwittingly, and perhaps accidentally, given in to this silent shift in our culture.

Most parents would be aghast at the idea of feeding their children only chips, soft drinks, and dessert. They're constantly aware of the impact of the children's diet on their health, self-image, energy, and future. Yet these same parents will allow their children's lives to be dominated by fun activities rather than meaningful activities that build joy. As fun gains prominence in our culture, joy dwindles in many children's lives.

Kids have a pretty good idea of what would be fun for them to do. In contrast, most kids we have met know little about what would give them joy.

Let's look at the definition of fun and joy as we use them in this chapter. The words *fun* and *joy* are not synonymous. Almost universally, people *sense* that there is a huge difference between fun and joy. Imagine saying to someone in parting, "Have joy," instead of saying, "Have fun." What a different meaning that would have! Fun and joy are different in character, in form, in content, and, above all, in intent.

Fun is morally indifferent and spiritually detached. Joy is morally grounded and spiritually aware. Fun has a bent toward excitement, while joy has a bent toward peace. Fun is enjoyable but often fleeting. Joy is far more enduring. There is a sense of meaning in joy. There is depth, gratitude, or perhaps wonder. Joy reminds us that life is worthwhile in a way that fun cannot.

What's Wrong with a Little Fun?

This high priority on having fun is a huge shift from past generations. Among Western youth there is a goal or even an expectation they should be entertained nearly every day. Little wonder entertainment is no longer something saved for special festivals, holidays, or weekends. "Let's have fun!" The prevailing thought is: *What's wrong with it? Life is short. Have fun, live a little, be good to yourself!*

For many kids, the pursuit of fun has become their primary focus. Teens say the word *fun* more than almost any other word. Having fun is a highly valued and popular goal. When kids part from each other or end a phone call, very often they'll give this message: "Have fun; don't work too hard."

Teens often talk together about how much fun they had at an activity or event. We suspect that if they were asked, "Did you experience any joy?" the typical response would be: "Joy? What do you mean? I just had fun."

Young children grow and learn from play and fun activities. But as a child hits his or her early teens, it's time to move from fun-dominated activities toward those with the potential to build joy.

Almost everyone is in favor of kids having fun and hardly anyone is against it. But why should we have fun? The answer is, "Because it's fun!" Fun has become its own justification.

Fun has a fleeting and momentary nature. It expires fifteen minutes after a great comedy movie or the morning after an amazing party. The pursuit process starts again as the person experiencing the fun returns to his or her life before the movie or the party. The movie was a two-hour escape and this may be all that's desired, but an escape inherently does not endure. It is entertaining or funny or crazy or suspenseful, and then it is over and nothing has changed. More importantly, we haven't changed anything in our world.

In our teen culture, kids are compensating for the fleeting nature of fun by pursuing it relentlessly. With such a short expiration date on fun, it must be purchased anew over and over. Fun used to be a wonderful seasoning for life. For some, it has become the main course. It was never meant to be the whole meal. As the main driving force of life, it is not very attractive.

Fun has become mainstream as a value. There are a few

coaches and mentors who challenge fun as a valued outcome, but they seem few and far between. Likewise, there are few books, sermons, speakers, or advertising messages that dare challenge the merits of fun.

Many adults have bought into this personal quest. For these adults, chasing fun becomes a goal and a preoccupation. Fortunately, the responsibilities and commitments of most adults don't allow them to succumb to this. Others find it not as satisfying as they had hoped. But we've all seen adults who have become chasers of fun and live lives that resemble an extended and unattractive midlife crisis.

The Benefits of Pursuing Joy

Joy doesn't show up as easily as fun. There is not much fun in being honest or in hard work, and little fun at all in self-discipline. What fun is there in being a kind grandchild, a good sibling, or a young person of your word? What is fun about being grateful for what you have, or sacrificing for someone with less? Not very much fun. Then why pursue joy? Because joy is more peace filled and enduring than fun. Those who pursue joy don't have dull or uninteresting lives. They just value joy more than fun. Joy usually costs a little more and lasts a lot longer, and it will give experiences that focusing on fun will never produce.

Individuals who relentlessly pursue fun might not be giving much thought to joy. This is not a conscious trade-off. They are simply unclear about the differences between fun and joy and what they really want. It's common for people to pursue fun when it may be joy that they really desire. Joy tends to cultivate a depth to life and a sturdier form of happiness that fun cannot produce.

Fun-focused kids rarely experience the happiness that comes from real joy. Serving at a food pantry during the holidays may not seem fun or exciting or even convenient. Yet, something happens in a child's heart when he sees tears well up in a woman's eyes as she smiles and says: "Thank you so much! This will change the holidays for my family!"

How about cutting into an afternoon of fun by cooking a meal with your child to take to a sick neighbor? Often we overlook or discount the joy that time spent in meaningful activity with our kids can bring.

Joyful activities don't need to be focused on someone else, but they do require some kind of investment. They can be completely selfish. Participating in Tough Mudder or losing thirty pounds can bring joy, and these are self-serving events. A real adventure requires a real investment and usually produces joy. An artificial or counterfeit adventure, which is what all video games are, brings only fun.

Young people are inherently drawn to adventure. Girls and boys alike are instinctively drawn to heroes, competition, and challenges. If they aren't allowed or encouraged to pay the price of a true adventure, they will likely substitute it with virtual adventure or a fabricated drama. This counterfeit adventure will not satisfy their yearning and will bring only fun at best, and perhaps not even that.

Is Fun a Parent's Responsibility?

We see an increasing number of parents who have taken on the weight of this cultural shift. They feel responsible for helping their kids have fun and facilitating its endless pursuit. Some parents have bought into the notion that fun should be expected and frequent. Some parents even feel guilty if they haven't provided a steady diet of fun for their kids. They try to present fun options on a regular basis, feeling that this is part of the modern parent's job description. Consciously or subconsciously, the progression sounds something like this in the parent's head:

- I love my children.
- I want my kids to have a happy childhood.
- My kids seem to need fun regularly to be happy.
- My younger kids have trouble coming up with ways to have fun.
- If I interfere with my teenager's fun, I will interfere with his happiness.
- My children have enough challenges in life, so I need to facilitate their fun.

If we as parents mentor our children's fun, we will mentor them into a repeated chase and endless pursuit. These kids wonder as soon as they wake up, *What are we doing for fun today?* Because fun is by nature brief, kids schooled in fun will want to find it every day of the week. If we mentor our children in joy, we teach them to find something that has meaning and depth, something that is more enduring.

Here are some thoughts that consciously or subconsciously can help parents rethink this shift in our culture:

- Fun is fine, but joy is deeper and less fleeting.
- Joy usually requires creativity, achievement, self-discipline, or effort.
- Creativity is often birthed from passion, sacrifice, or boredom.

- Creativity or passion often leads to achievement.
- When my child finds joy in something, it will last awhile and will contribute to his or her self-esteem.

Ironically, searching for fun can be an accomplishment that brings joy. This is why there is immense value in having young children discover their own fun. They find joy in the process of looking for fun. This is the primary difference between setting a child up with a game or fun activity and patiently waiting for the child to discover or invent an activity to play. When parents constantly find fun for their children, they are *stealing* the opportunity for those children to find joy in their own pursuit of fun. Be patient—creativity is often birthed from boredom.

Sarah's Story

Sarah was fifteen and very excited about going to Disney World. She was not too old nor too cool to enjoy a family vacation. She had wanted to go about three years ago, when her family had first talked about it. But, each spring, either money or time was in short supply. This year Sarah's little brother was seven and old enough to enjoy the Disney experience along with another sister in the middle.

This was to be a once-in-a-lifetime trip and had taken much effort and time to pull together. The kids had spring breaks a week apart. The parents coincided the trip dates with the seven-year-old boy's vacation time. Sarah would miss a week of school and have four days left of vacation after they arrived home.

Their eight-day trip included the Magic Kingdom, SeaWorld Orlando, Busch Gardens Tampa Bay, Universal

Studios Florida, Discovery Cove, and Epcot. Plus the family was going to stay at one of the Walt Disney World Resorts. Sheer stamina may have been the biggest obstacle to perfection. But the week went wonderfully and actually exceeded the family's lofty expectations.

Sarah and her family got home early on a Monday night, and Sarah went to bed that night reveling in the fact that she didn't have school the next morning. *How great was that?*

Tuesday morning all the family except Sarah kicked into function mode and dispersed to the individual demands of a normal week. Sarah slept in and didn't roll out of bed until nearly 11:00 a.m. She promptly found something to eat in the fridge, and checked to see if there was anything good on TV. There wasn't, so she settled into a casual Facebook update.

At 2:30 p.m., Sarah's mom got a text from Sarah. It didn't say, "Mom, thanks for the amazing vacation!" It didn't say, "Mom, I'm exhausted from seeing the best theme parks in the Western Hemisphere in one week." It didn't even say, "It's nice to be home." No, her short-and-to-the-point text simply read: "I'm bored. There's nothing fun to do here."

A Word about Truths

Joy is often richer than fun—this is the truth. The wonder of truths is that they can be signposts to help us navigate life. Truths are guides proven over time to help us know whether to turn left or right when we get to the next fork in the road. Advice tells us what to do in a particular situation, whereas truths give us a foundation from which we can advise ourselves.

Too often these truths are not passed down to our kids. Perhaps this happens, in part, because there are always exceptions to a truth. At the same time, there are some generalizations in life that hold true most of the time, and we can benefit from remembering these and using them as a platform to make choices in life. We can teach these to our children so they can learn, before they turn sixty, that there is value in understanding how things usually work and what decisions typically pay off.

Here are a few truths that we believe. Understanding your truths will help you choose left or right when you face the next fork in your life's road:

- Joy is usually more fulfilling than fun.

- Learning is more elevating than knowledge.

- Courage is ultimately safer than fear.

- "Meaningful" is typically a better choice than "comfortable."

- A challenge is inherently more rewarding than the familiar.

- Having compassion for others is usually more mature than judging others.

- Gray thinking is usually more honest than black-and-white thinking.

- Generosity and giving are often a hedge against taking.

These are not facts—they are guides for the journey. Though we or our children may find exceptions to these truths, they still merit being valued because they will usually serve us well. Our children will need these truths when they come to forks in the road, since left or right is not always easy to distinguish.

The GIST of It

- A significant challenge for today's millennial parent is raising kids with a balanced perspective on fun and joy. Most forces in our culture push the "fun agenda," which leaves kids wanting escalating experiences that don't satisfy for long.

- Introducing and exposing our children to joy is important.

- Think about what gives your child joy. Then try to balance their yearning for fun with experiences that build joy.

- Children will come to forks in the road of life where one path leads to fun and the other leads to joy. Help them turn toward the path of joy. In our culture, this is truly the road less traveled.

- The difference between joy and fun captures just one of many truths that we can remind ourselves of and teach to our children as they grow.

5

CHECKLIST
FOR ADULTHOOD

One does not become fully human painlessly.

ROLLO MAY

IMAGINE WHAT IT WOULD BE LIKE to have a checklist for adulthood—a list of prerequisites for young people to complete before they would be considered adult. To our knowledge, a list has not been compiled and most likely will never be. But it is a great thought.

The book *1,000 Places to See before You Die* lists many places to visit, including Machu Picchu in Peru, the Eiffel Tower, and the Grand Canyon. Seeing such incredible sights gives us the type of wonderful experience we often associate with a checklist or a "bucket list." These are lists intended to be peak events providing unforgettable memories. We make lists like these when we prioritize our lives and our travels.

What might be on a list of things that we would love for our kids to experience before they become adults? Everyone's list would be different, but some things that would probably be included are:

- going to the Caribbean for spring break
- getting the newest smartphone
- hosting a birthday party
- having the "best Christmas ever"
- planting a tree
- writing a paper on global warming
- making the varsity team
- having great friends
- going to camp
- seeing Europe
- buying that first car

The list could be endless. Most of us would probably include positive experiences for our children, experiences that would fill them with wonder, thrills, happiness, and pleasant feelings.

In contrast to this list of positive experiences, there are things that most parents would never want their child to endure. In fact, if it were up to parents, items on this list would be avoided as much as possible. Yet this list exists, whether you are aware of it or not.

Kids need to have a certain number of these not-so-positive experiences in order to mature and gain wisdom and perspective. Without these kinds of experiences, children may grow up unprepared for adult life. We see this all the time in our respective practices—young adults whose maturity levels are sluggishly behind their chronological ages, and who have little ability to function as emancipated adults.

This second list is far more important to our children than the first. The experiences on this list are different from the first and perhaps obscure enough that we wouldn't typically think of them. Here is a list of experiences a child *should have* before he or she becomes an adult:

- not being invited to a birthday party
- experiencing the death of a pet
- breaking something valuable
- working hard on a paper and still getting a poor grade
- having a car break down away from home
- seeing the tree he planted die
- being told that a class or a camp is full
- getting detention
- missing a show because she was helping Grandma
- being blamed for something he or she didn't do
- having an event canceled because someone else misbehaved
- being fired from a job
- not making the varsity team
- coming in last at something
- being hit by another kid
- rejecting something he had been taught
- deeply regretting saying something she can't take back
- not being invited when friends are going out
- being picked last for neighborhood kickball

To some extent, any child who has not experienced the bulk of these or similar events will not be ready to be an adult.

Part of parenting your children well is learning to see events you might otherwise dread or try to avoid in your children's lives as *growth-producing* events. The main task for parents is to keep their children safe while preparing them for adulthood. There seems to be a lot of agreement on this goal. The misperception is about how to reach that goal. In many homes, safety is out of balance with preparation. Today there is more concern about safety, followed by an emphasis on performance, but not nearly enough focus on preparation.

While it could go either way, getting fired from a job is usually a good thing to happen to a teenager, especially if he or she was fired for giving free product to a friend or for not arriving at work on time. When a young boy gets a bad math teacher or has his skateboard stolen, parents don't usually think, *Perfect, that's perfect—it's just what he needed to happen at least once in his childhood.*

When Something Bad Is Good

Recently, a parent called saying that his teenage daughter, a fairly scattered and unfocused driver, had just been in a car accident. The crash was severe enough that the old car was totaled. No one was hurt in either car, the car was insured, and the daughter was remorseful. Not only did she feel terrible, she was immediately repentant about not paying better attention to the road.

These parents had some training in the "checklist to adulthood" way of thinking about their daughter's life experiences. The dad found it remarkable how radically differently he and his wife perceived and processed the entire event than they would have a year earlier. They were able to be calm, objective, and supportive throughout the whole ordeal. Why? Because they had concluded, after numerous talks with their daughter about her driving, that it was likely going to take an accident, or at least a close call, to finally get her attention. As their daughter sat crying on the couch that night, there was no doubt they had her attention. They had crossed something off her checklist to adulthood, without irreversible damage. Their daughter had taken a huge step toward driving more responsibly.

Of course, we would never wish a car accident on anyone. The variables are too risky and unpredictable. Likewise, parents wouldn't wish for a bad coach or math teacher for their son or daughter. It is only after the fact that we can be grateful for the learning that comes from any unpleasant incident or experience. It is an irrefutable fact of life that events that we might try to avoid are, in retrospect, the very events that produce important growth in our lives. Especially later in life, we can look back and see that almost all our growth is from something that was difficult or unpleasant.

We must teach our children to see that the things unwished for in their lives play a powerful role in forming their strength, their character, and their ability to deal with adversity in constructive ways. *Growth is the unintended benefit of the things in our lives that disappoint us.* It doesn't matter if our children are too young to understand this; it is important that we as parents understand this.

The Best Teachers

The best teachers for our children are not obedience, modeling, instruction, or habit. Contrary to popular parenting principles, we consider these to be "pseudo-teachers." Instead, *experience* in life is the best teacher, and wisdom and maturity are the end result of having experience as a teacher. Experiences that involve failure, disappointment, uncertainty, unfairness, and sacrifice will teach your child the deeper lessons of life.

A four-year-old child can and should be obedient. He can follow instructions, take on a habit, or copy what's modeled to him. But a four-year-old child cannot be mature because a four-year-old has not had enough life experience.

"My Daughter Has Changed!"

A couple came to the counseling office with their daughter for help. As the father described the dilemma, he said, "My daughter has changed so much in just sixty days that I barely recognize her. She does whatever her friends tell her to do. They have talked her into smoking, skipping school, lying, and smoking pot. If they asked her to jump in the river off a high bridge, she would probably do it."

Knowing that it is uncommon for anyone to change that much in sixty days, I asked, "Really? How has she changed?"

He said, "Sixty days ago she was an A student, she was trustworthy, she was a leader in our church's high school group, and she was helpful around the house. Back then she would do anything we asked her to do."

His phrasing caught my ear and piqued my curiosity. I said, "I guess she hasn't changed all that much."

"What do you mean?" asked the father with a surprised look on his face.

"Sixty days ago she was a kid who did what you and other adults asked her to do. Now she is a kid who does what her friends ask her to do," I said. "She isn't thinking for herself or following her own convictions. The only difference is that she has changed who she is listening to."

What's Wrong with Obedience?

Obedience, modeling, instruction, and habit are all useful tools for helping us raise kids, but they are not ideal. Independent thinking and self-discipline are the reasons to celebrate a child's completion of a task. It is our hope that someday a child will shovel the snow from the front steps— not for reasons of obedience, modeling, instruction, or habit, but for another's safety. Any other reason is a different form of playing "follow the leader."

Obedience looks good, especially when children are being obedient. But it's just a way to describe a child who is behaving the way the adult wants him to behave. Most of the time, obedience has a *deal* underneath it. The child behaves obediently to avoid the consequences, not because he truly wants to behave that way. An external force requires a child to conform to an expectation.

Obedience is the most overrated "false teacher," yet parents love to see it. It has nothing to do with real maturation, and everything to do with acting a certain way in a particular environment. A child who is obedient 90 percent of the time may not be 90 percent mature for his age, but he outwardly looks good to his parents and most people around them. Obedience is a wonderful stopgap or transitional form of learning, but it is not a definitive answer. When the environment changes, or when Mom and Dad are not around and no one is watching, obedience will likely dissipate. Only what has been internalized will survive.

Granted, obedience is an important skill for every child to learn. We all have people in authority over us, and we all (even adults) must at times do what we're told. The importance of this cannot be overstated. The point, however, is that while obedience is a necessary skill, it does not contribute as much as we think toward maturity.

The Downside of Modeling

Modeling has been another overemphasized parenting concept for the past thirty years. Yet there are several problems with modeling. First, modeling shows the child exactly what to do and how to do it, but it doesn't let him or her independently try something different that might be successful—or might be a failure. Modeling is an externally motivated way of conforming to one way of doing something. It's difficult to learn how to solve problems on your own if the only way you've done things in your life is through someone else's modeling.

Second, modeling creates an entire menu of options for the child to use to frustrate parents when tasks aren't completed as modeled. If you model loading the dishwasher or vacuuming or cleaning up after the dog in the backyard and your child does it differently, to you the result might look incomplete, insufficient, or lazy. If you use modeling, you will have equity in situations where equity is unnecessary. Your child's deviation from the modeled procedure may create an unnecessary and avoidable confrontation.

Modeling can be helpful in brief and limited situations. It is fine to model how to fold a shirt or mow the lawn. It can be helpful to model how to drive up an icy hill. But once a task or skill has been modeled concisely, the best scenario is your child deciding how he or she wants to do the task. Your child can decide to do it the way you demonstrated or figure out his or her own way to do it.

Parents whose kids have significant problems with maturity and behavior have said to us, "We have modeled a good marriage and a loving family." Our question to them is, "How's modeling working for you?" Our experience is that modeling has very limited value in helping kids grow up.

When Instruction Fails

Instruction for the child isn't a bad thing, but it usually involves the parent too much. It's obvious if instruction has been overused with a particular child. When asked to do anything, the child looks like a deer in the headlights— paralyzed as to where to start. That's because someone has always started things for the child. This learned dependence and reliance on the adult cripples the child when he or she gets to a point of needing to do things independently. Parents who instruct excessively usually go into great detail about what they want their child to do and give a step-by-step way for them to accomplish the task.

Please don't hear us wrong. Instruction for our kids is a good thing. It is merely overrated and not as powerful as we might think in the long run.

We should instruct our kids in everything from how to meet an adult, to how to care for a pocketknife, to how to apply for their first job. All of this is good and highly recommended. Often instruction works better to create maturity if you ask the kids for their thoughts before giving them instruction. Try asking, "What are you thinking would be a good outfit for you to wear to your job interview?" After you hear your child's idea, then instruction can be of value.

The Habit Trail

We all agree that good habits are better than bad habits. However, having no habits is even better than having good habits. That is more mature. It is a fine thing to say "Thank you" out of habit, but it's far better to say "Thank you" out of gratitude. Habits tend to be automatic, things that become part of us without our remembering why we even do them. There are good habits—like brushing your teeth twice a day or locking the car when you go into a store. But habits that are imposed on the child can quickly lose their impact. Too often parents use habits to force behaviors they feel are valuable, and then the child has no internal motivation to do what might be considered proper.

Thinking, self-discipline, and experience are the best teachers. They are the first choice when applicable.

The GIST of It

- Always keep the goal of adulthood in mind. Without this focus, you will lose your way in the turbulent journey of raising children.

- You may overvalue things like bedtime, vegetables, homework, sports, birthdays, music practice, and compliance. In doing this, you may accidentally undervalue lessons in failure, disappointment, forgiveness, resilience, injustice, personal responsibility, and kindness.

- Allowing your child the opportunity to collide with life in wonderful and painful ways will teach him much more than protecting him all the time. This is the easiest and most efficient way to raise your child.

6

THE EAGLE STORY

Two baby eagles hatch in an eagle's nest in southern Ontario in early May. For this first season of life, their home is a five-foot-wide nest, high up in a stable tree. Born needy and vulnerable, they are well protected in this haven. They have no predators except at night when a few nocturnal owls present danger if an adult eagle is not nearby.

In one short season, the young eaglets need to become emancipated young adult birds of prey. There is no time to waste. Within four months, these fledglings will change and have the appearance of an adult eagle except for the color of the plumage on their heads and tails, which will not turn white for a few more years. By early fall, the eaglets are as big as they will ever get. Although strong, they have now entered the time of their youth that is the most dangerous, even more dangerous than when they had just hatched.

Their vulnerability during this time is great, as the young ones do not yet know how to fly. The time for them to leave the nest is coming soon but they lack many skills, particularly the skills associated with flying. To learn this, the young birds will practice flying over the nest. They spread their wings, catch updrafts and downdrafts, and flap their wings, all while hovering safely over the nest. After they have mastered this, they take tiny flights to nearby branches and then return to the nest. The adult eagles stay nearby during this month for good reason: If a young one falls, it has no chance to survive without protection. The fully grown eagle watches with concern but is silent.

Eagles relive this story annually. Many young ones do not survive their first year. Many fall from the nest long before they are prepared to fly. Those that can fly may not be able to fend for themselves in the wild. They can't yet hunt by themselves and will become weak and undernourished. Occasionally a young eagle is fairly good at flying, but its ability to navigate has not been developed. In 1987, a juvenile eagle crossed the ocean from North America and landed in Ireland, weak and exhausted. No one knows how many young eagles die after being blown off course in the first year of life.

The eagles that survive that first year are the ones that hone their skills over the nest and near home. It doesn't matter how big or how old they are; it only matters how well they can fly and navigate. The birds that leave the nest before they have proven their prowess almost certainly do not survive. There are plenty of winds and storms close to the nest, and the skills that they have developed hovering over it will save their lives when they are on their own in the wild.

The GIST of It

- Allow your child to experience the ups and downs of life with you around.

- Let your child hover and be tossed by updrafts and downdrafts. Let him or her try and fail, over and over again.

- By trying, your child will gain just the right amount of prowess to survive away from you.

- When your children aren't learning to live life on their own, watch and wait with patience. Don't rescue them; instead, balance your presence as a source of wisdom and knowledge.

- Always first wait to see what they are capable of doing.

- The best place for your child to learn the skills needed for college life and beyond is in your home.

PART II

Core Development

7

THE EASY WAY OUT

The path of development is a journey of discovery that is
clear only in retrospect, and it's rarely a straight line.

EILEEN KENNEDY-MOORE

AFTER ONE OF Michael's GIST presentations, a mother was waiting to talk with him and said, "I heard you speak nine months ago and you mentioned that parents should only offer critical comments when absolutely necessary. So nine months ago, my husband and I sat down with our fourth-grade daughter and told her that we had been parenting her without seeing how she could do things on her own, and that from now on, we would only talk about the things she needed to do if necessary. We wanted to see how she would do life without us reminding her all the time." They also told the daughter that they weren't going to abandon her and would step in if she needed them.

The mother went on to say that parenting through this new "filter" had stopped the vast majority of reminders and critical comments she had been saying. One day went by, then five days and ten days went by, and her daughter was doing most everything she needed to do on her own. The mom said, "Last night we were watching *The Voice* as a family, and our daughter asked us to DVR the rest because she had homework to do." With tears in her eyes, this mom said, "I shudder to think how much unnecessary parenting we would have done with our daughter had we not changed our approach."

Changing a parenting approach doesn't always go this smoothly. But once you understand it, a new parenting approach is much easier to use than you might imagine because you'll focus on what's important and what works. If it's not important or doesn't work, you don't need to be doing it. Much parenting energy is spent on a failing approach that doesn't work, serves no purpose, or engages in battles that don't need to be fought. Once you learn to see a situation differently, many parenting challenges will go away on their own and without effort.

However, if you misperceive a situation, a simple problem may never go away. Always remember that if your premise is wrong, most likely everything you do after that could be wrong.

Laddie

I (Michael) once picked out a puppy at a local humane society. I didn't know the story of where Laddie came from, but he was a beautiful dog. He was also absolutely terrified. He trembled constantly for the first few days after my family brought him home. We speculated about what type of terrible abuse he must have suffered earlier in his life. Within a few days, his trembling changed to cowering. I assumed, as frightened as he was, he must have been abused and needed attention and reassurance to heal. I concluded that with his unknown nightmarish past, he needed to know that he was safe and loved in our home to be able to stop cowering.

Reassuring Laddie did not work, and the cowering did not go away. For months he would lower his head, slouch, and even roll over on his back in a submissive posture when anyone came near. We obviously weren't making any progress with the cowering. Whatever we were trying to do to help seemed to be the wrong approach.

One day I was talking with a Welsh woman who raised champion herding dogs. I hadn't called her about this problem, but while she was on the phone, I mentioned Laddie's cowering to see if she had any ideas for me.

Immediately she said, "You are thinking about it backwards. You aren't reassuring your dog at all as you think. You are rewarding his cowering. Just simply walk away with no words or eye contact the second Laddie starts to cower. Leave when he drops his head."

Within three days, and with no effort at all, my puppy stopped cowering. It was so easy it was almost embarrassing. I later learned that I had been thinking about this situation wrong and had continued to see it wrong for some time. I thought he needed reassurance to stop this behavior (which I was growing tired of quickly). All this reassuring was frustrating, ineffective, and making me weary. My initial premise was faulty. As long as I was thinking about the problem wrong, I was never going to solve the issue. But when I thought about it the right way, it almost solved itself.

Laddie has never gone back to cowering.

An Easier Approach

One reason parenting is so difficult is that parents are repeatedly trying to fix something that isn't broken. We believe the following principles will make parenting easier than you can imagine.

1. If Kids Are Thriving, Stop Parenting

Life is the best teacher. As long as we don't protect our kids from life, life will show up over and over again just in time to tutor our kids in the lessons they need. Life is by far the best trainer of our children.

When your child is thriving, wear your parenting hat as little as possible. With a thriving child, you may need to parent only a few hours a month. During these times of thriving, your child is consumed with growing and with life. Adventure and creativity are abundant, and as parents, we have front-row seats. It's an easy and wonderful place to be.

A thriving child is one who:

- follows the important rules
- gets along with others to an acceptable extent
- performs in school at an appropriate level for his abilities
- is honest and cooperative
- shows creativity and passion for life
- demonstrates obedience when obedience is important
- lives with age-appropriate courage to face new adventures
- refrains from breaking any laws or acting reckless in any way

If this describes one or more of your children during a specific time in his or her life, just take it easy. Watch your child with amazement and enjoy—without needless parenting banter. Needless banter is all the things parents say that are unnecessary. If they had waited a few minutes, the child would have handled the situation independently.

When your children are thriving, give them time to remember to brush their teeth, time to call Grandma when she is sick, or time to clean up a mess they made. Too often, good parents with good kids talk too much, using words that are not good and are unneeded.

It's okay to tell your child: "You are living your life so well right now that I want to just sit back and watch you learn. When I can, I will try to back off so you can continue to grow. If, in the future, I see something that concerns me, I will step in and intervene when it is needed."

If or when you are in this sweet spot with your child, stop talking down to him or her and stop making obvious or insignificant comments. Give your child a few minutes and then see if you need to say anything. It is much easier that way. While this season will not last forever, it will last longer if you give your kids space. Kids in this stage just need the smallest of nudging, and that is how they should be handled.

How easy is that?

Someday the thriving will end, the sweet spot will be over, school assignments will be unfinished, and the arguing will resume. After all, your child needs to push back some to do that "growing up work." Then you need to immediately re-involve yourself in the process. But in the meantime, you and your child will have had a nice break and you'll be reminded that parenting is not something you need to do every day.

2. Stay Interpersonally Connected and Emotionally Separate

Most parents are not even aware why parenting is difficult for them. When we ask them why it's so hard, they can't articulate the reason. They don't see how emotionally involved they are in the process of raising their child. They see the child's misbehavior or immaturity and don't know how not to take it personally. They are fatigued and don't know where it's coming from.

Parents often take way too much personally. When your son misses the bus, he doesn't miss the bus *at* you. He just misses the bus. When you are parenting, *take nothing personally*. Your daughter will do what she does and will likely do it for a predictable reason. When parents take something personally on an emotional level, they drastically diminish their competence.

For example, let's say a mother has a fifteen-year-old daughter and it's Mother's Day. On this morning, the daughter stays in her room and has no gift, no card, no kind words, and no breakfast in bed for her mom. So what? It doesn't mean anything. We don't know why the daughter acted like this. All we know is that in the fifteenth year of her life when Mother's Day rolled around, this girl was unable or unwilling to celebrate her mom. She may love her mom or she may not that year. It doesn't matter. That is how she feels that day, and a Hallmark card is not going to change it.

Some parents subconsciously believe their love will change their children. These parents want their kids to know how much they love them, but they also want their kids to know how much they have hurt or disappointed them. This approach is a losing proposition. In fact, the more parents take things personally and emotionally, the more power they give their kids. Don Miguel Ruiz, in his book *The Four Agreements,* calls it "emotional poison" when we unnecessarily take on comments and behavior in a personal way.

Look, we have a job to do. It's to *teach* our kids to live, not to *make* them live a certain way. There is a big difference. It is more important than any job in any profession. The stakes are high.

Most adults have learned they are more effective in their jobs if they don't take things personally and don't get emotionally entangled with events at work. We need to take this awareness home. We will perform better as parents if we deal with things in a matter-of-fact way, without strong emotions (expressed or concealed). If there are muddy boots in the entry or cigarettes under the seat of the car, deal with it wisely and effectively, but don't take it personally.

If your son lies to you, it isn't really *you* he lied to. He lied, and you were standing in front of him. Your son simply lied because he has not fully learned the importance and value of honesty. If he is going through a lying stage of his life, he will lie to anyone he can, not just you. It doesn't matter who they are. It matters who he is and where he is developmentally. Deal with the lying in some definitive way. Decide what you are going to do and do it. Teach him the importance of honesty. But don't take it personally or respond emotionally. He is not lying at you in a personal way.

When you learn to love your kids and stay involved in their lives without taking their misbehavior personally, your job will feel completely different. It's so much easier that way. When you take things personally, you will feel offended and your reaction will be to defend yourself. This causes needless conflict, and you will make something big out of a nonevent.

3. Let Life Play Itself Out

The first question parents should ask themselves when faced with a parenting situation is this: *Is this a situation I should do something about, or is it one that will take care of itself if I'm patient?* It would be smart to ask yourself this one question a thousand times a year. When the answer to that question is *It will take care of itself,* then you have nothing to do. It doesn't get any easier than *nothing.*

We can't tell you which situations will take care of themselves without knowing your family or your child. However, we are confident that you will recognize them. If your two kids get into an argument about a common situation, you'll know if they have a track record of working things out in twenty minutes. In that case, you need not do or say anything. Or you'll realize there is a differential of power between your kids and the weaker one may need some help.

That said, here are some situations that typically require no parental involvement:

- Your child gets detention for being rowdy on the bus.
- Your son loses his new Atlanta Braves cap.
- Your child breaks a neighbor's window by throwing a water balloon.
- Your daughter forgets to buy a present for her friend's birthday.
- Your daughter left her cheeseburger on the deck and the dog ate it.
- Your late teen threw her cell phone in a rage and broke it.
- Your ten-year-old won't come in for dinner.
- Your eighteen-year-old lost his paycheck.

- Your seventeen-year-old hasn't returned a DVD (rented on his debit card) for five days.
- Your fifth grader hates his science teacher.
- Your four-year-old left his action figure at McDonald's.
- Your young soccer player left her spikes out in the rain.

In most families and on most days, all you need to do with any of these happenings is nothing. Maybe show a little empathy, but that is it. There is nothing else to do. Don't talk and don't get involved—just watch it play out.

Learning this principle starts with repeatedly asking this crucial question: *Do I really need to do anything here?* This parenting gig is hard enough without creating extra work, especially when the extra effort is invested in a mediocre approach. Jumping in unnecessarily is a mediocre approach.

4. Practice Joyful Parenting

Now, let's up the ante. Let's move from easy parenting to joyful parenting. Notice the third example in the bulleted list above—the broken window. The easy thing to do is nothing. The joyful thing to do is wonder how this whole broken window thing is going to play out. What is your daughter going to do? What will she say when she knocks on the neighbors' door to tell them? What will it cost and who will your daughter suggest to fix it? Some of the most joyous situations we have had as parents started with the thought, *Wow, this is going to be interesting!* Taking a few days to let a situation play out and reveling in the anticipation of how it will be handled is a fun way to parent.

Suppose your son desperately wants a new state-of-the-art

aluminum bat for his fall baseball league. You figure out with him that he can easily earn the money by simply mowing the lawn each Saturday during the summer. During the summer he repeatedly forgets, procrastinates, or complains, and does not mow the lawn. Perhaps you go ahead and mow it two or three times because it is fun to be outside on a nice day, and twice you hire a sibling or neighbor to mow the lawn. In this situation, the easy part is doing nothing. The joyful part is in wondering what your son is going to do. You don't need to talk, remind, or even teach him a lesson. Life will have that part covered. Just watch.

Months later, the season is starting, and he realizes he doesn't have the money for the bat. Remember, you're just watching. Then he has a plan. He asks his older sister to lend him the money for the bat. She says she will lend it at 7 percent interest a month. You say nothing. He agrees and races out to get the bat. Two months later he hasn't made a bat payment and you hear the kids arguing in the next room about the debt.

Better yet, imagine that he's at a tournament and the bat disappears after he leaves it in the dugout!

Why would you want to interfere with any aspect of this situation? It's going perfectly. Anything you do to get involved will just contaminate the perfect balance of life playing out before your very eyes. Even if your daughter comes to you and says, "It's been two months and Joe won't pay me!" you still don't need to do anything.

You may simply and unemotionally say, "I'm guessing you knew that was a possibility when you lent him the money."

As time goes on, you may find it necessary to get involved.

But don't get involved until you need to and until you have given the situation plenty of time to play itself out.

You might tell small children you will take them to the beach as soon as they change into their swimsuits and pick up their toys. They are excited to go to the beach and quickly change into their suits, but they haven't picked up one toy. Instead of encouraging or lecturing the kids, you think, *Wow, this is going to be interesting.* You hold your car keys and your beach bag and sit down and do nothing. Just wait for it to play out. How easy is that? Even if Anna picks up her toys and Emma doesn't, you still don't need to say anything. Even if Anna picks up Emma's toys for her, you still don't need to say anything. Calmly and silently let it play out.

There will be little or no monotony or tedium when you parent this way.

5. Family Time Can Be Overrated

Again and again, when middle-aged adults are asked about their favorite memories from childhood, the memory often starts with, "The times my dad and I . . ." or "The day my mom and I . . ." Far less frequently the memory will start with, "When my whole family . . ." This is because doing things one-on-one is so important to our development.

One-on-one time can simply make parenting easier. Doing something, anything, one-on-one with your child is effective, enjoyable, and usually easier than loading up the entire family to go somewhere. This is a great strategy for parents to keep foremost in their minds. Going to breakfast, Grandma's house, a ball game, or even a vacation is usually fairly easy when it's with just one child. And it's usually more effective for connecting and building memories.

As a family unit, younger kids often compete for Mom or Dad's attention. Consciously or subconsciously, kids keep track of which child is getting the most notice. Sometimes kids just accept this, but they often fight back to win the attention battle. They may speak louder and louder in the car, or they may spill a drink or tattle or even wander off. Kids can be very creative when they feel their siblings are stealing some of their rightful attention.

Have you had one or more of your kids being peculiarly disobedient at Target, grabbing items off the shelf, wandering away, or pretending to be unaware that they were drifting out of an acceptable radius? The culprit may be competition for interest, affirmation, or attention. Often these same kids would act wonderfully on their own.

A teen may withdraw, wear earbuds, or answer questions with single-syllable answers. It may look like the teen doesn't want attention, but she is usually acting out hurt because she feels misunderstood. She wants attention, but she has lost track of how to get it in a productive way.

If you have two kids in your family, it will be productive and efficient for you to repeatedly break up the family activities into pairs. This can't always be done and the family needs to learn to function as a whole, but breaking up into twos (which is not done often enough) can really help the parenting process go easier.

6. High-Maintenance Kids: It's Not Okay

It's not acceptable for kids in a family to be high maintenance. A high-maintenance kid is one who engages in draining behavior. They are high maintenance because they are *talked to* about draining behaviors but nothing is really done about them. This kind of child's misbehavior falls just short of being disobedient but is exhausting. Parents may find themselves caught trying to manage an annoying situation, all the while unable to spot what is really wrong.

In young kids, these behaviors might be interrupting, wiggling while their car seat is being secured, touching fragile items, whining, complaining about being bored, only wearing certain clothes, etc. For older kids it might be a demanding "I need the car," changing the TV channel when someone else is watching, leaving a pizza box in the family room, or just acting distant and annoyed.

Most kids who behave this way continue to behave this way because this issue has not been effectively dealt with. Kids need and deserve adult attention. But it's unacceptable for them to steal it or get it by pouting, acting in a high-maintenance manner, or shaming their parents. There is a right way and a wrong way to argue about getting permission to go to a friend's house for a sleepover. There is a right way and a wrong way to interrupt someone.

Politeness and manners are important for our kids. If your son got in trouble on the bus, it is usually more important that he talked to the bus driver with respect than that he followed some rule about standing while the bus is moving. An interpersonal and social education is as important as anything our kids have before them.

Implementing this principle will not make your life immediately easier, as some of the other changes we've suggested will do. But your life will improve when your kids learn that being rude or difficult won't pay off for them.

Unfortunately, parents are prone to overtalking, with comments such as, "Don't talk to me in that tone of voice,"

"Stop touching . . . ," "I've told you not to interrupt me while I'm on the phone," or "Don't text while I'm talking to you." These behavior problems cannot be handled verbally. Of course, if they could be handled with words, they wouldn't be problems anymore because they have been talked about so many times.

First, tell your daughter, for example, that she is entitled to your attention, but not all of your attention. She has to get your attention through proper means. Second, and most important, you must make it costly for her when she is rude or inappropriately demanding. This needs to be done calmly. It will be unconvincing to your child if you behave rudely or are inappropriately demanding when you are trying to get her to stop her rude and inappropriate behavior.

Soon after this behavior stops paying off for her, she will use a more tolerable approach. When you quietly take the keys, or stop helping with a science project, or turn the car around and drive home, or disable the TV (especially if you aren't angry), it won't be long before your home is a much more pleasant place to live.

Parents can come up with unique explanations for their child's misbehavior. "My child is hyperactive . . . exceptionally creative . . . special . . . gifted . . . adopted." They use these explanations as an excuse to accept otherwise unacceptable behavior. Some parents almost carry these excuses as a badge of honor or as a reason to get sympathy from their friends.

A difficult child might call you out to be a more effective parent and might demand you gain a higher level of expertise, but he or she shouldn't require more energy. Your child takes as much energy as you give. Often, the most poignant question is not why your first child requires so much more energy to parent than your other kids. The question is, why are you giving this child more energy than is needed or helpful? It likely dilutes the energy you have for another child or your spouse or parent or other parts of your life.

Whether your child has attention deficit disorder, is adopted, or is exceptionally bright, he is going to need to learn how to be polite and not be unreasonably demanding to survive in life. As a parent, you are the person who is most able to help that happen.

Here is a test: Think about the amount of time and energy you'd ideally want to give your child to convey your love and involvement. Now ask yourself, has my child found a way to demand more time and energy from me than I intended? Is one of my kids taking a disproportionate share of the parental energy in the home away from his siblings? If he or she has, then you have a high-maintenance kid and something needs to be done.

7. Anticipate the Problem and Plan a Strategy

Even though our kids often surprise us, we really do know what they are like. We know how our kids react in certain situations, and we tend to be good at predicting what's about to happen. We know which kids are likely to pull in the driveway late, oversleep, or leave the kitchen a mess, and which one will fuss in the aisle at the store. We won't usually know which day these things will happen, but we do know what is likely to occur.

A parent might say, "If I leave the house, he'll turn the TV on before I'm at the end of the block." From bedtime to road trips to picky eating to renting a movie on Netflix, as parents we often can anticipate what is going to happen. Even so, we often do little to prevent a possible problem. This is a lost opportunity for many parents. Instead of just anticipating the problem behavior, parents need to develop a plan of action when they anticipate something is going to go wrong. Parenting is always easier when we have a plan tucked neatly in our hip pocket, just waiting to implement if needed.

If we take some moments on a Tuesday night to plan a response to what we anticipate happening on Wednesday, then we'll think better and won't find the whole dilemma troubling to handle.

A dad was taking his four kids out for a fast-food dinner one night. He anticipated there would be extensive arguments about where to eat. He could have just simply chosen their destination, but that wouldn't have stopped the complaining. No matter which place he selected, two or more kids would have complained and argued about the restaurant choice during the entire meal.

Suspecting this would happen, he developed a plan ahead of time that he could use if needed. When the five of them jumped in the car, the dad didn't start the engine. Instead, he turned to the kids and said, "You have seven minutes to agree on a place to go for dinner. In seven minutes, I will ask you for your collective decision. If you haven't agreed on a place in seven minutes, we are going to stay home tonight and you can all make yourselves sandwiches."

"Six minutes and forty seconds, six minutes and fifty seconds, seven minutes," Dad calmly counted down. "Well, what is your answer?"

Simultaneously, the answer came back, "Wendy's, KFC, Subway, McDonald's!" Just as Dad had anticipated, they couldn't agree on a plan. But this time, Dad had not only anticipated the problem, he had come up with a plan to respond to the problem. He simply said, "No problem. You guys are on your own for dinner tonight. We will try this again next week." And he jumped out of the car.

The next week, all four kids packed into the car to go to dinner. Again, Dad told them the seven-minute rule and listened as the kids tried to come up with a solution.

It was fascinating. This time, instead of arguing, they started negotiating. One of the middle kids said, "I'll go to Wendy's this week if we can go to KFC next week." That was quickly agreed to. Within five minutes, the kids had, on their own, developed a fair and equitable rotation of who would decide each week based on birthdays, birth order, and other creative factors. Soon the oldest said, "Dad, we don't need the whole seven minutes. We all agreed on Wendy's for tonight." Off they went with no complaining.

How easy was that? The problem solved itself creatively and the kids learned an important life skill. It all started with Dad anticipating a problem and using that insight to develop a strategy. He didn't know for sure he would need the plan because they might have agreed the first week. But he knew his kids and guessed that they wouldn't agree, and he was right. He likely heard some complaining when he got out of the car that first week, but it was a small price to pay for the privilege of watching the kids come up with their own solution while practicing a needed life skill.

Why Parents Get Angry

Besides being easier, having a plan decreases parental anger. It doesn't seem like it, but much of parental anger arises from not knowing what to do. Mom may think she is angry because chores didn't get done, or Dad may believe he's angry because his son broke curfew again, but most of the anger usually comes from not knowing what to do. The situation feels helpless. It feels tiring. It can feel hopeless, especially if we are trying to discipline while maintaining a close relationship.

This is a bigger problem than you might think. When parents don't have a plan, they try to get their kids to behave using logic, lectures, and love. None of these tactics work. Deep inside, parents know these approaches won't work. But what will work?

Tired parents don't have the energy to look up some creative consequence for everything their kids do wrong. They know something must be done, but what? What the parent wants to say to the child is, "Why couldn't you just do what you are supposed to do? Now I don't know what to do, and I don't have the energy to fight you or be creative. I'm so angry you put me in this position!"

Having a plan ready to go will make life easier and drastically reduce anger in the home. In many homes, there are regular outbursts of anger and fights about kids being on an electronic device late at night. In some homes, fights occur about this issue several nights a week. Having a plan stops the fights, the discussions, and the anger.

The plan could simply be to have Wi-Fi on a timer that shuts off at 10:05 p.m. In a few days, the family will accept this new reality and find a way to get things done by that time. Even a mediocre plan is better than no plan. Not all plans work, but you will find yourself getting better at devising a plan as you become less tired and more creative.

Of all the myriad problems facing parents today in our complex world, fatigue should not be one of the biggest, yet it is. Parenting is an important and fun job, and we can't do it when we are exhausted. We hope you can see some ways to become more efficient by understanding these principles.

The GIST of It

- One of the best things you can do when your child is thriving is to take it easy and enjoy what you see.

- Taking what your child has done personally on an emotional level will dramatically diminish your competence. Stay emotionally separate when you wear your parenting hat.

- Learn how to be patient, letting life play itself out. Many times the best thing for a parent to do is nothing.

- Take the opportunity regularly to spend as much one-on-one time with each of your children as you can. Those memories will last a lifetime.

- Many times parents keep doing things the same way with no positive results or change. If it's not working, try something else. This may be the most frustrating thing in parenthood. Mix it up, change the strategy, decide on a new plan, and then implement it.

8

JUST SHUT UP!

It's good to shut up sometimes.

MARCEL MARCEAU

A BOY IN HIS EARLY TEENS glared at his dad. Without saying a word, the boy spoke volumes in that moment. He wasn't searching for the right words to say; he knew what he wanted to say. He also knew better than to say it. Speaking with just his face and eyes, he said to his dad, "You are pathetic, I can't stand you, and please just *shut up.*"

"Just shut up!" may be the words most frequently circulating in kids' brains. They hear it in their heads all the time. They might blurt it out with every ounce of contempt they can muster, but usually they don't. It just remains a pounding thought in the silent recesses of their minds. Over and over again, they whisper it to themselves: *Would you just shut up?* They don't say it aloud because saying it could trigger another discussion that would produce twenty more thoughts of *Just shut up!* Hence, they remain mute.

Loving parents can talk too much. Conscientious parents can talk too much. Involved parents can talk too much. And absentee parents can talk too much. This is an equal opportunity error. Whether a child thinks *Just shut up!* or accidentally blurts it out, he is probably wiser than he knows.

Parents who talk too much often destroy their relationships with their children. It does no good to talk too much *at* your kids. In fact, it makes learning a lesson more difficult than it needs to be and creates shame.

This does not mean that you shouldn't talk to your kids! Talk to your kids all you want. Talk about anything *except* their mistakes—past, present, and future. When we talk about what they've done wrong, we are talking about their past mistakes. When we use warnings and reminders, we are talking to our kids about their future mistakes.

The Consequences of Talking Too Much

When a parent talks too much it is very difficult to keep what a child did wrong separate from who he or she is. Shame is the first consequence of a parent talking too much. Shame is the overcorrelation between what the child has done and who the child is. There is a big difference between parents identifying a fact and parents commenting about who the child is.

Coming home late is what the teenage boy did. A mess is the condition of his room. In a shame-based home, when he comes home late or his room is a mess, shame tells him he is irresponsible and a slob. Parents who talk too much tend to make this overcorrelation for their child. It is very difficult and takes great skill to be able to talk to your child for more than a minute or two about what he has done wrong without perpetuating shame. Soon the child learns to take on a shame-based existence on his own.

The Speeding Ticket

Picture yourself out driving some night very near your home. There is no traffic, the visibility is clear, and without really thinking about it, you begin to speed. A local police officer clocks you going twelve miles an hour over the speed limit and turns on those flashing lights. As you see the police car in your rearview mirror, you glance at your speedometer and see that you're over the speed limit.

At that moment, you know it's too late to slow down. You wonder for a brief moment if there is a way to reverse the past one or two minutes and slow down, but you realize that can't be done. You can't undo something you have already done. As the officer approaches, you roll down the window hoping you will just get a warning, but you know that's unlikely. As you hear the officer's steps approach, your more realistic plan is to get the ticket, get it fast, and get it over with. You can pay the eighty-five dollars and deal with the insurance ramifications later. You're glad it wasn't a serious problem. You just want to hear the damages and move on with your life.

The policeman comes up to the window and says, "I hope you're not in a hurry, because I think we need to sit here and have a good long talk about what you just did and who you've become. I expect some people around here to speed, but I really expected more from you. You live around here and you know there might be kids outside in the dark. You even have kids in this neighborhood. You know, I saw you go by two weeks ago about eight miles an hour over the limit and I let it go, hoping you would learn a lesson. But I was wrong about you. You are the type of person who needs a ticket to learn a lesson." On and on it goes. Then the officer adds, "While I've got you here, I've noticed your dog out in the street unleashed on occasion, and I've observed your garage getting more and more untidy ever since you got involved with that investment club you're in."

Slowly at first, then more rapidly, a rage starts building in you. There are little kids out at night in this neighborhood, but you weren't going to hit a kid—the visibility was perfect. And what did the officer mean when he said, "You are the type of person who needs a ticket"? *How does this police officer know what kind of person I am?* Soon you are thinking about all the burglaries and DUIs that have happened in your municipality in the past year that the officer should be concerning himself with. Your defenses kick in, resentment fills your mind, and the words form in your head, just the way they did when you were a kid: *Just shut up!*

What just happened in that interchange? Let's break it down. When you first saw the lights in your mirror, your first emotion was regret. You were sorry for the choice you had made, wishing and hoping that you might not get what you deserved and that the officer might have grace. That wish lasted only a few seconds. An acceptance and an "owning" of what you had done and a healthy willingness to pay the fee followed. Finally, you had a brief awareness that despite great visibility, a minor distraction could have resulted in a mistake with dire consequences, one much more costly than the expense of a ticket. This was the best possible outcome from a speeding incident: just a speeding ticket, healthy regret, and an adequate wake-up call about paying more attention while driving.

But you also got a long lecture that boiled your blood. This lecture changed the dynamic of the whole event. What if the officer had simply said, "Hello, did you know you were speeding? You may be a very careful driver, but at twelve over I just can't let it pass this time"? What if he or she handed you the ticket and said, "Have a good evening and please be careful on this road in the future"? There! It could have been done in twenty-five seconds with nothing more needing to be said.

The officer's "good long talk" pretty much guaranteed that the outcome was going to go in a different direction. Think about blame alone. At first, in the privacy of your own heart, you blamed yourself in a healthy way. By the time the officer was done talking, you had reversed that whole process—you were blaming the officer and defending yourself. Sound familiar? Just about every wonderful and healthy lesson from the speeding ticket dissolved as the officer kept talking. That officer did what many parents do—expanded the crime. Soon the topic rolled into dogs and garages. What do dogs and garages have to do with speeding?

Many parents think that talking is part of parenting. Without reflecting on the topic, they believe that if they aren't talking, they aren't parenting. Some parents don't even seem to realize they are talking excessively. They may be in the car, in the kitchen making dinner, or at the grocery store, and they just talk. Sometimes it's about mistakes, but it can also be nothing more than white noise filling the air with unnecessary words.

Envision this common scenario: While waiting in an optometrist's lobby, a mother comes in with her two children, about ages five and three. The kids behave well, except for reaching for a few low-hanging frames on a display. In thirty-five minutes, the mother never stops talking to her children. Ninety-nine percent of what she says is unnecessary and quite destructive. She continuously offers commentary about where they walk or sit, what they say or eat—and two dozen other topics. There are continuous threats, warnings, and even some encouragement from this well-intentioned mom. Yet most of what she says to her kids is a message of shame and inadequacy. Most likely, this mother is unaware of the negative impact of her excessive words.

In Garrison Keillor's classic book *Lake Wobegon Days*, he writes of Harold, a middle-aged man raised in Lake Wobegon who left town and returned home twenty years later, nailing his own personal ninety-five theses to the door of the Lutheran church. It was a brief manifesto written as a formal complaint against his childhood. It contained the ninety-five things he had learned growing up. He likely had a mother similar to the one in the optometrist's office. Harold concludes his document with this summary:

> My posture, facial expression (if any), tone of voice, gait, all were of constant critical interest as you strove to achieve a perfect balance in me.
>
> "Sit up. Don't slouch." Then, "Relax. You make me nervous just to look at you."
>
> "Why such a gloomy look?" Then, "Wipe that smirk off your face."
>
> "Pick up your feet." Then, "Can't you walk without sounding like a herd of elephants?"
>
> "Speak up. Don't mumble." "Keep your voice down."

Now you call me on the phone to ask, "Why
don't you ever call us?"[1]

Harold points out that when he does call his parents,
they are mostly disinterested in hearing about his life—they
are just hurt that he hasn't called. Harold concludes that he
doesn't need to call home anymore because every day he still
hears his parents' critical messages in his head. He even leaves
the radio on to block out their voices, but to no avail. He
assumes that he will hear their voices until the day he dies.

It would be hard to measure the actual percentage of parents who talk too much. For some parents, this is not really
an issue. We just know that it's quite common in both of our
professional practices to see parents who talk far too much
at their children when most of what they say is unnecessary,
repetitive, and destructive.

It's certainly a great thing to talk to your kids about their
dreams, accomplishments, friends, and imagination. But too
much talking about their behavior—including their mistakes
and failures—along with corrections and meaningless comments, serves no purpose except to inflict shame and resentment. You don't need to say something to your child that he
or she already knows, and you don't need to engage in meaningless banter or parent-talk with your child when you're
buckling him in a car seat or she's riding in a grocery cart. It
just hurts your relationship with your child.

One night, a twenty-eight-year-old professional woman
was sitting in a pub in Chicago with eight of her friends.
These highly educated and successful young adults were
well into their careers. Their conversation morphed into
how most of them still heard their parents' critical voices in

their heads, sometimes daily and even ten years after leaving home. This dynamic stemmed from parents who talked too much. The consensus was that most of their parents' excessive talking had to do with correcting. On this night, the most frequent comment echoing in their heads was *Have you done your homework?* It really doesn't matter what the echo was. An adult who has been out of the home for a decade should not still hear a parent's critical voice.

Parents should use a chart, a consequence, a nod of the head, a wink, a sticky note, or any other creative response— anything but incessant talking about chores, corrections, warnings, or failures. Say what you need to say, say it once, and move on. This will help reduce shame in your children.

The "What Have I Done Wrong?" Trap

Don't be fooled if your child says, "Mom, tell me what I have done wrong." Be warned: It could be a clever strategy on the part of your child. If your child wants to talk about why she was an hour late coming home or why she saw a movie different from the one agreed upon, she is most likely setting up her defense. If you talk, you're falling into the trap. When she asks, "What have I done wrong?" she really wants to find out:

- how much you know about what happened,

- if you have weakness in your position as a parent,

- if she can blame someone or something else, or

- if she can wear you down. Exhausting a parent is one of a child's greatest strategies. Amen?

Your daughter may want to talk about what happened to her missing assignments. But most likely, her goal is to argue that it's the teacher's fault, the teacher didn't explain the assignment well enough, or the assignment was done but then was lost. The poorest response to this situation is to get caught up in your child's excuses, blaming, or justifications. It would only be marginally better to tell the child to take responsibility for herself and that the situation is her fault. The best (and easiest) response would be to say, "That may be. The teacher might be at fault, but you need to get your assignments in. It really doesn't matter to me whose fault it is. Your assignments have to be turned in."

Very seldom does a child or teen ever want to talk about something he or she has done with genuine contrition or repentance as the goal. If it does happen, you are fortunate and it will likely be a short conversation. Most of the time kids know exactly what they have done wrong. Don't be fooled.

The GIST of It

- Parents need to change how they think about talking to their kids. Too much talking about behavior—whether good or bad—fosters shame.

- Talk to your child about their dreams, friends, and imagination.

- Parenting does not equal talking.

9

SELF-PROTECTION

The walls that we build for self-protection become
the walls of self-imprisonment later.

ATTRIBUTED TO HARRISH SAIRAMAN

JUSTIN, FOURTEEN, HAD BECOME progressively more irritable over the past six months, and his parents were concerned. His dad thought he might be going through "early hormonal change," and his mom wasn't sure. All they knew is that Justin and his friends were spending a lot of time on *League of Legends*.

Justin was obsessed with playing on his Xbox either with friends or alone. He would come home after school, immediately start playing the game, and continue playing until dinnertime, when it always was a big battle to get him to the kitchen table.

One evening Justin was told to stop playing the video game and he lost it. He threw the controller at his parents. "Just leave me alone! I never get to do anything I want!" he screamed at his parents in a rage. "All my friends can play as long as they want and you have all these rules. I hate this house!" Then he stormed off and slammed his bedroom door.

Little did his parents know that there was another fear driving Justin's anger. In this particular game, he knew other players would berate him if he shut off the video game. He had also purchased additional game weaponry three weeks previously on his mother's credit card without her knowledge. This terrified him. Justin's mom and dad thought they were seeing a new aspect to his personality when, in fact, Justin was scared and trying to protect himself through rage behavior. The next night Justin's parents did not tell him to stop playing. Instead, they just told him to go to bed when he was tired. They had become afraid of their son, and he had trained them to not interfere.

Parents' understanding of how their child uses self-protection will help them parent that child more effectively. Just as importantly, parents' understanding of their own use of self-protection and how it intersects with their child's strategy will make them better parents. Usually what we are protecting ourselves from is fear or shame. Shame is the sense of having lost value as a person because of mistakes, failures, or rejection.

We as parents may sense a loss of value as a person when certain things happen to us. We may receive a glare from an angry child, a mumbled profanity, or a poor "report card" from the child. Anything can trigger the belief that we have partially failed as a parent or as a person, which in turn feels like fear. Yet it's hard to differentiate between fear and shame because often shame feels like fear. For both children and adults, fear and shame are at the root of self-protection.

I (Michael) have learned about fear from looking at myself. Observing families, parents, and kids has taught me a lot, but I needed to observe no one but myself to understand the role fear plays in life. I can think back to mornings in my life when fear was one of my first emotions in the day. On those particular days, fear lay around me like morning dew, waiting for the sun or the wind to remove the damp.

On those days, my thoughts and my courage awakened more slowly than my fear. I wasn't always aware that some form of fear was present since I was prone to call it something other than fear. It sometimes showed up as feeling that I was way behind, or I was inadequate for the challenges of the day. Maybe I felt defensive. Or it sometimes appeared as just asking, *Why is it raining again?* I seldom even thought of the role fear played in my life because I didn't care to identify it. I would rather eradicate the feeling before stopping to take its pulse.

Whatever my specific thoughts or behaviors might have been on these days, they undoubtedly fit nicely into the categories of self-protection, busyness, or courage. Courage is the only solution that takes the time to stare at the problem long enough to face it. My experience with fear is not unique. In part, many of us create our own fears through the way we look at the world and the way we see things. If we see something as a threat, we feel fear. The fear could be from almost anything: Fear of the unknown, fear of rejection, and fear of failure are just a few, but truly there are thousands of fears that impact our lives.

Unfortunately, we often use self-protection and busyness to deal with the fears that we carry. When we do this, we don't take the time to look at the way we see the world or the thoughts that generated the fear in the first place. In effect, we try to eliminate fear's impact before we look at its composition.

When we don't notice the role fear is playing in our lives, we also don't notice when we are self-protecting from the fear. Our goal for dealing with the whole mess is to neatly keep it all in our subconscious. This dynamic is common in families and in adults and kids alike. People try to manage unexamined fears. This, in turn, drives thousands of unexamined behaviors. We see and describe ourselves, and others, by these behaviors.

"He's full of rage!" "She is withdrawn." "I am a perfectionist." "You blame everybody."

We can parent (and exist together) in healthier ways if we can learn to understand some of these behaviors in the light of what they are: self-protection strategies. These are simply tools we all use to manage a world that can feel too frightening at times. Self-protection drives many of the behaviors that kids engage in that are annoying and ineffective. When a child believes he or she has failed at something, that child senses a loss of value as a person and will usually initiate one or more of the six self-protection strategies.

How Self-Protection Looks

There are six major types of self-protection. There may be more, but just about every self-protection strategy fits nicely into one of these six categories. Most people use one or two primary strategies to protect themselves. Most often, these are skills learned in childhood that served their purpose well for a while. All of these strategies work, but each can be costly in our lives and in our relationships if they are overused.

Learning about self-protection will be as helpful for understanding yourself as it is for understanding your child.

First we'll talk about the six ways we, and our children, self-protect, and then we'll look at the cost of each strategy on our relationships. No strategy is worse or better to have—they are just different.

1. Withdrawal

Withdrawal is the first form of self-protection. It involves protecting the soul by just pulling back. It says, "I want to be alone, so don't bother me." People using this strategy decide that sharing their thoughts, emotions, or story is just too dangerous and risky. They keep everything inside and refuse to tell anyone what's going on. The easiest way for them to accomplish this is to escape and check out of everyone else's life.

Kids will use TV, video games, headphones, pot, or just about anything else to help them not be interpersonally present. A teen might spend excessive amounts of time in his room "wired in." No one is going to know what this teen is feeling or thinking. Wearing headphones helps that teen project the message, "Don't bother me!" Many who use this form of self-protection may not even be aware of it. It becomes their way of functioning.

Adults use this as well. A mom might watch a lot of TV or spend endless hours in the garden. She likely won't argue much or share her opinions with any regularity. A dad who uses withdrawal may work late or spend endless hours under the car, or in the garage, emotionally engaged with a Harley Davidson or his tool collection. Or he may be the dad who has four beers every night and sits with his remote glued to his index finger.

2. Rage

The second self-protection strategy is rage. Rage usually functions as a way of saying to another person, "Get away from me!" Even more accurately, it says, "Get away from my emotions!" Rage is a warning to others: "Don't bring up that topic again; don't do that behavior again; don't make me feel this way again." Or it may be saying, "I don't want to feel this fear right now." All of these are subconscious thoughts of rage.

Rage is different from anger, which is more of an inward emotion. Anger is a frequently mislabeled emotion. It usually connotes frustration. Rage (at least interpersonally) is meant to make someone get away or get back. Rage is essentially a maladaptive way for someone to handle anger.

Children (and adults) who use rage are trying to train those around them to act in a certain manner. Training is a major goal of rage. This is why there is so much rage in alcoholic homes. Family members are trying to train each other.

Let's imagine a parent who walks by a teen's phone lying on the table and sees that Instagram is open. Out of curiosity, the mom or dad looks at a couple of photos. The teenage son returns to the room and totally blows up. His rage is designed, in part, to train the parent to never look at his Instagram page again. If a teen uses rage after his parents have just searched his room, the rage is not anger that the room was searched. The teen's purpose is to warn the parents they better never ever do that again, otherwise he will "lose it." The teen is training his parents to stay out. This is usually carried out on a subconscious level of thinking.

In the same way, an older brother might go ballistic when his younger brother picks up the video game controller and starts to play. He yells and screams, throws things, and physically pushes his brother, all the while "training" his little brother to never interrupt one of his video games again.

Those on the receiving end of rage pull away from the person because interacting isn't safe. The impact on relationships can be significant, and entire family systems can end up "walking on eggshells" around the rage-prone family member, whether child or adult. When we see that rage has little to do with anger, we can clearly see that it is really a self-protective strategy to train people around us. In fact, looking at rage this way causes it to lose power and can even make it intriguing.

3. Blame

Blame is a form of self-protection that is probably the easiest to understand and describe. Blame simply means that the person self-protects by making whatever his problem is somebody else's fault. Children can be very creative in the excuses they fabricate. At times, this strategy could be downright funny if it weren't so heartbreaking.

A teen may say, "It isn't my fault that my assignment isn't done. Mr. Jones didn't explain it at all in class, and when I went to his room during study hall he wasn't there." Or maybe she'll say, "Those aren't my cigarettes. I'm just keeping them for a friend." Any adversity, problem, or mistake is always somebody else's fault.

Adults use this strategy as well. A dad may say, "I'm sorry I got mad, but when I saw all the mess in this room, I just lost it." The dad is not taking responsibility for getting mad because it's his kid's fault. A mom may say: "It's not my fault I'm late picking you up. I had to go to the grocery store first and the checkout person was pathetically slow." Or she may say: "Sorry I burned the lasagna. Grandma called right when I was about to take it out of the oven." All of this is so unnecessary. All a parent needs to say is: "I'm sorry. It's my fault."

Kids who are blamers need their parents to give them this message: "The world really doesn't care who's to blame." Many parents would recoil at the thought of saying such a thing to their child, but children need to know that in this world, blaming eventually is ignored.

4. Perfectionism

The fourth strategy of self-protection is doing it perfectly. This is particularly appealing to people who are already doing life 95 percent perfectly. Then the thought strikes them: *I am only 5 percent away from being perfect.* They might become immune from fault, criticism, or shame if they do everything perfectly. With a little extra effort, they feel they can handle that 5 percent and they will be safe. Working at being perfect helps them avoid the pain of life, feeling defective, having a lapse, or overlooking something. It protects them from criticism and avoids fault. They're always thinking of ways to do things more perfectly.

This might be the twelve-year-old girl who is stressed if she doesn't wear the "right" outfit or the skinny teenager who becomes horrified when she jumps on the scale and has gained four pounds. Students may act depressed if they get only a 93 percent on their English papers. Perfectionists want their Instagram pictures perfect, their hair perfect, and their car perfect. This may not manifest necessarily in being perfectly neat. They may want it perfectly messy, just as long as it is perfect to them. Because they tend to function at a high level, we see teen perfectionists far less often in therapy than the users of other strategies.

Kids who strive for perfection tend to be unaware of the law of diminishing returns. They can spend an inordinate amount of extra time on grades, sports, music, or dance to gain little in outcome. Perfectionists work themselves to the bone and burn both ends of the candle. They eventually run out of energy to keep the facade going.

A girl perfectionist wants others to like her. She becomes very troubled if anyone is angry with her or misunderstands her, even if it's someone who is insignificant in her life. Being perfect to her means, *Nobody dislikes me.*

5. Self-Contempt

Self-contempt is another strategy of self-protection. It might be the hardest to describe, but if you know someone who uses it, you will recognize this strategy quickly. The goal of self-contempt is to lower your own expectations every time you are about to fail. The message to those around is, "Don't expect much from me." It essentially is a way to deal with anticipated or impending failure.

Imagine a tenth grader who is asked in August what level of grades she would like to get for the upcoming school year. She answers, "I would like to make the B honor roll." By October, she is asked again about her grades and this time she answers, "I would like to get Cs." When asked again in early December, her answer is, "I just want to pass." This teen lowered her expectations month by month to avoid facing the pain of failure. Lowering expectations is the hallmark trait of this strategy. It's not typically an issue of incapability; it's an issue of anticipated failure. Past failures have taken a toll on those who have self-contempt, and failure becomes a self-fulfilling reality of their daily experience.

"I just won't get a driver's license," or "I won't drive to the mall anymore because last time I got lost" is how this might sound from a teen. Younger kids might stop skateboarding after a bad fall or quit a sport after not making the "A" team. A child with self-contempt may prefer transferring to the lowest math class rather than working hard on her homework. These children self-protect by expecting less of themselves and take on the mantra of "Why should I even try?"

Parents may unknowingly collaborate with this agenda. They may start backing off on expectations they have for their son when they see he is obviously demoralized and drowning in the responsibilities before him. This is a misguided effort to try to keep a child feeling good about himself. By doing this, a parent cosigns with this lowering of expectations for their child. A mom or dad will become hesitant or frightened to hold their child to nearly any expectation if they see he is barely coping with the stress of life. There is an understandable and natural instinct in this perception.

One solid strategy that can be used effectively to help an overwhelmed child is to lower expectations to a reasonable level. However, lowering expectations to zero will not help at all. Stressed and overwhelmed kids need the tasks facing them to be pared down at times to increase hope when they feel too dejected. The difficulty here is that a child starts feeling another form of hopelessness when he has no achievements to count as his own. Parents are called upon at times to lighten a load for a child, but overlightening the load will contribute to self-contempt in the child and won't provide the safety or self-love you hoped to achieve.

As a parent, lowering your expectations for yourself will

usually not lead you to a better place with your child, though the desire for a break can be completely understandable. One of the unique traits of parenting is that you can't quit. We have heard frustrated and depleted parents exclaim, "I quit!" Sometimes this is followed by a slight grin as they realize (short of a court hearing) that this is a job where quitting isn't an option. We've seen exasperated parents who can't go on anymore simply decide to take some time off and just let their teenager run wild for a week or two. This usually doesn't produce anything positive for the parent or the child—or give them a break either.

6. Using Power to Protect

Striving for power can look like rage, but it's very different. Remember the goal of rage is to communicate, "Get away from me" or "Don't ever do that again." The goal of striving for power is twofold—to make sure the other person doesn't get too close, but also not too far away. It's a combination of a coexistent force field and magnet between two parties. Striving for power has a unique energy. The one who strives for power sends constant reminders to the other person of who really has the power. The message is, "You can't confront me because you need me."

Here is an absurd example of this. Imagine that the owner of a company arrives thirty minutes late for an important meeting, sits down, and makes the following statement: "I know I'm late to the meeting, and I welcome anyone who wants to confront me on that, but first I would like to remind you who signs your paycheck."

In our professions, we see this in families where there is emotional abuse. There might be a statement like this: "You can file for divorce if you want, but I will get the best attorney in the county, I'll make sure everyone knows about your drinking, and you'll never see your children again." You can see how this statement conveys, "You cannot get close to me and you also can't get away."

Not every example of power is this obvious. It can just be the control someone has over another. Imagine a home with a single-parent mom whose job involves working some late evenings. Suppose this mom has three children, ages eleven, fourteen, and seventeen. The mom depends on her seventeen-year-old son to drive his siblings places when she has to work late. The son violates some family rule or acts out in some way. With an arrogant smirk, he looks at his mom and says, "So, why don't you take my car away?" He knows very well that she can't do that because he's a taxi driver for the younger kids and she needs him.

The Price of Overusing Self-Protection

Each of these self-protection strategies has its own consequence. Unfortunately, our strategies do more than help us avoid pain. When the strategies are overused, they come with a price for the self-protecting people and those around them. Whether medically or emotionally, there is always a price to pay for avoiding pain. Whether we self-protect by using oxycodone, playing endless hours of video games, or not looking for work, there is always a cost.

1. Withdrawal

People who overuse this strategy will most likely be lonely. They may or may not be aware of it. Those who have used withdrawal since they were young are not aware they are lonely. Those around them will recognize this because there will be a lack of closeness in their relationships. Withdrawing to self-protect usually starts for kids between ages eleven and fourteen, but people can adopt this strategy all through life. Men and women in a bad marriage or a bad job will keep their thoughts and feelings to themselves. When it is not safe to talk, some people just stay quiet. When it is not safe to stay in a room, some people just leave the room. This is sad to see, but it's not complicated. Whether teen or adult, the person always leans toward isolation rather than community.

2. Rage

Children who use rage will become secluded. People around them learn quickly that it's not pleasant to be in their presence and will pull away because the relationships are too unsafe and difficult. It's sad that many children who use rage will find themselves without a mentor even in a parent. When a kid uses rage all the time, the parent essentially stays away. This becomes a problem when that child *does* want a parent involved, but is then left to face life on his or her own.

3. Blame

People overusing blame just never seem to grow up. A seventy-year-old blamer has never grown up. We all grow from our mistakes, but only from the mistakes that we don't blame on others. Think about it this way: If a person blames two thousand of his or her mistakes on someone else, two thousand growth-producing possibilities have been missed. Ultimately, passing up that many opportunities to grow will slow or stop anyone from maturing. A child who is a blamer will gradually fall behind his or her peers.

4. Perfection

Not being known by others and exhaustion are two costs to those who use perfection as a self-protection strategy. It's not easy trying to do everything right. Since no one can do everything right, the perfectionist will invariably be tired. Also, he or she will have to hide those things not perfectly done, coming across to others as shallow or elusive. Eventually, other people will feel as if they don't really know him or her.

5. Self-Contempt

Kids who use self-contempt to self-protect will experience a lowering of self-esteem. Children using this strategy have a lower self-esteem today than they had two years previously. Every time they lower what they expect from themselves, they lose respect for themselves. Even though they fail less, their self-expectations are diminished. It becomes impossible for them to like or respect themselves.

6. Power

Lack of intimacy in relationships is the cost to those overusing power to protect. They may have lots of acquaintances but few close and meaningful friends. If you're in relationship with someone like this, you will probably feel consistent "come close" and "get away" messages.

Give It a Rest

Here's an important tenet for parents to be aware of with self-protection: When a child is actively engaged in his or her mode of self-protection, all attempts to discipline, talk, and negotiate should be postponed. Kids in high arousal states do not learn or reason or receive guidance well. If your child is in the middle of a rage, do not try to reason with him. It won't work. If your daughter has withdrawn to her room, don't try to force yourself into her life to "talk about things." It won't work. If your son is going on about what a loser he is, don't try to convince him otherwise until he is out of that state of mind. It just won't work.

Here's a fascinating thought on self-protection. Think about how your child's primary mode(s) of self-protection intersects and interacts with your primary mode of self-protection. Imagine a mom or dad who has brought yelling and screaming into the family system. Put that together with their child who uses self-contempt. You have a problem. The raging parent will contribute greatly to the lowered self-esteem of his child, many times without even realizing it. Put a power-striving child in a home with a withdrawing parent, and see who runs the roost. The parent will feel steamrolled every day and live in fear of that child.

Everyone uses one or more of these strategies to avoid the pain that comes with life. Life is tough, and we need to have some protection from difficult times. All six of these can be used without too many consequences or problems as long as they are rarely used. But overusing any one of the self-protection strategies without being aware of the price can lead to interpersonal consequences. Those who occasionally use all six strategies at different times have an easier time growing up than someone who overuses one or two.

The GIST of It

- Remembering that fear drives behavior and emotion helps us understand each other.

- In our relationships, some of what we call misbehavior or personality is really a form of self-protection.

- There are innumerable ways to self-protect, but most of these fit nicely into one of six categories.

- While these six strategies work to protect, each has a predictable and undesirable cost that makes it an ineffective strategy for life.

- The self-protective strategies of family members will interact in unique ways with the differing strategies of other family members.

10

BECAUSE IT WORKS

Cause and effect are two sides of one fact.

RALPH WALDO EMERSON

ADULTS AND KIDS ALIKE do what they do, to an astonishing degree, because it works.

Here's an example from the adult world: A tenured university professor was giving a lecture in a large lecture hall. Over his decades of teaching, he had developed a habit of pacing left and right on the stage during his talk. Back and forth he would walk during his explanation of the material, stopping briefly at the podium to check his lecture notes.

One day, the professor was called out of the lecture hall to take an important phone call. While he was gone, a clever (or mischievous) student stood up to address the class. The student suggested a plan. The proposal was that when the professor returned, the class should subtly act interested and engaged whenever the professor walked to the right side of the stage, and should subtly act bored and tired when the professor walked to the left side of the stage. No particular reason—just to see what might happen.

The students did this well enough that the professor didn't pick up on the prank. Within five lectures, though, and without his conscious awareness, the professor was giving his entire talk from the right side of the stage. Why? Because it worked. See, adults and kids alike do what they do, to an astonishing degree, because it works.

Here's an example from the world of children: Aleah was becoming a real problem. At the age of four, her parents had been called again to take her out of daycare. This was the third daycare in the last year. Aleah had always been precocious and could talk circles around most adults in her life. She loved being the boss and controlling what her peers played and who got to play. She loved to control the adults in her life too.

When she didn't get her way, she would whine and protest until those around her gave in. She didn't have any friends because being around her was so hard. Aleah had become skilled at not letting other children get legitimate attention. She did this by whining and throwing tantrums anytime she wanted adults to focus on her.

She had become a monster of sorts, created to whine and cry to get her way. Her parents wondered if Aleah was a psychopath or had some undiagnosed psychiatric disorder. They also wondered how they would ever help her become easy to be around.

In most situations, the reason why a child repeatedly misbehaves is . . . *because it works.* It's as simple as that. Pouting works, whining works, forgetting works, anger works, hitting works, and arguing works. If some of these things worked for us when we were growing up, it's not surprising they continue to work for our own kids. It doesn't matter if your child is two or twenty-two. Most problem behaviors happen because they work or have worked for years.

Why does two-year-old Joshua whine so much? The answer is because whining works in Joshua's family and life. When a five-year-old "picky eater" says she hates pork chops and broccoli, she usually gets macaroni and cheese. It works for her. A ten-year-old gamer who throws and breaks things when told to stop the video game doesn't get told to stop anymore. Throwing and breaking things works for him.

It is the same for older kids. Why does a twenty-year-old young woman argue so much? The most likely answer is because arguing works in her life and in the family. Teens learn that if they wear earbuds in the car, Mom won't ask if they finished a science project. They learn if they sleep in on Saturday, they might not have to clean the garage. Sometimes they have learned that if they make a big mess making a sandwich, Mom will make the sandwich for them. Many seventeen-year-olds have learned this well. Arguing can work, being quiet can work, flattery can work, and—one of the most prevalent—staying up until 3:30 a.m. can work. If you live in the Midwest and your teen is living on Hawaii time, you can be sure that this arrangement won't work for you. But it can work for teens. Sleeping in works to get them out of doing housework, give them more Internet time, or help them avoid relationships in the house. They might even sleep in just so they can wear an outfit that Mom and Dad find objectionable.

It makes sense that one of the first strategies of efficient parenting is to make sure that poor choices stop paying off. Sometimes the payoff is easy to spot. A toddler girl asks for orange juice or a snack by whining. You feel exhausted from her whining, so you pour her a glass of juice or get her crackers. She has once again been reinforced to whine. Even though you know what's happening, you do it anyway—just to stop the whining. Her payoff is getting what she wants by whining.

Other times the payoff is harder to spot. A ten-year-old boy swears at his mom and pulls his little sister's hair. Mom tries to make him apologize to his sister and the boy refuses. Mom yells at the boy and sends him to his room without supper. The boy goes to his room crying and yelling "I hate you" at his mother all the way up the stairs. The mom might wonder what her son's payoff was for this encounter. Surely there wasn't any, right? The boy is in his room crying with no dinner. The problem stems from the fact that what looks like a disheartening situation to an adult is really a payoff for the child.

Actually, the payoffs are significant in this story if you know where to look, and there are two likely payoffs in this situation.

First, it is common for ten-year-old boys to feel powerless in their world. They may have no power with their peers, none in the family, and none in the classroom. Even the dog won't obey them. Yet what an amazing sense of power this boy would have if he could get his college-educated, forty-year-old mother to cry, yell, or throw something! That scenario would be proof positive he has considerable power in his world, a world that is significantly short on power.

Second, this boy probably finds great comfort in a story that he tells himself. He has carried this story with him for years. It comforts him when he is down and relieves him of responsibility when he is overwhelmed. The story he creates might have something to do with a little sister his parents have always liked better. He is less liked, less noticed, and less tolerated. His sister is the chosen one. He is the black sheep. He orchestrated the whole "yelling" event to secure his ability to retell his story. Kids (and adults) find great comfort in having a familiar story about their lives. In fact, many people of all ages will choose something familiar over something better if the option presents itself.

This may seem counterintuitive, but much of parenting is counterintuitive. As adults, what we would view as a consequence or bad outcome could actually be a payoff for a child. Negative attention, a power trip, a familiar story, and revenge are just a few of the things that kids can have as their payoff. Some kids just are wired to retaliate if they feel they're wronged. The kid thinks, *You hurt me, now I'm going to hurt you.* It's that simple. This is one reason why parental anger is so unproductive.

Understanding the payoff isn't the most important thing. Most of us aren't smart enough to figure that out. If we tried, we might even be guilty of overdiagnosing our child. No, determining the payoff isn't what's important. What's critical is making sure the cost of behaving badly is expensive enough to get the child's attention. Parents can do this without ever understanding the nuances of the payoff.

Let's go back to the story of the ten-year-old boy who

pulled his sister's hair and screamed at his mother. What thing or things could be used to make his misbehavior too costly to continue? One needs to ask, *What is my child really into?* For some kids, missing dinner and going to bed works. If your kid is like this, you're probably not reading this book. The list could include privileges like TV, outside playtime, video games, bike riding, a cell phone, having friends over, Legos, or swimming at the health club. Simply taking away one or more of these for a day or two, combined with not rewarding the behavior, almost guarantees that whatever this boy's payoff is for hair pulling, it wouldn't be worth doing again. Most kids change after two or three interventions for a particular behavior.

Unfortunately, many parents focus too much on trying to understand why their child is doing a certain behavior. That's a waste of time and energy for all and will be of no help in parenting. The behavior you don't want to see again needs to receive quick and calm consequences with no negotiation. When this is implemented correctly, your child learns that your *yes means yes* and your *no means no*. Emotions are out of the picture: no arguing and no drawn-out negotiations, just a follow-through.

If part of the payoff for your child is power or revenge, much of that will be mitigated by simply not reacting to the child's behavior. Revenge isn't much fun for a kid if the parent doesn't react. Striving for power feels hollow if Mom and Dad are unaffected by the behavior.

We believe it's most important to calm down and recognize that your child is simply implementing a familiar strategy that has worked for years. Greater clarification than that is usually unnecessary. You wouldn't be mad at your dog for sleeping on the couch if the dog doesn't know it's wrong. The couch is a great place to sleep on a cold winter night, especially if sleeping there has always worked in the past. Similarly, we shouldn't get angry with our kids for doing what works. Why would you be angry with your daughter who comes downstairs an hour after bedtime saying she is scared if this strategy has worked her whole life?

The Invisible Game

Bedtime is a nightmare in many homes for this very reason. Kids are geniuses at figuring out how to get a little extra time, attention, food, or mischief out of the last sixty minutes of their day. Parents who are unaware of this strategy are no match for a creative kid who has nothing better to do than to try to get some needs and wants met after "lights out." Some kids are difficult and some kids are easy. Most of the time, a strategy called "the invisible game" will work beautifully to eliminate a child's pattern of excessive bedtime stalling. This is not something that you would use his or her entire childhood.

Obviously, you will want to start by extinguishing the overt and covert payoffs for your child not going to bed. That is simple enough. The difficulty is in understanding payoffs. Some things are obvious payoffs like a drink of water, or a snack, or one more kiss or snuggle. One of the most overlooked rewards for children is eye contact. When you look at your child you are, in a sense, providing a reward. Kids are motivated by fun, power, revenge, and attention, but they are also motivated by engagement. When parents make eye contact with their child, they engage their child. This is part of your child's plan. Eye contact is the earliest point of contact in human interaction. Usually the no-eye-contact strategy is very difficult to use. This is because no eye contact is so unnatural and counter to the parenting voices that echo throughout our culture.

The invisible game is a great way to defuse the because-it-works strategies your child may have mastered. This bedtime strategy involves the house functioning exactly as if the child had gone to bed, or as if the child were invisible. Half an hour before the child's bedtime, the parents need to dim the lights in the house as though the household is winding down for the night. Parents need to go through the normal pre-bedtime rituals of brushing teeth, reading a book, tucking under the covers, and giving a kiss on the forehead.

From this moment on, the child is invisible. The child who calls out for parents should be ignored. The little girl who comes out of her bedroom should not be seen or looked at. The parents should check their emails, go through some mail, read a magazine or book, and straighten up in the kitchen—all without looking at the child or responding to any question or activity by the child. Don't answer a question, and don't be a parent anymore, asking questions such as "Have you brushed your teeth?"

In some situations, the parents can watch TV, but in other cases this creates added complications. If the dad is using the "invisible game" strategy and is watching the third quarter of a *Monday Night Football* game, watching the game might be a reward for the little guy. If this is the case, Dad should simply and quietly turn off the TV without a word. If the child has no interest in football, the plan might work perfectly. It's important that all this be done with no emotion, no approval or disapproval being conveyed. It would be acceptable for a parent to say with no eye contact, "I can't talk to you now . . . you're not supposed to be up."

Here are a couple of tips to increase the likelihood of a good outcome. Quietly disable any foreseeable problem. Take the cords for the video games, turn off the Wi-Fi, or use any other simple and quiet way to disrupt the child's stalling routine. Then don't talk about it. No threats, reminders, or warnings. With some older kids, it can even work to flip the circuit breaker for your child's bedroom. Almost all the time this simple and silent plan will solve the epidemic problem of bedtime. If you lost this round today, don't worry. Just regroup with the added wisdom and try again tomorrow. That would be better than falling into a power struggle or implementing a plan that is half developed.

Where's the Moral Compass?

Kids function differently from how most parents might assume. There often is not as big a moral component to their decisions or behaviors as we might think. They simply lie if lying has worked for them in the past. Can we really blame them for that? They don't pick up their coats if dropping their coats on the floor has worked for them in the past.

It's easy for parents to partially misperceive certain "unethical" or "dishonest" behaviors in kids. Things like lying, cheating at school, shoplifting, stealing, and other behaviors of that ilk can be misinterpreted if we see them through adult eyes instead of a child's eyes. All of these behaviors are troubling, and they are all semiserious. However, they are not catastrophic and do not mean a child is totally void of a "moral compass." Parents do not need to feel devastated or hopeless because their child dabbled in an immoral choice.

An adult who did the same things would have made a decision on some level to trade integrity for these types of corrupt behaviors. For a kid, it's not so much an integrity issue as it is a way of trying out the breaking of a moral code of ethics. It's more likely a reflection of peer pressure, feeling trapped, taking a short cut, trying out a wrong behavior, or, again, doing something *because it works.*

All of these wrong behaviors are serious enough to be dealt with, and dealt with in a strong and decisive way. Kids need to know rapidly that cheating won't pay off. But there is no need to overreact or to emotionally panic. Your child is not sliding down a slippery slope into an abyss that is void of a moral compass. He or she is just growing up.

A frequent question from parents in the counseling setting is, "How long do I take something away?" Well, it depends on the child's age, developmental stage, degree of negative behavior, and natural receptivity to being disciplined. Whatever decision the parent makes, however, should not be negotiated or discussed. It is what it is. Remember, the sooner you give back the Xbox, the sooner you can take it away again. Sometimes not disclosing the time frame for a lost privilege is a good strategy. That tends to work well with the "negotiator child." Sometimes it works to tell these types of kids that if they try to argue or negotiate, the time will double. Whatever your decision, stick to it. If a parent is confused about what and how long to take something away, they should err on the side of *severity* and *brevity.* Do not back down, no matter how obnoxious the tantrum. Do not get hooked into an argument. Be calm and assertive.

Often children have legitimate needs they try to meet with maladaptive strategies. Children need to hear their parents tell them that they are loved. This is normal and healthy. It would be appropriate for a child to say, "Mommy, do you love me?" That would be a healthy way to address that need for reassurance. A maladaptive approach to getting this need met is for the child to say, "You hate me, don't you? Why don't you just admit it?" Most kids don't think about what is unsuitable or dysfunctional for a given situation. They subconsciously simply keep track of what works. If saying, "You hate me, don't you?" works to get an "I love you," or works to get a cookie, or works to get attention or a shortened time-out, a child will undoubtedly use that strategy over and over.

Sammy's Story

An eight-year-old girl named Sammy wore out her mother by repeatedly saying, "You hate me; I know you hate me," every time she was ordered to her room for a time-out. Mom, on cue, recited back, "No, I love you very much." Sammy would respond, "No, you don't—you're just saying that." This resulted in further reassurances, arguing, and attention. The strategy worked perfectly for Sammy. Reassurances and attention were what she wanted in the first place. Her maladaptive strategy was working flawlessly.

Sammy's mom asked for help with this issue. She was told that the next time Sammy implemented this approach, she was to say, "I am not talking to you right now about whether I love you or whether I don't. Right now, you need to go to your room. If you're still wondering about my love for you on Saturday, ask me then and I will gladly talk to you about it." Within five days, all of the "you hate me" comments had ceased. Sammy chose not to talk about her mom's love on Saturday when the topic came up. Mom was blown away with how simple the solution was to a problem that had been going on for four years. Plain and simple, Sammy's maladaptive strategy for her legitimate need had stopped working. She stopped using it in just five days.

This may sound like an insignificant and trivial issue. You may ask, "Why not just reassure Sammy of Mom's love each time Sammy feels the need for that?" Actually, there are many reasons not to affirm this strategy, not the least of which is exhaustion. Sammy's mother was exhausted by this whole routine. In addition to fatigue, there were other issues—like Sammy's manipulation of her mom. Sammy was "pulling her mom's strings" and stealing control of the situation. When kids learn maladaptive strategies as children, they can carry that approach with them right into adulthood. Fast-forward seventeen years and you can almost hear Sammy talking to her husband, who has just conveyed to her that he needs to go into work for part of a Saturday. Sammy: "I know why you work on Saturdays—you don't love me—it's obvious." We can expect that Sammy would use that approach even as an adult—because it works.

The extent to which kids use what works is amazing. A deaf couple had two normal-hearing children, ages eighteen months and three-and-a-half years old. There were many unique challenges facing this family. Because of the safety concerns in a family with two deaf adults and two small children, the social services office was contacted and a social worker would occasionally stop by to make sure everything was going smoothly.

Whenever a social worker stopped by the house, she would walk into complete silence. Crying, whining, and fussing were not effective for these children to get their parents' attention. The three-and-a-half-year-old could talk perfectly, and both children could hear and function as normal children away from home or when visitors were at the house. Both children simply pounded on a table or high chair to get their parents' attention. They had learned that crying or whining didn't work in this house, but that their parents could feel the vibration of the pounding and would look up to meet the children's needs. This is a powerful example of just how adaptive kids are, and it captures the extent to which kids will simply use what works.

The GIST of It

- Most of the continued misbehavior we see in kids is carried out simply *because it works*.

- We can't really blame kids for doing what works. It's natural and instinctual. Whining, hitting, stealing, getting out of bed, lying, and jumping on the couch can all usually be traced back to that behavior working. It's usually not driven by a moral violation or bad intent.

- Making good choices pay off and bad choices costly is the simplest way to try to alter a child's behavior.

- Adults also often use what works. So be understanding and gracious when you address troubling behaviors in your children.

11

CASE STUDY: JENNA

JENNA WAS A VERY DIFFICULT YOUNG LADY. At fifteen years of age, she was filled with rage and shame. Her life had been tough, so it was not surprising that she was angry.

Her parents were divorced and she lived with her mother and stepfather. Because she had moved several times in her life, Jenna struggled with having consistent friends. Her family's financial situation made it hard for her to participate in sports or extracurricular activities, so she felt empty. Like many young women her age, Jenna didn't have a positive body image.

Jenna liked to act tough and talk back, she liked angry music, and she liked her privacy. She showed her anger in violent, destructive ways like slamming doors, stomping, and punching walls. Jenna was very good at "hooking" her mom into long and drawn-out arguments, which did not end well. This gave Jenna a sense of control and power, but she had fallen behind in knowing how to disagree in mature and age-appropriate ways.

It was clear to her parents that she needed to work on managing her temper. It wasn't that she didn't have the right to be angry. Anyone with her history had a right to be angry. But she really needed to figure out how to express her anger in more acceptable ways.

With our coaching, her parents decided they would take a different approach. On a Friday they had a brief talk with Jenna and told her they were going to start focusing on a couple of things starting Monday morning. One of those things was her anger, which often turned into destructive outbursts. Starting Monday, punching walls, kicking chairs, slamming doors, stomping her feet, and slamming books down on the coffee table were all behaviors that were going to cost her something. Calmly and lovingly, her parents told her that they were not angry with her. They said they understood it might take her some time to change her patterns of reacting to things that made her angry.

As expected, Jenna wanted to get angry right away. No kid likes the rules changed in the middle of the game. She asked, "What is going to happen if I break something?" Her parents responded that they weren't sure; it would depend on the offense, but she was assured that it wouldn't be too bad. Her parents concluded: "It's just teaching. It isn't something designed to hurt you."

Right on cue, on Monday night Jenna was told that she needed to get off the phone and go to bed since it was a school night. Jenna was a child who wanted what she wanted, and what she wanted that night was to finish her phone call. Predictably, Jenna blew up, swore at her parents, stomped upstairs, and then crossed the line. She walked in her room, punched the walls a few times, and violently slammed the door.

Jenna waited and listened. Was anything going to happen, or had her parents forgotten about the new focus? Nothing happened. Nothing was said. Jenna wasn't surprised. She had slammed her door a hundred times before and nothing had ever happened. So she just figured everything was back to normal—just the way she liked it.

The next morning nothing was said as Jenna got ready for another day in ninth grade. But while she was at school, her stepfather came home from work at noon and took her bedroom door off its hinges; he moved the door downstairs, behind the furnace. To avoid a power struggle, it's important for parents to implement a "cost" without their child present whenever possible. Nothing was said about it.

At 3:10 p.m., Jenna came home from school in a surprisingly good mood. She greeted her mom and headed up to her room as she always did. Thirty seconds later, there was a violent explosion as Jenna realized that her door was missing. She started stomping around, yelling down the stairs to her mother that she was an idiot and demanding her door back.

Mom, uncharacteristically, said nothing and simply did not respond. Jenna came down the stairs and demanded: "Where is my door? I want it back right now!"

Mom said nothing.

"What did I do? This family stinks. You said the consequence wouldn't be too bad."

Mom said nothing.

"Fine, I will just wreck the house then. You think you can just take my door and not pay for it?"

Mom said nothing.

"Why won't you talk to me?"

Her mom said, "I will talk to you, but I won't answer your question."

"This is crazy! My friends think you and Dad are psycho."

"I am going to make one comment about your door and one comment only," her mom said.

"What? I suppose this has to do with slamming my door last night?"

"Jenna, I am not mad at you and you will get your door back on Thursday. That is all I am going to say about it."

"Fine, then I will just destroy the whole house!"

"That is your choice." And her mom turned and walked away.

In the next forty-eight hours, Jenna brought up the topic of the door several times and also threatened to make her parents pay for what they had done. Each time, her mom and stepdad just said nothing. Thursday afternoon at 3:10 p.m., Jenna got off the bus and went up to her room where her door was hanging, as it always had, on the doorframe.

This family had almost no issues with Jenna damaging the house after that day. After years of fighting her on this issue, it was over in six days.

About two weeks after Jenna got her door back she accidentally, more out of habit than anything, mildly slammed her door. She immediately opened the door and yelled down the stairs, "Sorry, sorry, sorry . . . I didn't mean to do that!"

There were no consequences added. She had learned this lesson.

The GIST of It

- Scripting a short talk with your child who is behaving in maladaptive ways is a useful way to start a new reality for him or her. The plan needs to focus on one or two specific behaviors.

- It's important to let your child know you are not angry and want to see him or her grow up in these specific ways. Be patient; it may take a while for your child to learn a new behavior.

- It's sometimes advantageous to keep a consequence a secret (like removing the bedroom door for a few days).

- Once the plan is employed, it's important to say nothing and not engage in argument or negotiations. Just keep quiet.

12

THE TWO THINGS

Order and simplification are the first steps
toward mastery of a subject.

THOMAS MANN

SOME WOULD SAY Maggie was a pretty typical teenager. She was the kind of kid who didn't really excel at much, earned average grades, and had a few good friends. Her mother described her as "lazy" and unmotivated.

Her brother, on the other hand, excelled at all the things parents love to see in their child. Schoolwork, responsibility, and self-sufficiency all came easily for Jared. At the age of sixteen, Maggie's room was always a mess, she didn't help around the house with any chores, and she had to be awakened every morning for school. She slept through her alarm nearly an hour after Jared was already up and ready. She usually missed the bus for school, so her angry and disgruntled mom ended up driving her. Once again, Maggie was a failure.

When asked about what Maggie needed to learn to do at her age, Maggie's mom recited a long list of things she felt were important. Maggie's mom stated she had been frantically working on as many of these as possible because "Maggie isn't going to be ready for college someday."

Yet the more her mom pushed for her to learn these skills, the less motivated Maggie became. Maggie just didn't seem to care about growing up, but the truth was, there were too many things on her mom's list. The mom couldn't readily think of anything Jared needed to work on, but she missed the fact that Jared was falling behind socially and frequently worried about things that he didn't need to worry about.

As different as Maggie and Jared were, they had one thing in common: They both had two things they most needed to work on next.

Do you ever think of all the things your children need to learn about life, about themselves, and about others? Have you wondered why they never seem to learn anything?

You've been good at letting them know all the things they should be doing right or better. "Get good grades. Clean your room. Pick up your coat. Stop playing that video game. Hold your fork right. Have you done your homework? Don't talk like that. Don't wear that outfit. Did you send a thank-you note? Stop eating so much junk food. Get off the phone. Help out a little around the house. Eat some salad. Clean up the stuff you left in the family room—now!"

This could be the soundtrack inside the head of even the best kid. It might sound like this to them, even if nothing is being said in the house. If you are thinking these types of things, your kids will know. Biting your tongue won't help. Leaving the room won't help. Watching TV won't help. They just always seem to know what you're thinking.

If you see thirty different things a week that your daughter could do to improve her life or to grow up, she will know it. For a "bad" or troubled kid this can actually become overwhelming. Now add these messages onto the messages that may already be in her head about shoplifting, bad friends, lost faith, secrets, drugs, and truancy. Understandably, the burden of all the areas in her life she needs to improve can crush her spirit.

The problem is that parents panic when their child gets behind. A fifteen-year-old boy should not have to be told, "Do your homework." This is the conundrum a parent can feel: *My child is already behind where he should be. I don't want to nag, but how on earth am I going to get him caught up to where he should be if I don't get on him about things?*

This becomes a vicious cycle for many parents and their children. Time goes on. Every month that goes by with no growth means your daughter is falling further behind where she needs to be at her age. As a parent, you know she's falling behind. Knowing that she needs to grow even faster in order to catch up adds pressure to your days. Combine that with your awareness that she isn't going to grow very much by hanging out with the kids she is currently friends with. It's love and concern that motivates this tension. If your child is like this, you feel the stress.

What's Next?

What can parents do when they realize that a child has fallen behind in his or her growth? They should do the exact same thing they would do if their child hadn't fallen behind. At least that part is simple. We believe in a concept that forces parents to identify the *two things* their child or teen most needs to learn next. Every kid always has two things he or she most needs to learn next. It doesn't matter if the child is a four-year-old daughter or a seventeen-year-old son. It doesn't matter if this kid is heading to Harvard or to juvenile detention. Parents need to ask the same question about each child as he or she grows up—from toddlers to high-school seniors and beyond: "What are two things my child most needs to learn at this time in his life?"

It's pretty easy since most parents can put a list together of twenty or thirty specific things they think their child most needs to learn. They want their kids to:

- turn in assignments on time
- do a good job vacuuming
- go to bed without whining
- stop talking back
- come home on time
- cut back on video games
- stay home two nights a week

And the list goes on. What can be difficult for many parents is to decide on which next two things their child needs to learn—and then to remain focused on only those two things until they are resolved.

Sometimes the list is more countercultural, which would be the case with Jared. A brother and sister may have opposite goals. One child may need to learn to:

- be more social
- study less
- lighten up
- be less responsible
- dress like a slob now and then

These messages would be given less frequently, but for the right kid, these unusual messages could be just as powerful and important as those on the first list. Just know it's a universal truth that every child has two things they most need to work on next.

A mom who raised her hand in a parenting workshop said: "I can't think of two things my daughter needs to work on. She is an honor student, a leader in her school, an award-winning violinist, a great sister, and a leader in her church's youth group. She is also an outstanding athlete." As she continued with this impressive resume, she paused. It was a long pause as something occurred to her. She continued softly, "My daughter has never learned to fail at anything."

That's exactly the point. This daughter may need to experience what it is like to miss the varsity cut or get anything but an A. In this way, we are all in the same boat. We all have two things we could learn next.

Pause for a moment and think of each of your kids. Without too much deliberation, think of several things that are uniquely germane to each child's next season of growth. Most parents start with more practical aspects of their child's life, such as turning in all math assignments and practicing the cello. Some parents may decide to focus on the more social aspects of their child—for example, talking nicely to the little sister or calling grandparents each week to say "Hi."

What makes the current list of two things is up to the parent. As much as is realistically possible, these two things are what you will be focused on and working on with your child. For instance, you determine that your son is going to work on bedtime and remembering his soccer games and practices. Then one night he hits his sister. Obviously, some things still need to be addressed. As much as possible though, let the other stuff go.

The Two Things concept is a powerful one that speaks to the nature of how humans learn. Working on two things at a time is ultimately the most efficient way to grow. A golfer will learn much more about his golf game by hitting a hundred four irons at the practice range than by playing a round of golf. In ninety shots on the golf course, a golfer might hit his four iron twice. A baseball pitcher learning to throw a new pitch, like a slider, would be better off going to the practice mound and throwing a slider repeatedly. Trying to throw all five of his pitches in practice will not help him learn the new pitch.

Tennis players have long known that focusing on the topspin backhand down the line is a great goal. If they work on their whole game, they won't learn the backhand as well. The only efficient way to learn any shot is to focus on that shot until you learn it well. It is too unfocused to just "work on your game." In the same way, it is too unfocused to just "work on life." If we really want to teach our kids new life skills, social skills, or organizational skills, we will be much more effective parents by focusing on two things at a time.

Once you have focused on a couple of behaviors to work on, the question always seems to emerge, "How do I overlook the things we are not working on? Do I just drop all other expectations for my son?" We don't recommend just saying and doing nothing about problem behaviors that are not currently being worked on. Over time, we have found another approach far more effective. This suggestion may not sound like much, but it is extremely effective. To illustrate we will use a simple example.

Jordan's Two Things

Jordan is fourteen, and his behavior has been slipping for six months. After a difficult review of his grades and conduct, Jordan's parents determine that he is going to work on two things. He must attend school every day and get caught up on every assignment. Also, he must be exactly where he says he is and come home on time. (We consider this list for Jordan *two things*, school and curfew, even though it could be argued that it is actually four things. It's okay to connect two closely related expectations and count it as one thing.)

Jordan is told that if he violates either of these rules his privileges will be completely shut down. This means no cell phone, no texting, no rides, no money, no Internet in his room, no video games, no time with friends, and no TV.

It has always been part of Jordan's daily responsibilities to empty the dishwasher and make his bed. So with the new rules in place, what happens when Jordan doesn't make his bed or empty the dishwasher?

We recommend this simple and powerful approach: Either parent can simply say to Jordan, "Jordan, I noticed you didn't make your bed or empty the dishwasher today. Those are still your responsibilities, but right now we are adamant about these other two issues. We want you to know how serious we are about your assignments and your curfew, so if you choose not to take care of your bed or the dishwasher we won't talk about it or give you any added consequence. All of your freedoms right now depend on how you do on those two areas of focus. We're going to solve those first. Maybe next month we will revisit the dishwasher job when we know you are keeping up in school and you are home on time."

A comment like this would take about forty-five seconds to say, and that is really all that needs to be said. It may seem like a surprising approach to let two of Jordan's responsibilities slide at this critical time. Well, it surprised us too. We discovered over time that there are four messages critical to the plan's success:

1. This strategy provides a clever and graceful way to send a warning to Jordan about how serious you are about the two focus areas. The crucial issues are not going to get lost in the chaos of the home.

2. This approach conveys to Jordan that you are pulling for him and that you are aware of the struggle the two things might be for him. A child needs to know that you are for him and that you are being reasonable. This will reduce resentment, which is a primary reason kids like Jordan fail.

3. His parents holding their course on just two issues will eliminate several of Jordan's excuses. He can't very well say that they have asked too much of him when they have pared their expectations down to two things.

4. This approach is wonderfully matter-of-fact. The parents aren't angry, nothing is confusing or subjective, and the stakes are high. This nonemotional approach communicates to Jordan that Mom and Dad are interested in seeing how this all turns out, but they have no emotional investment in the outcome.

Jordan's parents can check on the school website to see if he was in school and how many assignments are late. The clock on the microwave tells them what time he is home. We strongly favor not asking a child, "Is all your homework turned in?" or "What time did you get home?" Once you have established that a child is not honest in these areas—stop asking. Just figure it out for yourself.

For Parents in Crisis

If you read the first part of the chapter and thought, *I wish I were dealing with these issues with my daughter. Are you kidding? Write a thank-you note? Hold your fork right? Clean your room?*

If this sounds familiar, you might be one of the many parents who feel they are losing their kids altogether. The concerns that haunt these parents in the middle of the night are lying, drinking, smoking, using drugs, hooking up, failing school, or perhaps even dealing drugs. They're not thinking, *Will my child be ready for college in the fall?* but rather, *Will my child be alive in the fall?*

These are the parents whose fear for and anger at their child are only exceeded by the guilt and responsibility they feel in themselves. *How did this happen?* they wonder, and *Where did I go wrong?* They look at the family album and see the smiling face of a fourteen-year-old in a soccer team picture or at summer camp just two-and-a-half years ago. *That seems like an eternity ago.* Now the local police know their child's name and the thought of Mom and Dad going on vacation for five days by themselves is ridiculous.

What ever happened to the wonderful child who told the truth, did well in school, and was responsible and respectful? Those were the days when school conferences were joyful occasions. If this resembles your situation, you are undoubtedly scared, confused, angry, and worn out. You may be thinking: *Where can we get some help? We are so far past getting our child to help shovel the snow from the driveway.* You may have even had a thought you never dreamed you'd ever have: *I can't wait until my teen leaves the house for good!*

This chapter is also for you. The Two Things concept works as effectively as a place to start in this situation as it does for the more benign issues. There are always two things that are the next two most important things for your child to learn.

Chances are if you have a child who is "running wild," you may end up with a showdown. Unfortunately, it is a showdown you may lose. If your child is on drugs, the first thing to address is the drug use. If your son or daughter is addicted, he or she may need treatment and may not stop until it gets to that point. Telling your child this will be a good place to start.

Parents Have Power

You may say, "The next two things my son needs is to stop using pot and to get up before 11:00 a.m." If that is true, then that is your focus. Do not focus on almost anything else. Your son may need treatment. He may need a drug test. You may need to call his friends and ask for their help. You may need to call his friends' parents and get them on board. Whatever you do, it will yield a better result if you are focused on just two things at a time.

"I can never do it well enough" is a lie kids love to tell themselves. There may be a morsel of truth to this, but usually it is self-deception. They may declare this deception with such conviction that you might be tempted to believe it yourself. Majoring on two things will eliminate this excuse and add a focus that will alter the dynamic of the whole confrontation.

Parents may feel underpowered to confront their child in a meaningful way. Most parents underestimate the amount of leverage they have. We see parents who feel their child has all the power. This might show up when a parent tells his son he is grounded, and then the kid swears at his parents and walks out the door. How much power would you have if this happened? You can't go out in the yard, tackle your son, and put him in his bed. He's too big. But almost always, parents have more power than they are aware of. They have more leverage than they realize. This influence is more powerful when only two things are being focused on.

When the two things start to improve, other things will also start to improve. This is a wonderful mystery. When working with a child on emptying the dishwasher, she may start turning in her missing math assignments or saving money. When a child starts to turn in her math assignments, she often starts treating her sister better. We suspect that reduced stress is some of the reason for this. The child knows that only a couple of things are the focus in her life. There seems to be a new "I can do that" attitude in kids who previously had an "I can never do it well enough" attitude. Perhaps she just feels more successful and, consequently, feels better about herself.

Getting Up

There's a life skill that should be one of the two things for many older children. It is one of the most pivotal, important, and significant things to work on. We see it all the time in families and it frustrates parents to no end. That issue is the child getting up in the morning for school completely on his or her own. Nothing we have found will make a more broad, sweeping, positive change in a child.

Sometime between nine and eleven years of age, your children should be self-sufficient to start their days. That means using the alarm, with no knocks on the bedroom door, no reminders, and no warnings. It is astounding and alarming how many parents are still waking up their seventeen- or eighteen-year-olds. It's very hard for teenagers to feel like adults when they are treated like children at the start of the day. Think about it: How could an eighteen-year-old feel like an adult if he or she has to be awakened in the morning just like in fourth grade? This teen would be starting the day in regression.

There may be a war in the beginning. There may be many detentions, profanity, tardiness, missed tests, etc. Recently we heard of a seventeen-year-old girl who wanted a medical doctor to write her a note for school saying that she had a sleep disorder and should not be expected to get to school on time. Kids can be so entertaining.

Somehow, parents must find a nonverbal way to get their child to wake up independently. *Do not wake your teenager in the morning.* Some parents have used four or five alarm clocks, some have used foghorns, and some have purchased high-tech alarms that shoot helicopters across the room that must be found and retrieved to shut off an alarm that is steadily increasing in volume. However you do it, you must find a nonverbal way for your children to wake up by themselves.

Here are examples from two different families of how a child's behavior might be confronted. Both of their situations started the same way: a short meeting during which the parents told each child that the way life had been going was not going to be tolerated, starting in a couple of days.

Colin's Story

Colin was a twelve-year-old boy in the sixth grade from a divorced family. In many ways, he was a wonderful kid. In other ways, he was a bit of a monster, especially to his mother. Colin's mom came in for help when she had tried everything she could think of and failed. This mom had read several books on parenting and books on nutrition, and she was very invested in being a good mom. It complicated things a little that Colin was going back and forth between his parents' homes.

The main reason the mom was not getting very far with Colin was that she was working on too many things at once. Her list was long. She wanted to work on Colin eating less junk food, vacuuming better, finishing a science project, talking nicely to Grandma, playing fewer video games, picking better friends, and not talking back to Mom, just to mention a few.

The first thing we did was to help this mom focus on two things. It wouldn't have mattered very much what we chose. The issues chosen were that Colin would get up in the morning on his own, and that he would discuss issues with his mom and not argue (speak respectfully). It would not matter if Colin complied or agreed, just that he didn't argue. His mother calmly told Colin that she was going to back off on her endless banter about how he should behave, eat, and study. She told him that in three days most of the focus was going to be on these two things. He would simply lose his Xbox, his iPod, and his cell phone if he didn't get up on his own and was late for school, or if he did not stop arguing with Mom. There would be no discussion and no anger—it would just happen.

Mom was instructed to take away the Xbox cables when Colin wasn't around. If Colin decided to hide the cables, she was to just shut off the circuit breaker that ran power to the television. She would do this all with no anger, no discussion, and no resentment.

Within a few days, there was a great improvement in Colin's behavior. But another problem arose. Colin's mom, after seeing the rapid improvement in the two focus areas, tried to add more things to work on too quickly. It wasn't long before Colin's behavior regressed back to the way it had been.

Some parents will group multiple things into one thing, such as being obedient, helping out around the house, and doing well in school. These are not specific behaviors; these are groupings of behaviors. Focusing on a grouping will usually limit your success.

Jason's Story

Jason was a totally out-of-control high school junior. After coaching, Jason's parents told him, "Jason, there are so many areas in your life that we would like to see some improvement in: grades, lying, how you treat your brother, how you talk to us, getting up on time, and many others. We have decided that we are going to start with two things that we deem to be the most important at this moment. We want you to stay off drugs and we want you to go to school every day. The other things we mentioned can wait a little while as we narrow our focus to these two things.

"Starting Monday, we are going to shut you down if you

can't comply with these two basic requests. If you are not at school or you fail a drug test (or refuse to take one), we are going to shut off your cell phone, cancel your Internet, deny you use of the car, and search your room regularly.

"Because we love you, we can't with clear consciences allow you to keep living like this. We are willing to overlook numerous areas where you are falling short to make this clearer and make it easier for you to turn this around. But on these two points we are going to be as firm as concrete. No exceptions and no discussion. We won't ask you if you were at school. We will find out on our own, so you don't need to worry about that.

"We just cannot allow you to have a fun junior year of high school while you are functioning this poorly. This is your call. You have three days to think about how you want this to go down. Here are the drug tests we have ordered, and we will administer the first one on Monday evening. We hope it goes well for you. We love you very much, but if we don't do something we are facilitating your failure. We are not going to enable your poor choices any longer."

Jason's parents may be in for a knock-down-all-out battle with their son. But almost always, if this approach is handled firmly, quietly, briefly, and with unending resolve, it will work.

The Two Things concept is one of the most important parenting strategies we know of and is simple, doable, and focused. When kids start mastering life skills, relational skills, and family skills, they (and their parents) start to see progress and maturing. Trying to work on too many things at once results in failure and frustration for all. Keep it simple: Work on the two things that your child needs to learn next, and watch the change happen.

The GIST of It

- One of the most important things for a child of eleven or older to accomplish is to be able to get up independently in the morning.

- Choose two things that are tangible and attainable. Be sure not to group together multiple behaviors under a broad statement like "being good at home." Pick specific things that you want to work on.

- Keep this focus for about three weeks.

- The Two Things concept works whether your child is ahead, where he should be, or behind.

- Working on too many things at one time invites frustration and failure.

A Word about Secrets

The secret life of adolescents may be the biggest hindrance to their growing into mature young adults. Surprisingly, lies are usually not nearly as destructive as secrets. Though they often go together, it's the secret that impedes growth more than the lie.

A ninth-grade girl, with some encouragement from her friends, started to shoplift cosmetics and jewelry. Obviously this is not a good activity, but the disruption to the family occurred when the girl's energy was mostly spent on keeping her secret from her parents, not on growing up in normal age-appropriate ways.

To keep it a secret, she couldn't wear much of her "new stuff" because her mom might notice. She had to manage her stories, her purse, her makeup bag, her receipts, and probably her Facebook account. She had to remember what she had told to whom, who knew and who didn't know her secret. She had to have excuses ready in case the secret was discovered. She needed to keep track of what her sister and all her friends knew. Any of her shoplifting colleagues could have blown it for her at any time. With all this to manage, she wasn't going to hang out in the kitchen and chat with her mother or help out around the house. Too many discussions uncover secrets. Therefore, her whole existence had to be carefully managed. That didn't leave much time for her family.

Even the most deceptive kids have a hard time managing a spontaneous conversation when they are hiding something. Consequently, they will wear earbuds, use a harsh voice, avoid the main part of the house, act really tired, or adopt a hundred other strategies to avoid a normal, unguarded discussion.

If a child is avoiding his or her family in this way, the parents may be able to guess what the secret might be. Often they will have no clue, as it could be anything. It might be a new girlfriend or boyfriend or shoplifting. He or she may be failing a couple of classes or being deceptive about social outings. This behavior doesn't mean the child is hiding something, or that what he or she is hiding is serious. It's just a construct to help us interpret this new avoidant behavior.

If you sense a secret, it never hurts to say, "I feel there might be something going on in your life you haven't told me about." Notice that this is a statement and not a question. Questions are not helpful in this situation. Your son will not tell you something until he is ready. If he wants to tell you, he will bring it up in the next day or two.

13

CASE STUDY: KYLE

KYLE WAS A DIFFICULT KID, probably in the top 5 percent of difficulty. As a rowdy seven-year-old, he was becoming more of a handful every day. The short list of things he needed to change included arguing, name-calling, messiness in his room and throughout the house, talking in class (which led to numerous complaints from school), picky eating, fighting with his brother, riding his bike without a helmet, and refusing to go to bed at night.

Kyle's parents were exhausted, at a loss of what to do, and very discouraged when they first came in for help. It was hard to know where to start since the parents were so ready to quit (whatever that means when your child is seven). Kyle had been such a handful and his parents were so worn out that they couldn't stand the idea of trying one more thing that might not work. They assumed that, even in the best scenario, it would take years for his behavior to show even a little improvement.

When his parents agreed to give it a shot, the first step was for them to get quiet in their parenting. This couple was far too verbal, which often led to yelling matches. Then they were asked to target two things to focus on. They were assured that it didn't really matter which two things they chose. So they chose Kyle's behaviors of fighting with his brother and not wearing a helmet when he rode his bike.

Because Kyle's parents were at the end of their proverbial rope, the first evening was scripted for them more than we would normally have done. They were instructed to have a brief meeting with Kyle to inform him that they would be focusing on him wearing his helmet when he rode his bike and treating his brother better. They were to tell Kyle that if he chose to misbehave at school they were going to let the school handle those issues for the time being. At home, they were only going to focus on his bike helmet and the way he treated his brother.

Tuesday night the parents called Kyle into the family room. The meeting started with Dad saying, "Kyle, we have talked to you a lot about wearing your helmet when you ride your bike. Tonight is the last time we will ever talk about it. Starting tomorrow, you will lose your bike privileges every time you ride without a helmet. No arguments and no excuses. In addition, you are going to lose TV, video games, and computer time whenever you are mean to your brother. We aren't going to warn you anymore and we aren't going to discuss these topics with you anymore."

Few things in life were as predictable as Kyle. Wednesday

after school, Kyle came in the house, grabbed a snack, and went out to ride his bike. As expected, Kyle rode his bike helmet-less. Everyone knew this would happen, but this time his parents were prepared. They had screwed a large lag eye-bolt into the garage ceiling and bought a cable lock.

This also required getting his mom to a mind-set where she would be willing to wait—and to wait quietly. Up to now, Kyle's mom had taken it personally when he rode without his helmet. It was all she could do to sit in the house and watch Kyle flaunt his independence in front of her on that first day. Every fiber of her being wanted to yell at him as she had always done and run out to force him to stop riding. In the past, she used false warnings and idle threats. This is what Kyle expected on this Wednesday in late April. To Kyle's surprise, his mom did not get angry, did not warn him, and did not say a word. She didn't even go outside. She just waited.

For ninety minutes Kyle rode his bike up and down the street and around in his driveway without his helmet. Finally, he stopped to go to the bathroom. As soon as Mom heard the upstairs bathroom door close, she jumped into action, ran to the front yard, and wheeled Kyle's bike into the garage. She hoisted his bike on her shoulder, took a few steps up the ladder, and locked Kyle's bike to the eyebolt. (To avoid a power struggle, it was important for the bike to be locked away and unlocked without Kyle present.) She got down the ladder and was back inside before Kyle finished upstairs and returned to the front driveway.

Not seeing his bike, Kyle started looking around. He soon found it hanging from the garage ceiling. Immediately he tried to engage his mom in an argument, but she wouldn't talk. She simply told him twice, "Dad and I told you last night that we will not talk anymore about this helmet issue. You can try again on Friday." Kyle cried and went upstairs and started destroying his bedroom. Mom did nothing. He came down in about forty minutes and was quite civil the rest of the evening.

Kyle got his bike back on Friday, though he never saw it being unlocked. Within an hour, he was riding it without his helmet again. Again, his mother waited for her chance. This time Kyle wouldn't leave his bike to go to the bathroom. Eventually, one of the neighbor boys came over to play video games. As soon as the opportunity presented itself, Mom locked the bike to the garage ceiling again. This time, Kyle wouldn't see his bike until Tuesday.

That was the last time Kyle ever rode his bike without a bike helmet.

A similar plan was set up with Kyle anytime he fought with his brother. He would lose his screen and video-game time for two days, and no words were to be spoken. Two times that week Kyle was mean to his little brother, and each time he lost screen time for two days. Within a week, both these target behaviors had dramatically improved.

At the beginning of the week, Kyle's parents had no confidence that this simple plan would work with Kyle. He was too difficult and they had already tried dozens of ideas. One week later, Kyle had lost both his bike and video-game privileges twice. By the sixth day, he had started wearing his helmet, and by the seventh day, he was treating his brother better. Kyle's parents were amazed that he had also become much less messy in that week, he had started to eat a wider variety of foods, and his overall attitude at home and at school had improved—without them ever working on the other things or even mentioning them.

The GIST of It

- Some kids just love to argue. Parents of these kids need to "get quiet."

- Deciding on when the new reality will start is good to share with your child. This helps them think about what and when you are expecting the change.

- It's powerful to implement the "cost" (hanging up Kyle's bike) when your child is not around. This helps prevent a blowup or power struggle between you and your child.

14

TELL THE TRUTH

In a time of universal deceit, telling the truth
is a revolutionary act.

UNKNOWN

WHEN CONNOR WAS FOUR, he started his soccer career, haphazardly running around on the field with other four-year-olds. It was fun for all the parents to watch. And Connor seemed to be pretty good at soccer. Early on, his parents told him that he was the "best soccer player" on his team, which for the most part was accurate as far as four-year-old soccer players are concerned.

As Connor progressed through the school years, he continued playing soccer. He loved soccer. Noticing the passion Connor had for the game in middle school, his parents would say, "You're such a gifted soccer player; you will play in high school and college." Many of his mother's social network posts focused on Connor's soccer games, and his dad would brag to other dads about how good Connor was at soccer.

The problem was that Connor was just a little above average at soccer. By high school, his peers surpassed him, and Connor was unable to make the varsity team with his friends. He was confused and depressed at the thought of giving up soccer, wondering why he believed he was so good.

What is the truth about your child—the real truth? What is the truth about how outgoing or popular he or she is? What are his real chances of making it in the NBA or her chances of singing on Broadway?

It can be tempting to tell children or teens anything that will help manage a current situation. We want to lift their spirits when they're sad or give them hope when they're discouraged. Often this includes some type of compliment, encouragement, or exaggeration. Parents may say things like:

"You played great!"

"Everyone likes you."

"Your picture is beautiful."

"Daddy isn't mad."

"Our divorce won't change the holidays."

These words are said to make the moment better. It's not clear whether these untruths are for the child's benefit, to help the parents with guilt, or to preserve an illusion they carry with them. While this type of comment can be helpful to manage the situation in front of you, you and your child will pay a high price for handling it that way.

How could there be a price for words of kindness and encouragement even if they are not true? Could words like that really hurt someone? Wouldn't everyone like a little encouragement?

Comments like these can have a cumulative and devastatingly negative effect on children. Try to imagine a kind grandmother who offers her chubby grandson a double chocolate brownie to erase his discouragement about being overweight. The child may be down because he's not doing well on a diet or is too overweight to play sports. Grandma's plea, "Here, have a brownie. That's better now, isn't it?" may sound and feel good, but it's doing harm.

Look at it from another perspective. The real questions are these: How can it ever help a child to see a situation differently from how it really exists? Could promoting a distorted view of the world and of himself or herself ever benefit that child? How could it ever help that child to lose trust in what his or her own radar shows or in the feedback of a loved and credible adult?

A crucial, yet often overlooked, aspect of maturing kids (and adults, for that matter) is for them to see themselves as they truly are, and to see the world as it truly is. This is a fundamental feature in any treatment or counseling. In fact, the core problem in mental illness is not seeing oneself and the world as they are. Whether the problem is grandiosity, narcissism, or a paralyzing fear—at its core there is an inability to see self and the world as they are.

Encouragement is a beautiful-sounding word, but if it isn't precisely true, it is short-lived. At best, false encouragement serves to temporarily alter a situation in order to ease the pain of normal or real life.

No matter how many untruthful statements are made to kids for encouragement, untrue encouragement provides nothing more than false hope. To genuinely help your child with his or her feelings, the feelings discussion must always follow truth. Trying to manage a child's feelings apart from the truth will be counterproductive.

Distorting the truth to make kids feel better has a negative counterpart. It can be just as tempting to negatively distort the truth for the purpose of discouragement. A parent might use this type of statement to shame or guilt the child in order to manipulate a situation or change his or her behavior: "If you go to school without showering, you will smell and no one will like you." Though less common in the world of conscientious parents, these untruthful statements will also delay the child's ability to accurately read a situation. Loving and accurate encouragement is great, but the power is in the loving and accurate part, not in the encouragement.

A teenage daughter mopes around, depressed, because she was not chosen for a part in a high school play. She might mutter, "I'm terrible at everything! I may as well just quit trying because the director will always pick somebody else instead of me." The main thing for parents to do in this situation is to simply say the truth. What the truth is will depend on your child and the situation he or she is in, and that will be up to the parent to decipher. The most important thing is to accurately and lovingly say the truth with honesty and candor.

Naturally, parents must know how to see life as it is to tell their child the truth about seeing life as it is. This is one of the worthy challenges of being a parent.

What to Do

Let's start with the basics. On its most rudimentary level, if your son is a slow runner, don't tell him he is a fast runner. If your daughter missed half the spelling words, don't tell her she's really a good speller. If your daughter just had a terrible softball game, don't tell her she played great. Instead, tell her that this was not one of her good games. Or, if it is the case, tell her that softball is not one of her strengths. Be accurate and say it lovingly. What we say to our children needs to match the reality of the situation.

Telling the truth goes far beyond this. The next level of honesty is to tell your child what strength or weakness you see in him or her. It might sound like this: "Dillon, let me tell you what I am seeing in you. I checked your grades online today and it seems you are doing well on all your assignments, and they all seem to be turned in on time. Your test scores are not as good, though. Is that how you see yourself doing this semester?" Or, "You seem to be popular at school, but this year it seems you don't like your teacher as much as last year. How do you think this year is going?" Or, "At church you seem less confident with your friends. That is just how I see it. How do you see your time at church?"

Here are some examples of truthful statements:

- "You are one of the twenty best basketball players in your grade."
- "You are drawing pretty well for your age."
- "Fourth chair clarinet seems pretty accurate for your playing ability right now."
- "You are very nice to your friends, but you don't act nice to your brother."
- "Yes, your sister is better than you at playing the piano."
- "No one's that special."
- "You're a little overweight."

These statements are not going to hurt your child. In fact, they are going to position your child on solid footing to face a world that is real. Wisdom can only come from seeing the world as it is and seeing ourselves as we are. You may take some flak for handling your kids this way, especially from people who still believe they can affirm a child into happiness and success. Don't worry about them because your kids will be better off when they know who they are. Just tell them the truth as lovingly as possible.

Trying to manage someone else's emotions by changing their reality is not kind at all. It really amounts to codependency. It's often true that we want our children to feel better. But we also know that if they feel better, we will feel better, and we want to stop feeling bad ourselves.

We also recommend that you tell the truth about yourself and your own motivations and opinions. Tell your teen that you're going to try to manipulate her into trying out for a school play. Yes, that's right! Tell her your agenda. Tell your child you weren't listening if you weren't. Tell your son you don't know yet if you like his new friend Jeff. It drives kids crazy when their parents won't simply admit what they are thinking or doing.

Growing up is scary. Deep inside, almost all kids are scared about growing up even if it appears as if they are not. Even kids who have a brash or cocky style may be scared they won't be ready for adulthood when that time comes. Knowing they have someone older and wiser in their life who will be honest with them makes growing up a lot less frightening. All children need someone who loves them enough to tell them the truth, not someone who loves them in a way that protects them from the truth.

This relates to why love must evolve and change as time goes by. As children get older, it can be frightening to realize they can't trust their own radar or read a situation accurately. As they transition into adulthood, this missing life skill creates anxiety and confusion, and it can lead to unfortunate situations like following the wrong career path, passing up opportunities, or ending important relationships. Life becomes an intimidating experience if you cannot accurately assess your life or know "the person in the mirror." It's hard enough to be fired from a job; it's worse not to be able to understand why you were fired. Without a developed skill of self-truth, life is unpredictable and difficult to navigate.

Over the long term, the failure to be honest with your child about who he or she is will result in your child growing into an adult who is either delusional or fearful. Many young people believe the accolades they have been given and create for themselves a world that doesn't exist. A perfect example of this is the hit TV show *American Idol*. In the first few weeks of each season, the show is full of deluded contestants who have been fraudulently affirmed their whole lives. Their false reality becomes embarrassing for them when real life collides with their fictitious world.

There are a few exceptions to this rule. First, if you don't like your child or you like one of your children less than another, you should *not* say that. This kind of honesty would be far too damaging. Second, do not tell your children how much they hurt you or hurt your feelings. This is usually passive-aggressive and can also give the child a way to have power over you. It's like handing them the arrows in your quiver when they have the bow. Just tell them what you didn't like.

The Rationale for Telling the Truth

In the 1980s, experts proclaimed that affirmations were going to be the saving strategy for solving many of the problems that young people faced. The remnant of this thinking is evident even today in schools, preschools, and homes across America. This was either a very poor hypothesis or one that was implemented beyond its intent. It doesn't help children to hear exaggerated affirmations and untrue declarations about themselves. Telling kids things that aren't true will not help them long-term. Avoid making comments like these to children over five years old:

- "You are a gifted actress."
- "You are exceptionally intelligent."
- "You're the best pitcher ever."
- "You can be anything you want to be."

None of these affirmations are helpful for a child's development unless they are actually true. As professionals, we're seeing an epidemic of "giftedness" in our society. Sixty percent of kids can't belong in the top 1 percent.

A man who played football in high school tells about the day he stopped trusting his dad, at least with respect to football. He had a terrible game. He knew he had played poorly and he knew why he had played poorly. When he saw his dad after the game, his dad said, "Great game, Son!" This teen knew he hadn't played well; therefore, he knew at that moment he could not trust his dad's assessment of him again when it came to playing football. That was too high a price to pay for an affirmation. It's significant that this teen knew he hadn't played well.

Recently, we spoke to a well-known sports psychologist who affirmed this. He marveled at how many kids he works with do not know or are not sure how good they really are at their featured sport. Sometimes they believe they are worse than they are, but most often these kids see themselves as much better than they really are. This perspective can significantly impact the choices a child makes in sports and life. With each decade, more children have become less able to even know how they perform.

It's sad when an elite, all-American athlete or superstar makes a public service announcement telling kids that they can be anything they want to be. We wish another Division I athlete would create a PSA like this: "I thought I was a big-time athlete so I went to a big-time school to play ball. I wasn't really as good as I thought. As a result, I never played one minute of varsity in my entire college career. No matter how hard I worked or how low I got my body fat, I was never going to play at the university I chose. I wish I had had a more accurate view of myself. I probably could have started for two or three years in a good Division III program."

A fourth grader was asked recently what he wanted to be when he grows up. This boy was an average student, not an exceptional one. He answered, "I'm going to play a few years in the NBA, retire early and become an Air Force fighter pilot landing planes on aircraft carriers, and then retire from that and serve two terms as president of the United States." He said that his parents and his teachers thought this was a great plan. When asked why he thought he could do all these things, he replied, "Because I'm the third-fastest kid in my class!"

The adults in his life think they are giving him a benefit by not telling him the truth, but the cost of this thinking is too high. There is a difference between adults who support the realistic dreams a child might have and adults who cultivate unrealistic life plans for a child.

Probability and the Joy of Being Average

Many parents love to dream big things for their children. It seems no mother wants her child to be average. The truth is, most kids are average. The distribution of many human characteristics follows a predictable, normal bell curve. For example, height, weight, and length of life follow a normal, bell-shaped curve of distribution. The measure of certain mental characteristics also assumes the same kind of distribution. Intelligence measures are a typical example: The average intelligence quotient (IQ) of a population is one hundred points with a standard deviation of fifteen points. We use these statistics to point out that the vast majority of kids are normal (which is to say they are within two standard deviations from the mean). Yet today, it seems almost socially taboo to say this about a child.

It's fine to be average. In fact, nothing is wrong with being average. It's okay to not get the lead in the play. Maybe the person who was given the part is a better actress and singer than you are. It's fine to play on the JV basketball team as a senior when the varsity team starts underclassmen. Maybe you're an average basketball player and not good enough to play varsity. That's okay, and it's not the end of the world. If six kids are trying out for quarterback, the truth is that five will not be the starting quarterback. Part of life is just probability. Part of life is talent and ability. Part of life is timing. A big part of life is knowing what's true and what isn't. Parents have a role to play in that process.

We live in a culture that is, for the most part, probability ignorant. The failure to accept, understand, and process probability results in a failure to see the world properly. We seem to be passing on this probability unawareness to the next generation. If we truly understood likelihood and chance, we wouldn't talk like we do, and we wouldn't live the way we do.

If a thousand qualified candidates apply for something with three hundred openings, seven hundred people are not going to be accepted. This does not mean that "It wasn't meant to be" or "Everything happens for a reason." This means that chance played a huge role in the selection of those three hundred people.

The chances of winning the Powerball jackpot are about one in 175 million. People cannot even imagine that probability. Our minds are tapped out just trying to imagine odds of one in ten thousand. Any more than that involves "funny numbers" that we can't even grasp. It adds to our distortions when we see lottery winners in the news every month or two. It is distorted even more if we once drove by the convenience store where the winning lottery ticket was sold. It makes us think that maybe we were close to winning too.

Why write about probability in a parenting book? Because we cannot understand life without an accurate understanding of probability. A teen needs to understand why a friend died in a car accident, why he or she didn't get into the University of Michigan, or why Grandma has Alzheimer's. Without some awareness of probability, we may end up thinking that these people brought on the circumstances of their lives when they didn't. Or we may think they didn't bring on the circumstances when they had everything to do with them.

Perhaps the teen's friend died in a car accident because he was going eighty-five miles per hour around a tight curve in the road. Therefore, the friend was totally responsible for his own death, tragic as it was. Another person may have been hit by a drunk driver and totally *not* responsible for his own death. This same teen may have been totally qualified to get into the University of Michigan and didn't, simply because there were too many freshmen applicants.

Kids must know and understand that a lot of life is managing probabilities.

- What are the odds of getting in trouble if I hang with this group versus that group?

- What are the odds of passing a driver's test if I study versus if I don't study?

- What are the odds of me losing my virginity if I go to parties where friends are drinking?

- What are the odds of breaking a leg if I snowboard down this mountain versus that mountain?

- What are the odds of a camping disaster if we are sober and the trip is well planned versus if we are stoned and have no plan?

The point here is not just to live safely but also to live life alive while managing the risks we do take. How can kids know what risks to take without a respect for probability? This skill needs to be developed over time.

There is a far greater chance you could be hit by a drunk driver late at night on New Year's Eve than driving home today. Managing that risk is part of seeing life the way it is. That doesn't mean you should go out or stay home; it just means that you have an idea of the risk involved. In rationalizing risky behavior, kids will just say something like, "We did the same thing last year and no one got hurt." When our kids understand probability, they will understand that this statement means nothing since an aspect of risk and reward is random and unpredictable. They also will know that other aspects of risk and reward are manageable and alterable.

If you think about teen tragedies, you may think of drowning, rape, fatal car accidents, or suicide. The chance of any of these happening is far greater if alcohol or drugs are involved. Therefore, sobriety is a large part of risk management for your child.

Tell the truth to your children. Tell it accurately and lovingly, and make sure you include the truth about probability. You will have wiser and safer kids if they have been prepared to see the world and themselves as they really are.

The GIST of It

- Kids need to grow up with accurate and intact radar about themselves and others. Without this trait, a child will probably live with unnecessary fear and self-doubt.

- Inaccurate feedback can be either too positive or too negative.

- Repeated, untruthful, and exaggerated feedback will block accurate self-understanding from developing. It may seem supportive to overstate a compliment or give encouragement to make a child feel better. This will have a short-term effect on lifting his or her spirits but will contribute to inaccurate self-assessment. That is too high a price for such a short-term gain.

- If truthful feedback is given lovingly, it will not hurt your child. Remember that most kids are normal in most ways. Truthful feedback will help kids accept the areas of life in which they are not exceptional. Kids need to know they are wonderful, but not exceptional.

- Feeling a need to be exceptional is very stressful on kids. This can contribute to kids giving up on life when they actually aren't doing that poorly.

- Not as many kids as we think are truly exceptional. Our country is paying a high price for this arrogance.

- An understanding of probability and the likelihood of something happening is part of speaking honestly to your kids. Some chances can be highly affected by choices we make, and some exist outside the realm of our influence.

15

THE ORIGINS OF
SELF-ESTEEM

Self-love is not only necessary and good,
it is a prerequisite for loving others.

ROLLO MAY

MARCIE GREW UP in a loving family that had the best intentions for her. Her parents loved telling her how special she was to them and what an awesome person she was. When Marcie would do something kind for someone else, her parents would make a big deal about it, telling their friends and relatives what an incredible young person she was.

Marcie liked all the attention she got for what she did, and she became accustomed to others' feedback. As she entered the teen years, the exposure to social media fueled her ability to glean positive feedback from all her friends and relatives. She became obsessed with creating a persona that fed on other people's compliments and affirmations.

By the end of high school, Marcie was doing most everything to get a response from others and keep up her perceptions of who she should be. When she felt the feedback didn't fit her actions, Marcie became frantic at the lack of positive accolades. Her parents couldn't believe that this sent Marcie into a depression. They had convinced Marcie she was loved, but Marcie had never learned to love herself.

Webster's dictionary defines *esteem* as "to set a high value on: regard highly and prize accordingly."[1] So self-esteem is your ability to esteem yourself. It's your own ability to highly value yourself, to have great regard for yourself, to prize yourself, and to respect yourself. Self-esteem is your journey toward liking who you are.

Self-esteem cannot come from others; it must ultimately come from one's self. If a teenage girl only likes herself when she is popular and others like her, that is others' esteem, not self-esteem. The esteem of others may feel like self-esteem, but it's not rooted inside the person. Celebrities and athletes may have millions of people cheering for them and yet feel inadequate when the cheering stops. The problem is that these people do not like themselves.

The topic of self-esteem is about as important as anything in life, and certainly one of the most important topics in this book. Given its significance, how does a person lay a foundation in his life worthy of building self-esteem?

Some theories on how to build self-esteem are distorted or unproven. They couldn't be further from the truth, but over the years they have taken on a life of their own.

Do compliments and affirmations from others build self-esteem? Does it come from accomplishments? Does it come from a combination of other people's esteem for us and how we perform? If enough people think I am great and I perform well enough, then will I like myself and have high self-esteem?

We call the perception that self-esteem comes from these things the Great Myth. Like every other myth, there is a little truth in it.

Exceptionally Wrong Thinking

Worse than not knowing where self-esteem comes from is thinking we know and being wrong. Many parents believe if their child feels exceptional, their child will like himself or herself. Yet we often see insecurity and self-hatred in exceptional people. Pop stars, athletes, and geniuses all frequently struggle with even basic self-love. So it can't come from feeling that one is better or more gifted than others are.

Being esteemed by others can be addictive for children and young adults. When they achieve it regularly, any dislike they have for themselves is temporarily anesthetized. In truth, performing for others and hearing their affirmations can temporarily take away the pain of not being satisfied with oneself. Nevertheless, the core problem of not being pleased with oneself is still there. Being esteemed, accepted, and valued by others is like a Band-Aid for a cut and Tylenol for a headache. The esteem of others never leads to self-esteem; it just temporarily helps people feel better.

How many of our children actually value themselves highly? Do they have great regard for themselves? Or are they just tuned in to the accolades that go along with high functioning and high performance levels? Often, children who are popular, good-looking, smart, and involved in good activities have no ability to see themselves apart from what everyone tells them. Their heads are filled with hundreds of compliments and affirmations, yet they can have a low opinion of themselves because they are constantly expecting others to define them. High-functioning kids may be secretly afraid that if others knew the truth about them, others would see past their performances and realize that there is nothing much there.

Child or adult, in order to grow, we need to like ourselves. We must like ourselves separate from others' opinions. *Self-esteem is what you think of yourself in spite of your performance and other people's opinions.*

There are no shortcuts here. Many people have tried to get around this journey by being nice, generous, successful, or well-liked, or by reading books about how much God loves them, in hopes that something will build their self-esteem. This just doesn't work long-term. These people usually just become more impressed that God could love someone as unlikable as they are, but they usually don't start liking themselves. It just doesn't translate into self-esteem. Remember the iconic old hymn?

"Amazing grace, how sweet the sound that saved a wretch like me . . ."

If *wretch* in this context is a synonym for *broken* or *humbled,* it can be an important factor to the beginning of recovery from poor self-esteem. It's important to replace arrogance with humility in the process of growing and maturing. However, people must eventually find something to like about themselves. It might mean that they first need to hit bottom and be torn down, but then they need to be built up again with a new identity. "A wretch like me" has a theological foundation, but in the field of mental health, people who were once humbled need to see themselves as valuable and precious in order to grow or heal.

Ironically, seeing ourselves as exceptional does not seem

to help self-esteem. It's more helpful to consider ourselves as not extraordinary, but just *wonderful*. The terms *normal* and *wonderful* show the paradox needed for self-esteem to exist. A good way to think about it is this: *I love who I am, but I know I'm no better than anyone else.*

The Foundations of Self-Esteem

Here's what is needed for self-love: love from someone else, accurate self-assessment, resilience, achievement, and the belief that we are not exceptional. A healthy self-love leads to self-esteem. Let's look at these important foundations.

1. Love

The first requirement for self-esteem is for a child to know someone loves him or her. It's hard for kids who have never known love to make it out of childhood grounded. This is immensely important. The only reason we are not devoting more pages to this is that most parents do a good job of loving their kids. Probably even a higher percentage of those reading a book about parenting love their kids.

We've heard many various complaints from kids, but we have never heard a kid complain that his or her parent says "I love you" too much. The body language of kids may show indifference, but hearing this frequently still penetrates inside of them and fills their souls.

Loving your child immensely is definitely part of the self-esteem foundation.

Love for a child happens in your heart. You know it's there but others may not be as sure. Kids can easily play the "no one loves me" tapes in their heads. This happens all the time. Just know it can take some artistry to convey the love you carry for your child. Love must be present, but it also must be convincing.

The most important factor in showing love is demonstrating utter joy that your child exists. This is also the most efficient way to show love, and efficiency is an important part of good parenting.

When your daughter gets up in the morning or your son comes home after school, do your face and eyes show joy and gratitude that this child is in your life? You'll have a tough time convincing your daughter that you love her if your face reflects a dislike or disdain for her. In fact, it likely won't happen. *You* might know you still love her, but your child is not going to believe it. It's nearly impossible for children to believe they are loved if they also believe a parent regrets they exist.

Start with the look in your eyes when you are conveying love. Then move on to other ways to show love for your kids:

- Spend time with them.
- Prove that you know who they are and what they are like.
- Give evidence that they are nearly always on your mind.
- Be firm and adult in your decisions.
- Look out for their best interests, not for their requests or demands.
- Value their opinions and privileges, but you don't need to agree.
- Find different ways to refer to them as one of the blessings of your life.

It's important that you decide how you are going to show love. Take into consideration who your child is and decide on your approach. As time goes on, it's okay for you to change your approach, but it won't work if you let your child change your approach. That will become a powerful and manipulative tool for your child's arsenal.

We want to say this as emphatically as we can: *Do not listen to what your child tells you he or she needs to feel loved.* This is a trap. You will be far better off following the list above, or any list you would like to make on your own.

The Love Trap

The simple love trap may sound like this: "If you loved me, you would let me sleep over at Donny's tomorrow night." A more complicated version would be: "If you loved me, you would get me back on Adderall so I can study." The most confusing love trap comes from a divorce situation: "If you loved me, you wouldn't make me go to Mom's for the weekend." (You may not want your son to go to his mom's place for various reasons, but that wouldn't be an "if you love me" issue.)

Somewhere inside your daughter, she wants you to be in charge. She knows she needs help growing up. Your son knows that left on his own, he would ruin his life or at least his high school experience. As much as it may appear to the contrary, your children want you to be an adult.

It's sad to hear a twenty-year-old say in counseling, "Looking back on it, I don't believe my parents loved me enough to stop me from smoking pot and sleeping around in high school." This is sad because this same young woman has probably forgotten that when she was sixteen she screamed at her parents, saying, "If you loved me you would get off my back." She probably said it with such power and conviction that her mom and dad might have partially believed she was right and gave her more space.

One of the most frequent themes in the love trap might sound similar to this: "If you loved me, you would respect me and my privacy and stay out of my room." This is one of today's adolescents' most familiar cries. We don't recommend checking your children's rooms if you have no reason to suspect them of anything. Don't just go in and read your daughter's journal. But definitely check her room if you have a reason to suspect something. Every day your child is living with a secret is another day she or he is not growing. Those days add up.

It's unwise to buy into your child's thinking on this issue. The "respect my privacy" argument, despite all the conviction and indignation it is expressed with, is mostly nonsense. Thousands of occupations require that an employee get tested, searched, watched, or recorded. Apartment landlords can go in and check a building they suspect to be in violation anytime they have cause. If an apartment manager hears a bark coming from a building where dogs aren't allowed, the manager may go in and check for a dog when the tenant is not home. Dishonest, disrespectful, and suspicious behavior erodes your child's right to privacy.

The problem here has nothing to do with love. It has to do with kids who want their rights respected when they don't want to respect the rights of others. If your son is worthy of respect, by all means respect every aspect of his life that you can. Checking a room has to do with respect, not love.

How are you going to express your love for your child? Take into account your child's interests and passions. If your son is on a diet, don't bake cookies to show your love for him. If your daughter is not athletic, don't take her on a strenuous hike. These expressions should be efficient and simple. You don't have to build a two-story tree house to express your love. The time increment that love comes in is moments. Commit to practicing these expressions. This is a commitment you make to yourself, not one you make to your child. Love your child in a way that is consistent with the commitment you have made to yourself.

As we've said before, love is best expressed one-on-one. As parents, we probably overvalue family time as it pertains to expressing love. For thirty years we have asked people about their best family memories, and usually their best memory has nothing to do with the entire family. Most often it involves time they spent alone with someone in the family. A son may say, "I remember the time my dad took me camping, just him and me." A daughter might say, "My mom and I went to a spa together and had the best time ever." Love penetrates a child best when his or her siblings are not around.

Focus more on your love for your child and less on your relationship with your child. Love is far more stable and predictable than relationships. Your daughter has the power to ruin her relationship with you, but she cannot ruin your love for her. Overfocusing on your relationship will hand your child too much power over you since you are valuing a dynamic she can choose to destroy. In desperate times, she will use this power to pillage your relationship because she knows how tightly you are clutching it.

You will make far better decisions as a parent if you focus

on love instead of relationship. It might surprise all of us to examine how many times the loving thing to do in a situation is the very thing that could cost us closeness. For example, it might be more loving to take your son out of college for a time when he has shown that he's not applying himself academically or socially. He might accuse you in that situation of not loving him, but you must be willing to risk the closeness of your relationship and love him in the way that is most beneficial for the long run.

Love your child enough to be willing to risk your relationship. You will be stronger and make better decisions, and the leverage your child could potentially have over you will be neutralized.

2. Self-Assessment

A second essential for building self-esteem is accurate self-assessment. Self-assessment is the skill of being able to accurately see yourself as you are apart from the input or opinions of others. Because of its importance to self-esteem, we devoted the previous chapter to discussion about accurate truth telling. It's extremely important that parents teach their children how to accurately assess themselves. This is not an ability parents think much about or usually teach their children. Many adults have no experience in using this skill in their own lives.

This takes practice, but it's a job perfectly suited for parents. Parents are there day and night and can ask, "How did you see yourself in this situation?" Or, "How do you think you did?"

When you look at your child's report card you can say, "This is what your teacher says about how you are doing.

However, I am more interested in how you think you're doing. Do you agree with your teacher's assessment?"

Or, "Do you see yourself as quiet in class?"

Or, you might ask, "How do you think you played today?"

Or, "How did your recital go? Would you say it was better or worse than your last performance?"

A child may say about a D on his report card, "I think I did fine." If that happens, the parent should just say, "I don't believe you are happy with this grade. I think you are just saying that to get out of work. But even if you are happy with a D, I'm not. That isn't going to be acceptable to me."

Kids should be able to roughly assess how well they did on a school presentation, how well they mowed the lawn, or even how in shape they are physically.

We are finding that kids are not adequately developing this skill. It's amazing how much of a child's life can go by without actually having many chances to accurately self-appraise, or having his or her accurate self-assessment noticed or confirmed by a parent. This is primarily because we live in a society that expects the adults in a child's life (parents, teachers, youth workers, etc.) to give an ongoing assessment of how a child is doing.

Allow and encourage your children to reflect on their performance, their diligence, or their perseverance in a particular situation. As a parent, celebrate any time your children assess anything accurately. We're not saying to get all excited and throw confetti when they accurately reflect on their experience. Instead, express to them your agreement with an assessment when it's "on target" in order to reinforce their self-evaluation skills.

This is a great thing for kids to hear from their parents.

Imagine you ask your seventh grader how the game went today and she accurately tells you that she scored several points but didn't get many rebounds. Your response should be, "It's really cool you saw your game that accurately."

Developing this trait is crucial to self-esteem. We believe it's far more important that your son can assess accurately how well he did on an English paper or how well he cleaned the bathroom than that he can do either of these tasks with proficiency.

As parents, we inherently assess our own children in ways that are inaccurate because we see them through biased eyes and rose-colored glasses. Having the ability and willingness to honestly give our children accurate feedback is the exception to the rule in most households. After all, we want desperately for our children to succeed, excel, and be the best. We will stretch the truth and even lie about their abilities, performance, and character in ways that attempt to self-fulfill some prophecy. Yet for our children to truly know how they performed in some area, we must know how they really did and then teach them the skill of seeing themselves accurately.

The exaggerated way parents see their kids may result in affirmations. Just as often, it results in parents being hypercritical because they see a higher potential in their children than is actually there.

People struggle with accepting the truth about themselves. It takes practice and grace to be willing to learn this skill. What deceives many parents is the myth of a self-fulfilling prophecy. Parents sometimes believe that if they pump up their children's self-esteem by telling them they are great and talented and able to do anything they want to do in life, then their children will miraculously become great and talented. This simply is not the case. In fact, it can back-fire. Overshooting your assessment of your child has a better chance of stifling his or her growth than it has of accelerating growth. An increasing number of kids do not have a clue about their true abilities because they are confused by what they have heard from their parents for years.

The truth is, most children do not grow up to become professional athletes, virtuoso musicians, brain surgeons, or CEOs of large corporations. That is okay.

Self-esteem suffers when a child's view of himself is different from what is true. It is easier for a kid to be frightened and turn against an unknown self than to turn against one who is known, liked, and viewed accurately. A child with an accurate view of himself or herself can go through rough waters.

3. Resilience

A child with healthy self-esteem can say after moments of failure, "I'll just try it again," or "I'll start over," or "I'll be more prepared next fall." Resilience is necessary for self-esteem. When kids don't have resilience, they become scared and tentative about life. We all need resilience to be able to effectively do life, with or without self-esteem.

It can be said that self-esteem is best measured when accolades have ceased, achievement has failed, friends are gone, and the path is unclear. It's unlikely any of us would get through such times without resilience. Resilience teaches us that failure does not mean defeat.

Practice allows your child to develop resilience. This happens naturally in normal family life. And a different mindset is needed to parent this way. Remember to be grateful when difficulties surround your child. Instead of showing discomfort as kids face setbacks, we can appreciate how needed these difficulties are for them to believe in themselves.

Resilience is one of the hardest lessons to learn because it so often involves covering the same ground twice. We try and fail, and then need to try the same thing again to succeed. Having to rewrite an essay after your computer loses what you've written is a good example of this. These situations in life involve achievement with disappointment—tough lessons for all of us. All you need to do to develop this trait is to celebrate resilience whenever it appears in your family. In homes where more energy goes into applauding someone who gets up again than into comforting someone after he or she falls down, resilience will find its own life and energy.

4. Achievement

Achievement is also an essential part of self-esteem. We wish this were not true, as it would really be a good progression if some kids could repair and raise their self-esteem first and then go out and tackle some achievement. However, achievement of some type must be part of self-esteem building. The most effective adolescent treatment programs we know of are programs that incorporate achievement into their treatment plan. The least effective are those that try to build self-esteem before achievement is established.

The achievements need to be personal. The kind of authentic self-esteem that can be built upon happens when a band member writes a good song, or a student perfects a role in a theater production. Any achievement that kids do solely to gain the approval of others has a more negligible effect on building self-esteem. In other words, an achievement that originates with your son's passion is going to be a building block of self-esteem. But an achievement that originates from his obedience, conformity, or submission will have a much smaller impact.

If you have a higher-functioning child, you may not relate to this because your child's life is full of achievements. Many others may not have a notable significant achievement. If you are the parent of one of these kids, you will know exactly how difficult this hurdle can be to clear. Innumerable kids have functioned so poorly in life—hanging out, using drugs, or skipping school—for so long they literally have not had an achievement in months.

Anyone attempting to help a child with low self-esteem needs to keep in mind that without an accomplishment of some type, this is an uphill struggle at best. These kids don't need to bring food to Haiti after an earthquake or spend two nights alone in the wilderness, even though these are noble ideas. Instead, fixing the family's computer, adding two new apps to Mom's smartphone, driving a little sister to swimming, or getting caught up on missing math assignments will qualify as small starting points.

If a child you love is stuck, make sure he or she has recently achieved something. If not, success in gaining self-esteem will be nominal.

5. *The Myth of Specialness*
There is an epidemic of *gifted* children in developed countries. The topic of gifted children shows up in hockey rinks, in math class, at Starbucks, in parent-teacher conferences, and in other places parents congregate. A growing percentage of kids today are thought to be gifted; however, that cannot be true.

Let's look at the discipline of probability theory. This theory again says there are a known number of gifted children out of every one hundred children. What is known and true is that about 68.27 percent of those measured on any trait lie within one standard deviation of the mean. Similarly, about 95.45 percent of the values lie within two standard deviations of the mean. So by definition, 4.55 percent of kids lie outside two standard deviations to the high and to the low end. Take out the half on the low end, and the remaining 2.27 percent of the population is above average in any measurable trait. Think of it this way: 97.73 percent of children fall below the gifted line. Bottom line: Most kids are not gifted.

Something has shifted in our culture. It has now become unacceptable in some vague way not to be gifted. To be normal is to be "below." We can deny it or argue about it, but anyone who works with kids can feel the undertow around them. Parents are baffled and angry that their child didn't make an elite traveling basketball team. Kids may feel disappointed because they only got a 92 percent on an English paper. Increasingly, parents see normal or average as an unacceptable reality for their children. There is no doubt the kids are feeling it. As a result, more kids than ever express the desire to give up if they don't excel at something.

Kids who are not exceptional in math feel they are less than those who are gifted. Girls without an exceptional figure hate the way they look. When kids today say, "I'm not good at anything," what they mean is that they are not exceptional at anything. These kids are finding it increasingly difficult to take comfort in being just like most of the rest of us.

This should be a wonderful reality. If I am ordinary, I fit in. I am no better or worse than anyone else. Most of the greatest people in history were not gifted people in any innate way; they were normal. From their normality they were able to achieve important and exceptional things. Normal kids need to embrace their normality, not fight it. If kids continue to feel defective because they are not exceptional, healthy self-esteem is going to be elusive and fleeting.

In our culture, when gifted becomes expected, normal becomes defective. It is an important aspect of growth, peace, and self-esteem that the core of who we are is good enough. Inside, people need to believe that their core self is something they can be happy with. It is actually all they have to be happy with. When kids feel that average is an insult, they will aspire to being gifted instead of working to be effective. Self-esteem takes an unnecessary hit when our kids carry this pointless weight.

What if your child is truly in the upper 2 percent of kids in a certain skill or trait? We still recommend you be careful about pushing this perception on your child. It's fine to mention this so your child understands that you expect him or her to work at a level commensurate with his or her ability. Any more than this will not be helpful. Here's why. If your child ends up going to MIT, most likely he or she will be quite average in that setting. What if your MIT candidate tries waterskiing? He or she might be quite average in that setting also. Being able to feel comfortable with being average is a great trait for us all to learn. Fortunately, most of us are average, so it is just a matter of accepting the truth.

It's an excellent idea to ask someone with average skills to do a credible and admirable job on something. Just do not expect this person to be gifted if he or she is not. There is so much unrest and such a tendency to quit among kids. A part of this is because they feel their family and culture only value the exceptional. Remember, only about 2.27 percent of the population is exceptional on any given identifiable trait. We, as a culture, need to start celebrating the wonderful achievements of normal kids.

The Story of Peter

Peter was behaving like a boy, even though he was about to turn twenty. During most of the previous five years of his life, Peter just existed as he smoked pot, drank alcohol, played video games, and used Adderall improperly. He slept in, skipped school, and hung out. To understand how Peter got to this condition would take about eighty pages of this book. Surprisingly to some, Peter got this way with two loving parents and a good home.

Peter could argue with the masters. He had a fierce temper. He had a much stronger persona than either parent. His parents primarily just wanted everyone to get along. "Why can't we get along?" they'd ask, and "Why can't Peter just do what he's supposed to do?" There were no answers on the horizon.

When he was fifteen, Peter realized that his athletic skills, which had served him well until this age, were no better than average. Kids with average athleticism have no place to go in organized sports after fifteen. He started vigorously pursuing video games. *World of Warcraft* became an obsession in tenth and eleventh grades. This contributed to his grades dropping. He began to lose friends in the real world, friends he replaced in cyberspace.

Early in the eleventh grade, Peter hit a plateau in his gaming. Though he was good at it, he realized that he wasn't exceptional in the video gaming world either. He had easily climbed levels in several games, but then he found it harder and harder to achieve *legend* status among his cyberfriends. In sports and in gaming, Peter wanted to be exceptional. When he realized he was just average, that would not do.

Peter got bored with the video experience and started watching movies incessantly. The few people he associated with were beginning to drink and smoke pot. Peer pressure got to him. In addition, the best stories going around school all involved someone being plastered or wasted. If you wanted to be in the best stories, you knew what you had to do.

Peter had distanced himself from his parents since his video gaming season. He had to. Initially, to keep playing four hours a day, he had to lie about his grades and his homework. Then he had to lie about the lies. Before long, he was vague about life in general, stayed secluded in his room, was angry with his parents, and was generally uncooperative.

His parents saw their son slipping away. When either parent tried to reach out to him, Peter would pull further away. When his dad asked Peter to help a little around the house, Peter would see it as an injustice and shut down even more. If his parents left him alone and asked nothing from him, he would hang out in the kitchen and make a snack, carry in some groceries, or watch an old *House* rerun with his mom and dad. This was all they had left of their relationship with Peter. They didn't want to do anything to jeopardize what little was left.

By then, Peter hated himself. He had alienated his parents, so he was unable to benefit from their love. He did not respect his loser friends. He often needed to medicate himself to face the day. He had not achieved anything of value for many months, and he had totally lost track of who he was. Peter's self-esteem was in a free fall, but it had never been high in the first place. He had created his own prison. While serving time in that prison, he had fallen far behind his well-functioning peers and had not learned the skills needed to embark on a different path.

Peter's story is common. He knew his parents loved him, but other than that, he had none of the building blocks needed for self-esteem. He had poor self-assessment, no resilience, and no achievements derived from his own passions. He didn't believe he was valued.

He quit sports and video games when he realized that he was average. His parents were average and they were fine with Peter being average, but in Peter's culture average was not okay. In the upper-middle-class suburb where he grew up, subtle messages everywhere implied that normal was not good enough. Signs about excellence hung over the school's entry and appeared in large print on his school yearbook's title page. With more than six hundred students in his graduating class, Peter felt that if he were not exceptional at something he would just be part of the masses walking the halls, and that made him feel desolate.

Fortunately, Peter was able to grow. In time, he learned to like himself. Peter gradually chipped away at his low self-esteem as his therapist listened to him and corrected his misperceptions about his world.

Peter was wrong when he believed that being exceptional was the only way life could be worthwhile and joyful. Really, what changed for Peter was perspective and forgiveness.

In counseling, he learned to see himself and others differently. He learned that very few people in life are truly exceptional and that he was fine the way he was. He began to see that as awkward and old-fashioned as his parents were, they loved him, they were trying to help him, and they would do nearly anything for him.

Fairly rapidly, three things happened: He accepted who he was, he accepted the family he was born into, and he began to see that many of his friends were self-centered and immature. While this approach to building self-esteem seemed to work for Peter, and he grew a lot in one year, it may not work for everyone in a similar situation.

"How Do You Think You Did?"

Some parents don't believe their child could accurately critique himself or herself, and they are probably right. We encourage parents to ask their child, "How do you think you did?" on a regular basis, whether it's regarding a report card, basketball game, crayon drawing, or mowing the lawn. A child with good self-esteem will gradually answer more honestly and accurately. The parent's job is to either confirm the child's assessment or guide the child to reassess if he or she is off track. If your son ever said, "I did an average job· on the lawn," you as the parent should pay more attention to the accuracy of his self-assessment than the quality of his mowing.

Ultimately, we do not create self-esteem in our children by affirming them to death. We only perpetuate their false sense of self, and we may even fuel their dependency on the esteem of others.

In America, it's hard to imagine young women having any self-esteem at all around an issue like body image. Hollywood, TV shows, and clothing models give girls the message they will be accepted only if they look like *that*. This reality impacts the self-esteem of most American young women.

If we are to teach our children self-assessment and how to look at themselves as they are, truthfully and realistically, it must begin with us. We must tell our kids the realities of their lives: their talents, their intelligence, their true abilities, and their weaknesses. Yes, even their weaknesses. This does not mean we should focus on what they cannot do; instead, it means we should guide them on a path that fits who they are.

The GIST of It

- The addictive nature of needing the esteem of others is at the core of our children's low self-esteem.

- The esteem of others feels like self-esteem, but it's significantly different.

- Love, accurate self-assessment, resilience, and achievement will instill self-esteem in your child.

- Don't buy into our culture's message that your children need to be exceptional and gifted. It simply is not true. Normal kids are unique and wonderfully made.

16

SHAME

The difference between guilt and shame is very clear—in theory.
We feel guilty for what we do. *We feel shame for what we* are.

LEWIS B. SMEDES

JOSÉ WAS NOT VERY GOOD at anything. He didn't have much in the way of natural athletic ability, book smarts, or looks. As he grew up, it seemed everybody else had something they excelled at, but not José.

It didn't help that his younger brother was a really good basketball player and his older sister was getting college scholarships for her brains. José was just average at most things. His parents regularly compared him with his brother and sister, asking him to study harder, go out and get some exercise, lose some weight, and clean his bedroom better—just to name a few requests.

José started to believe that he was a bad kid and not good at much of anything. Messages started to play over and over again in his head, messages that told him he was a loser and would never succeed. The only time José felt happy was when he was eating. He loved to eat, and eat he did. Over the few years of middle school, José gained seventy-five pounds. This reinforced José's self-perception of being unacceptable and a loser. José believed this story he told himself, and eating would keep that story alive.

Shame silently destroys families in our country and around the world. We define it as the painful sense that we have lost value as a person because of poor performance, bad behavior, or a mistake. Shame is the primary reason that so few kids live a balanced life. Everyone, to some degree, will battle shame in his or her life.

The spectrum of shame goes from mild to severe and can vary in its effect. Mild shame causes tears and anger. It makes apologizing difficult and defensiveness a certainty. In younger kids, it is at the core of bullying and teasing. It is at the heart of what drives a class clown. Shame is why a teen might squeal his tires or fail a test.

More significant shame drives anorexia nervosa, much drug use, and sexual misconduct, and it's a significant contributor to obesity. It can be the reason someone joins a gang, drops out of school, stays in an abusive relationship, or becomes the abuser in a relationship. Shame is at the center of chemical and alcohol addiction, and it's a primary reason for experimenting with and using drugs.

Understanding the origins of shame is critical to effective and healthy parenting. From our perspective, a major goal of parenting is to raise what we call "shame-reduced" kids. We say *shame-reduced* because it is doubtful that a child can grow up "shame-free" in our culture. The goal is to parent without adding to cultural shame, and ideally, to even neutralize some of it.

The Good Old Days

Shame has been around for a long time. To understand the role that shame plays in our history, let's look at parenting back in what some call the "good old days." Those good old days—back two, three, and four generations—were good for some reasons. In a more rural and agrarian society, kids felt needed. Not necessarily special, just needed. They were essential to the care of the farm. In urban society, teens would work long hours and turn their paychecks in to the family to help pay bills and buy food, maybe keeping 5 percent for themselves. Kids grew up respecting their elders and knew what a hard day of work felt like. Years ago, kids saw higher levels of school as a privilege instead of a requirement or an entitlement. They knew it was a blessing to be able to go to school past the eighth grade. Generations ago, a variety of body types were seen as beautiful or acceptable.

That said, the good old days were rife with shame. Kids were hit and belittled. Teasing was as bad as it is today; it just took a different form. Kids spoke respectfully to their elders, but they often didn't respect those elders. They just spoke respectfully out of fear of being slapped if they didn't. Kids of previous generations did much of what they did because they didn't think they deserved any better. It was not uncommon for adults to work their whole lives in a coal mine, farm a hopeless piece of clay soil, or stay in a relationship that was painful and doomed from the beginning.

There have been extensive and far-reaching changes to life in the past thirty years just as there have been far-reaching changes to childhood. One thing that hasn't changed is shame. Shame looked different in our grandparents' era, but in studying history we see that deep shame has been around forever. This is not a new battle. It has just taken on a new face with new technology and the passing of time.

It may be more appropriate to define the good old days as just different days. Glamorizing the past serves no purpose; it's just rewriting history.

The Impact of Shame

An understanding of shame is critically important to good parenting. Shame often controls what we do and how we see ourselves. Shame is often behind the following traits:

- Low self-esteem and low self-worth. When you believe you are bad at your core, it's hard to feel good about yourself.

- Feeling like you're not good enough. When you live in shame, you do not feel you deserve success, caring friends, or other good things.

- Low self-confidence. When you believe that you're not capable, you will hold back, not believing you can achieve your dreams.

- Believing you are bad. When you have identified punishment with being bad at your core, you believe you are no good.

We live in a shame-based culture, with significant amounts of overt and covert shaming going on. This makes it a challenge to have a shame-free childhood or be shame-free as an adult. Commercials tell us we deserve the best. This message shames those who can't get the best or don't have the best. The media endlessly project thin and beautiful women with perfect complexions, shaming young women for their variety of shapes and looks. Mutual fund commercials show a newly retired sixty-year-old man pulling up in front of his multimillion-dollar home or sailing a $400,000 sailboat. These media messages all contain shaming messages, but it's a passive sort of shame.

A shaming message makes someone feel defective when that person is just fine the way he or she is. Passive shame is sneaky. Everyone who doesn't have what everyone else has, look how they're "supposed" to look, act like they're "supposed" to act, or dress like they're "supposed" to dress is covertly shamed. Of course, it's up to the individual to fend off that message, but it isn't always easy unless he or she understands what's happening.

Our culture clearly defines the *haves* and the *have-nots*. We have private schools for the affluent. Yet even in public schools, the differences are obvious. Some kids get $7,000 four-wheelers for their birthdays or new cars when they turn sixteen, not to mention an iPad or trips to Mexico and Europe. These kids may sit next to a boy in math class who still watches a tube TV at home and gets some of his clothes from a consignment shop. There is nothing wrong with any of these life situations. But teens who "don't have" can feel perpetually faulty and deficient.

We see kids in our professional practices who feel they need certain possessions to avoid humiliation at school. All that parents and educators can do is to play a role in minimizing shame.

Shame is different from remorse in the way it is being used here. Remorse, or healthy guilt, is an appropriate sense that "I have done something wrong." It would be great if a student who cheated on a science test felt guilty about what he or she did. In fact, it's of great concern if the student doesn't feel remorse or have a bad conscience about it.

It's healthy to

- feel remorse that I made the family late,
- feel regret that I didn't keep a promise, or
- feel contrite that I lied about turning in an assignment.

How Shame Works in the Mind

Everyone is partly good and partly bad. All people can be giving at times and remarkably selfish at other times. We all have some attractive features, but we all know somebody better looking than we are. Everyone has let a friend down and, at some other point, come through big-time for a friend. Everyone at some point has lost his or her temper, yet has also exhibited incredible grace and forgiveness.

Those who work with prison inmates may be amazed by the kindness and intelligence of some of those men and women. Contrast that with the ignorance and control that CEOs or religious leaders can exhibit. We all live somewhere in the middle. The bottom line is: You're not as good as you think you are on your best days, and you're not as bad as you think you are on your worst days. We need to recognize that reality and admit it.

Yes, we all live in the middle. Sometimes we fall on our faces, and sometimes we bring a much-needed ray of light to a situation. That is the nature of life and the nature of self-honesty. But knowing and accepting this is difficult for someone haunted by shame.

Shame: Living in the Extremes

At the core of most people's shame is a sense of feeling somewhat defective. When children mix up what they have done with who they are, they come away feeling either arrogant or defective. They may feel as if they have passed the test, beat the odds, and become a model for what life should look like. Or they may feel they have fallen short, are inadequate, and are less than they need to be to have standing with others in their peer group.

By its nature, shame is extreme. Shame will not let us live in the middle as a partly good and partly bad person. It tells us that falling short or making a mistake or having a bad trait is evidence we are not good enough. This sense of feeling defective causes us to hide and defend our mistakes.

Shame can look either positive or negative in different people. Those who live in a *positive shame cycle* endlessly try to live better, perform better, and not let others down. They frequently become perfectionists in order to hide how they really feel about themselves.

People in a positive shame cycle aspire to be kind, smart, attractive, responsible, giving, brave, competent, or whatever qualities they happen to value. This is always at the price of self-honesty. When they act these ways, they actually believe these behaviors accurately describe them. In this state, they ignore how controlling, angry, self-centered, unforgiving, and judgmental they are. Convinced they have made the grade, these individuals believe the world would be a better place with more people like them.

Conversely, shame-based people in a *negative shame cycle* believe or feel they are unattractive, stupid, disliked, afraid, lazy, or incompetent. In this state, they ignore their generosity, accomplishments, kindness, popularity, and any other aspect of "goodness." They deflect compliments and do not see any achievement as *good enough*. Those who live in a negative shame cycle try to hide, defend, and blame away their mistakes as a maladaptive way to fend off feeling defective.

People in a positive shame cycle and those in a negative shame cycle all are driven by shame. The starting quarterback and the valedictorian can be equally as shame-driven as a school dropout or gang member. In this environment, there is no rest and no peace. Why? Because the truth is, we all live in the middle. In shame cycles, shame has in effect taken away the middle, so life never feels quite right.

In a sense, shame whispers in our ear that we are either wonderful or awful, and we must decide each moment. This is why shame-based people can shift from feeling superior to feeling defective as fast as it takes to utter a foolish comment or slip on the ice.

The techniques and parenting approaches shared in this book are designed to minimize shame while still holding our kids to high standards and discipline. In life, shame usually comes from words, either self-talk or words from another source or person. Normally, change comes from our experiences, not from talking. *This is why we cannot emphasize enough the importance of a parenting approach that includes as little discussion about mistakes as possible.*

Many parents think it is profitable to have a "nice long talk" about what went wrong Friday night or why homework wasn't turned in. We believe these talks should be as short as possible, perhaps thirty seconds or less. Perhaps there should be no discussion at all. Here's an important point in good parenting: *For the most part, consequences change behavior and talking fosters shame.*

Molly's Story

Molly is a fourteen-year-old partly good and partly bad kid who is living life in the middle. She asked her mom if she could go to the mall with Lindsey and Steph. Her mother agreed, and Molly and her friends were off for the day. Molly promised her mom that she would not go anywhere else.

At the mall, Molly, Lindsey, and Steph met up with some boys. The five of them decided to go across the parking lot to a pizza place to connect with another group of friends they heard might be in the area. It might not sound like a big deal, but Molly had specifically guaranteed her mother she would only be at the mall and only with her two friends. She was to call home if there was any change in the plan, but she didn't call.

Molly's mom found out, of course. One of her friends called her and mentioned in passing, and with no malicious intent, that she had seen Molly with a group of friends at the pizza place. When Molly returned home, her mom confronted her. Caught off guard and not knowing of the call from her mother's friend, Molly lied about what happened. Her mom understandably felt disrespected by Molly's dishonesty and believed her deception merited a consequence. Molly's mom took her cell phone away and grounded her for four days, and then instructed Molly to meet her in the family office for a talk.

Once in the office, her mom explained the whole story of how she found out about the "deception." Then she talked about how Molly had changed in the last six months. She said another mom had made unflattering comments about Molly's hair and makeup. The friend also said: "Molly doesn't smile like she used to, and she's choosing different clothes. What's going on?"

Molly's mom went on: "You started changing a few months ago. Your grades started dropping, and you've been really mean to your little brother.

"I hoped you wouldn't lie to me when I asked you about the day," she said. "How could you sit there with a straight face and blatantly lie? How could you do that to me? I am so tired of all of this. I can't trust you anymore, and I feel so bad."

Molly stormed out of the "talk," exclaiming, "You are a ninja parent! I hate you, and you are ruining my whole life! Thanks a lot!"

This true story is typical. Some parenting books recommend having these talks. We believe these talks are unproductive and added shame to Molly's life. Molly walked away from this thirty-minute talk feeling like a complete failure. Her grades were bad, her room was a mess, she was a liar, and her friend choices were poor. She wasn't even smiling the right way anymore.

To minimize shame for Molly, her mom could have handled this situation differently. It might have sounded something like this:

"Molly, my friend mentioned she saw you with a bunch of friends at the pizza shack yesterday. I don't know that you were or weren't doing anything wrong there. I just know that isn't what we agreed would happen yesterday. As I recall, we agreed that any change in the plan would need to include calling me. This isn't a big deal to me, but you are going to need to stay home this weekend. Then starting Monday morning we'll be back to normal."

This message is saying: "I'm not commenting on whether I do or don't trust you. I'm just saying you broke our agreement yesterday."

This response simply addresses what Molly did to receive a consequence. There is no grouping of issues, no speculation about wrongdoing, and no discussion about Molly's whole life becoming a disaster. Besides minimizing shame, this approach is simply a more efficient and effective way to parent. This type of comment will result in the greatest likelihood Molly will change for the positive.

Molly's mom is a loving mother, but she was fooled into thinking that Molly would be more likely to change if she heard all the areas of failure in her life over the past couple of months. This is a common mistake. It happens when loving, conscientious, but misguided parents aren't sure what is happening before their very eyes. In addition, Molly's mom believed that Molly didn't feel badly enough about who she had become for her to change.

It's understandable that Molly's mom would conclude this. Molly didn't look sorry—and indeed wasn't sorry—for anything she did that day. In triggering Molly's shame, Mom caused Molly to need to defend her soul and character. Molly's defensiveness reinforced her mother's belief that Molly didn't see what a different child she had become. So Mom tried to bring in the unrelated issues about her grades, her room, her honesty, her kindness, and her smile, all of which had declined.

This approach will never convince Molly to see things she should be concerned about. That isn't what Molly needed.

She needed to know that she broke the agreement and would be staying home for the weekend. That's all.

Minimizing Shame

Always remember that your kids live in a world that heaps shame on them from many directions. How you talk to them will either add to it or help reduce it. Honest, straightforward, simple, and brief communications regarding their mistakes is the best way to reduce shame in their lives. Keep it simple and to the point. Don't contaminate it with other unrelated issues. Stay with a reasonable consequence and follow through. Finally, be hopeful in what you say. Convey to them that what they did doesn't change your love for them. It's not the end of the world, and life will soon return to normal.

The GIST of It

- Shame is the painful feeling of having lost value as a person from a mistake, a comparison, a put-down, or a limitation. We feel *diminished* when we are doing just fine or when we have made a normal human mistake.

- Guilt involves healthy remorse. It's the appropriate feeling after an error. Guilt does not threaten our value or our worth the way shame does. With shame we feel diminished or *less than*.

- Most shame comes from careless words that contribute to people feeling defective and deficient.

- Shame usually functions as either a positive shame cycle or a negative shame cycle. In a positive shame cycle, people look and perform very well as a means to fend off the defectiveness they feel. In a negative shame cycle, people give up or make poor choices as they surrender to their perceived defectiveness.

- We are all partly good and partly bad; we all need to learn to live in the middle of that reality. Shame will not allow us to live in the middle.

- The only way to heal from shame is to simultaneously embrace our flaws and our wonder. We are never totally good or totally bad. We are never a total mess or totally together. When we learn to accept this, we have a chance of healing from shame and living with the peace that the middle brings.

17

OVERPARENTING

People tend to complicate their own lives,
as if living weren't already complicated enough.

CARLOS RUIZ ZAFÓN

THE CHILD CHARACTERS in the movie *Charlie and the Chocolate Factory* show us some interesting things about overparenting. Augustus is an obese candy addict who never stops obsessing about food. His plump mother is his source and supplies him on demand. His eating has become his identity, the way for his mom to keep him happy, and the only connection he has with her.

Violet is very cocky and a proud, world-champion gum chewer. Her trophy cases are filled with dozens of medals and trophies. Her mother has spent much time affirming her and has ingrained in Violet the idea that she "is the best."

Next is Veruca (which means "wart"), a very wealthy, spoiled girl whose father has never said "no" to her. She successfully demands anything and everything from her father. We quickly learn to dislike this entitled child for having no sense of delayed gratification.

And then there's Mike. He is addicted to media, especially video games. For him, stimulation is everything and violence is the outcome. While inside the factory, Mike destroys a pumpkin-shaped candy creation, taking great pleasure in the process. His father stands by watching, incapable of dealing with his son's show of unprovoked violence.

The last kid, and the main character, is Charlie, a sweet young boy from a very poor and destitute family. His father works hard and makes little. Charlie lives in a dilapidated house with his parents and four elderly grandparents. He shares a special relationship with all of them, especially one grandfather who used to work at the chocolate factory. His family is the most important thing he has. He has a gift of wisdom far beyond his years and shares all that he has with those he loves. He ties no conditions to these relationships and is grateful for what little he has, even cabbage soup.

Of course, the characters in the movie are all exaggerations. Charlie knows who he is and where he and his family fit into the world around him. All of the "things" the other children have or are given by their parents pale in comparison to what Charlie knows he has: a family who loves him, a heart for people, and a peace about his life's condition. He simply is himself, not trying to perform or impress, not trying to get more for himself. He needs no praise for his behavior.

The other children are examples of overparenting—one of the most common mistakes parents make. Just like when we overdo anything else, overparenting takes over our lives and results in an unhealthy family system. Too often our instinct to become involved, affirm, indulge, and protect becomes a mission to keep our children far away from the truth about themselves and the reality of their life and world.

The Mistake of Overinvolvement

We believe in parenting as little as possible. By this we mean to wear your parenting hat as little as possible. You may have a child who is polite enough, eats well enough, studies just enough, helps out around the house just barely enough, has pretty good friends, and goes to bed without a scene. This type of kid just needs you to sit back and enjoy his growth.

The first time your child won't come to the table when you call him or her for supper, just go ahead and eat without him. Until this pattern repeats itself and becomes a problem, there is no need to do anything.

We know numerous parents with pretty good kids who need parenting only a few hours a month; yet the adults are parenting eight to ten hours a day. This is overparenting.

It usually starts with a parent being overly critical for no apparent reason. When the mom senses intuitively that she has been picking on a relatively good kid, she may try to offset the critical comments with praise and affirmations. Praise will never offset our being critical. We need to stop pretending that it will.

Kids need to be left alone when they are functioning well. In our offices we have asked many parents these simple questions: "What grade point average would your child need to maintain in school for you to sign a contract saying you agree never to mention homework, studying, or school again?" Or, "Would you agree to never mention homework if your daughter or son maintained a 3.7 grade point average?" Nearly every time the answer is: "I would never agree to that. I don't care how well my child is doing; I want the right to talk to him about school."

This same pattern carries over to a dozen other areas,

including discussions about food choices, how clean a bedroom is, how the dishwasher is loaded, a situation on the school bus, a baseball breaking a neighbor's window, or who is to blame in a sibling squabble. Needlessly parenting when nothing needs to be done is overparenting, and it sometimes borders on harassment. It is parenting when nothing is wrong or parenting when the child has the situation well under control.

If the child needs your help, that's fine. But if your child is handling the broken window on his or her own, why get involved? That would be overparenting.

Let kids have their lives, their school, their friends, their dilemmas, and their solutions. If it isn't working, step in. A great comment would be, "About that window you broke next door—take it as far as you can with Mr. Johnson, and then if you need any help, you can ask me." If the child is managing the situation, back away and see what happens. To do anything else is to overparent.

In a given situation you could ask your kid, "What do you think you should do?" You'll never know how good an answer you might get if you don't ask.

The Mistake of Overaffirmation

One overparenting mistake we see many parents make is overaffirmation. Affirming our children is fine, but too much of a good thing creates problems. Too much of a bad thing creates problems too.

In the "Tell the Truth" chapter, we wrote about the risk of inaccurate affirmations. The caution about affirmations here focuses on simply overusing them. Even accurate affirmations can become too repetitive.

Early overaffirmations are found in and outside the home. Observe the posters often displayed in our elementary schools with their positive messages about how great every student is. When part of a child's world is saturated with affirmation, most of those affirmations become white noise and don't build self-esteem in children. Affirmation becomes an expected and repetitive part of each day.

Children track how many compliments and accolades they receive compared with the other kids in the class and compare them with what they have received before. When they hear a constant flow of accolades and admiration, particularly when they have achieved nothing out of the ordinary, children dismiss most of these comments and do not internalize anything beneficial. Children then need a silent or invisible quota of affirmation in order to get their attention. If a boy is told he did well at something, he puts it into a context of how many times he was told yesterday that he did that thing well. He also weighs it against the number of compliments the other children his age received at school or in social settings at that particular time. Then the child evaluates it all to see if anything is worth letting into his spirit.

Parents reduce the chances of their hoped-for outcome by inundating a child with too frequent encouragement. To improve the effect of an affirmation, briefly give praise when it is merited and accurate.

Overaffirmation is rooted in our need to nurture. Parents are hoping to develop their child's inner spirit when they overuse affirmation. The best way to accomplish this is to simply watch and enjoy your child with your full attention. Saying, "I had so much fun watching you build that fort," is a far better way to nurture than saying, "That is the best

fort ever!" This gives the child what he or she really wants—
to know he or she is important to you and brings you joy.
You can accomplish this with silence or minimal words. Your
child can see in your eyes that he or she is important to you.
Telling your child that a mediocre fort is the "best fort ever"
will not achieve this goal and will hurt your credibility.

Comparative words are often used instinctively in accolades. These are words like "best," "more than," or "better
than." It is easy to use these words in a compliment. But
over time, these comments can become more destructive
than helpful. Every person has the opportunity to learn,
train, practice, strive, and work toward goals in life. When
a child does anything worth noting, briefly mention that
you noticed something admirable about what he or she did,
without comparing it to other children or that child's past.

Overaffirmation can also be an attempt, subconsciously,
to offset being overly critical. The parent may realize that
he's been too critical of his child one evening and then tries
to balance the harsh remarks with affirmations. This strategy
doesn't work and will only cause "feedback overload." You
can't balance too much criticism. It's better to own your mistake, admit it to your daughter or son, and then apologize.

Remember, a constant flow of affirmations and encouragement is not helpful and doesn't even mean that much to
a child. Part of why precious metals are valuable is because
they are rare. Flooding the market with a million tons of
gold would depreciate its value. It works the same way with
constant, unfocused accolades given to kids on a normal day
when they have done nothing out of the ordinary: Too much
praise depreciates affirming comments.

Overaffirmation renders children unable to honestly

assess themselves. When parents overuse even accurate affirmations, kids will begin to expect them. If the frequency of those true affirmations decreases, the child begins to wonder what's wrong with him or her. "Why isn't Mom telling me how well I'm doing at school?" It's not just false affirmations that are harmful. Oversaying "I'm proud of you," even if it's true, is not helpful and adds stress to a child's life.

The Dangers of Overindulgence

Overindulgence is another form of overparenting and is rooted in our culture's inaccurate message that to be the best parents we need to give everything to our kids.

Our culture tells us that our children deserve it all and need it now. The list of indulgences is long enough to fill a book. A few of those things might be $300 video game systems, smartphones, American Girl dolls, iPods and iPads, motorized scooters, sports camps, dance lessons, $125 basketball shoes, Barbie cars, custom birthday parties, bedroom computers, limos to prom, and $90 jeans. The available choices today are staggering, and have created in us and in our kids an insatiable appetite for more. In our abundant society, it can be easy to forget that we *want* many things yet *need* little.

Overindulgence results in a child who feels entitled. This inability to delay gratification creates entitled young adults (and gets many of their parents into difficult financial situations). It's an ongoing battle not to buy for kids what everyone else already has. Jimmy just got a new Xbox in his bedroom. Kayla's mom bought her designer jeans. Corey's parents got him a car for his sixteenth birthday.

It's countercultural to teach our children that money

doesn't grow on trees and that waiting is a good thing. Having it all at a young age hinders natural creativity in our children. They spend a lot of time looking and pining for the next new thing. They play less and lose their natural ability to be creative. Overindulging our children steals the "child" out of childhood and creates the entitled generation we see today.

The Boredom Experiment

Imagine if parents actually allowed their children to get bored for five days over summer vacation. Let's say the parents decide to do the following experiment: no TV, no trips to the mall, no friends over, no technology, no swimming at the community center, and no video games for five days.

One family did this when their three kids were ages eleven, eight, and six. What happened was very interesting. For almost three days, the siblings complained and whined, but to no avail. On the third day, they decided to go outside and build a fort. And that's what they did. Together they searched for old two-by-fours and sheets of wood, tools, nails, screws, and glue. Then they found an acceptable tree in the woods across the street and started building. For two days they built. When they finished, it wasn't pretty, but it worked. It was sturdy and big enough. It was their creation, and they were very proud of what they had accomplished. Most creations, like forts, start from boredom.

Overprotection

Overprotection, the last piece of the overparenting quartet, seems to be the most common. Parents who overprotect rarely let their kids fall down in life. In essence, they are the cushions always hovering beneath their child. The goal is to protect their child from experiencing the pain of life when he or she gets in trouble, doesn't make the team, or fails in some way.

These parents make excuses for their children when there's a potential for disappointment. Sometimes the excuses are directed at the child: "The coach has it in for you." Or, "Your team lost because the ref was terrible." Or, "You didn't get the lead in the musical because the director is good friends with Melanie's parents."

The primary consequence of overprotection is dependency. These children are so conditioned to being bailed out that they are not able to cope with the adult world. Eventually their parents will not be there to protect them and they will crumble. Overprotection may even cause some kids to grow up with a skewed and fearful view of the world.

Which one teaches us more about ourselves: success or failure? Is wisdom learned from everything going as we think it should or from our collisions with life? When children grow up overprotected, their emotional growth is hindered, and their ability to deal with adversity is greatly reduced. The resulting dependency on their parents when things get a little rough will prevent them from being self-sufficient adults. Letting our kids fall down and feel disappointment and pain in life is an essential part of good parenting. They need to learn how to deal with the things life deals them. The wonderful experiences of disappointment are invaluable opportunities for growth.

Let's imagine your son, Luke, tries out for the school musical and really wants a particular part, but he doesn't get it. Instead, he's put in the chorus and now wants to quit. But quitting is not what your family would support. What should a parent say in this situation or any other situation of disappointment? If you feel like you need to say anything, here are a couple of options:

- "You are a good singer, Luke, but Miss Chadwick must think you will have a better experience in the chorus. I would trust her judgment."

- "I can see this didn't happen the way you hoped it would go. Life is often like that."

These types of acknowledging messages from a parent help children learn resilience and overcome disappointment. Swooping in to protect them from life's disappointments will have the opposite effect. If what just happened that disappointed your child reflects how life often works, not saying anything would also be one of your options.

The GIST of It
- The overparenting big four are: overinvolvement, over-affirmation, overindulgence, and overprotection.

- Kids with overinvolved parents end up feeling controlled and resentful.

- Overaffirmed kids end up with an inaccurate picture of who they are.

- Overindulged kids end up feeling entitled.

- Overprotected kids end up dependent.

- When your child is doing life well, just enjoy it. Compliments and criticism are simply not needed.

PART III

Unintended Parenting

18

BE CAREFUL WHAT YOU SAY

Words can be more hurtful than anything physically. I got little kids,
and it's common sense when you're raising them that the main thing
is how you talk to people, and how you treat people.

· ERIC CHURCH

AT TIMES WE ALL SPEAK IN CLICHÉS. We mindlessly repeat
unexamined platitudes or vent our frustrations without stopping to consider the effect of our words. As parents, we need
to become more careful of our use of certain words and messages, particularly the messages we repeatedly convey to our
kids or ourselves. Platitudes passed down from previous generations may need to be reassessed. To make sure we understand what it is we're communicating, we need to rethink the
messages we give our kids.

The first step in change is to be aware. First, we'll focus on
two statements commonly used by parents that can have serious negative consequences. Because these statements are so
pervasively used—although both are baseless—we'll address
them specifically.

Next, we will look at the ineffective consequences of the use of threats, warnings, and reminders. Too many parents have an arsenal made up primarily of these parenting "tools." We recommend this arsenal of tools be eliminated from every parent's parenting toolbox, or at least minimized.

Finally, we will look at the dynamic of lashing out at our kids, or unloading. We as parents need to recognize, prior to blowups or disappointments or moments of fear, what messages we can't afford to give our children. After we say them, we can't take them back. Parenting can be trying and exasperating. At those times, it is easy to do more damage than you're aware of if you aren't careful. We want to bring these messages to light so we as parents can make an internal decision, outside any emotional trigger, not to ever communicate certain messages that could scar our kids.

"Just Do Your Best"

Many parents think the phrase "Just do your best" is a useful expression or even a wonderful thing to say to their kids—a cross between accountability and grace. But saying this to your child is inviting him or her inside a riddle. It might even add unnecessary stress to your child's life.

We believe that it's not only ineffective to use this platitude, but it also can be damaging. Before you pass judgment on what we're saying and dismiss this as just semantics or an insignificant and unimportant distinction, please keep an open mind. Then decide what you think.

Try saying the statement "Just do your best" aloud a few times. It even sounds like a riddle. Wouldn't it make more sense to pair *just* with something that has to do with being average? "Just be mediocre" makes sense—"Just do your best" doesn't. Someone's best is the absolute limit of what he or she can do. Saying, "Just do the limit of what you can do" seems like an odd way to use the word *just.*

There are three major problems with telling your child "Just do your best."

1. It's Unachievable

First, it's an elusive, unachievable goal. *Best* is unachievable over time when you think about it. It requires us to always give a perfect effort.

When your teenage son has an English paper due in a week and you tell him, "Just do your best," he will inevitably fail to do his best. If your son watches any TV that week, goes to a movie or a high school football game, talks on the phone, or eats junk food that makes him lethargic, he won't do his best in writing the English paper. He could have written a better paper if he hadn't done any one of those things.

In other words, when parents say "Just do your best" to a child, they are really saying, "Just don't do anything that has any chance of negatively impacting your paper." You may be thinking, *That's not what I mean when I say that.* Exactly. Then don't say it at all, because that's what the child must respond to, whether she knows what you mean or not.

For brief periods in life, it's possible and perhaps a good idea to *do your best,* but those times are usually few and far between. A child doing his best on a four-hour test, doing her best at a tennis match, or doing his best in a job interview are all reasonable and perhaps helpful exceptions. All these examples encompass a short time frame in which a best effort is reasonable and helpful.

Ultimately, kids do better if a parent's expectations are well articulated and clearly defined.

2. It Opposes the Law of Diminishing Returns

Second, "Just do your best" messes with something called the law of diminishing returns. Our kids need to be trained in understanding the law of diminishing returns to work effectively in the world. But this law is in complete opposition to the maxim "Just do your best." The law of diminishing returns is an innate part of our everyday thinking. When it comes to any particular endeavor, we have to intuitively understand how to find the point of diminishing returns. If we think to ourselves, *Five minutes is enough time to spend on this email*, we are using the law of diminishing returns. If we don't implement this principle, our lives become inefficient and unbalanced.

Telling kids to "Just do your best" delays their learning this important law. It would be more effective to encourage them to find the point of diminishing returns. Ask them if they know the right amount of time to invest in a situation. If they don't know, help them with this. Mowing the lawn, emptying the dishwasher, washing the car, maybe even doing a math assignment, are all things kids should learn to do "good enough."

It's fine to have high expectations for our kids. It's our role as parents to encourage and instruct our children to commit to something, focus on something, or even carry out an extraordinary effort toward something. We are not advocating lowering expectations.

If your daughter has a part in the school play and is concerned about learning her lines, tell her to have Act I memorized by Saturday. Define what she needs to do in achievable steps. It's not important whether she memorized her lines by *doing her best*. It's simply important that she knows her part. Telling her to do her best gives her no road map to actually do what she needs to do.

To "do her best" might require a teen to live in isolation and have no other interests in order to earn a 3.8 GPA, while it would actually be better for her to have a 3.4 GPA, enjoy a social life, take pictures for the yearbook, and participate in a theater production.

It's also really hard to figure out how to do your best. Thousands of athletes are surprised to find that their game has not really improved after an intense off-season of conditioning and reducing body fat. Training year-round and repeated-motion injuries can be the result of an athlete attempting to "do his best" instead of finding the point of diminishing returns. The *do your best* mind-set is responsible for reduced accomplishments in many athletes. This is currently a major topic of discussion and study with sports trainers and sports psychologists. The merits of cross-training in different sports and taking a season off from a sport are gaining more support from the athletic community.

3. It Teaches Kids to Lie

A third reason we oppose "Just do your best" is that the whole dialogue around it is a breeding ground for lying and self-deception. Requesting this of your children puts them in a situation where they must lie to themselves to justify their efforts because they really didn't do their best. Children also end up lying to their parents to make them feel good.

If the emotional economy and the vocabulary in the home

support it, kids will start using that phrase without thinking. It becomes the accepted phraseology in the home. Kids learn what to say that will work for them in the family system. To diminish conflict they learn to say, "Leave me alone," or "I didn't mean to," or "She started it." They also learn that saying "But I did my best" gets people off their backs.

In a family where the vocabulary is all about doing one's best, only an unusually mature kid could say, "I didn't do my best; however I put about as much time into that as it merited, and I think I did pretty well."

Integrating this platitude into the family system brings a price. "Just do your best" statements are likely to lead to self-deception or stress. Either children will be dishonest about their efforts or, if they are honest, they will find it stressful because they will repeatedly have to admit that they *could* have done better. Giving something your best leaves nothing out, which takes a lot of focus and self-discipline. We need to do as much as possible to reduce stress and self-deception among our children, because self-deception is at the core of low self-esteem, fear, addiction, and delusional thinking.

How to Encourage Balance

Encourage balance by telling your child specifically what it is you want or expect. It's appropriate to tell your daughter that you expect her to get at least a 3.0 GPA this semester, if that's a reasonable expectation for her. Tell your daughter you want her to play with intensity and have fun at the basketball tournament. Tell your son that you'd like him to eat nutritious food at his friend's cabin, or that you want him to be in bed by 10:00 p.m. the night before his cross-country race.

Replace the phrase "Just do your best" with tangible or

balanced terms, and do not tell your child, "All we expect is your best." Your child doesn't know what that means. Nobody knows what that means.

"We Did That Stuff When We Were Kids!"

When parents say, "We did that stuff when we were kids," it's usually in reference to kids doing something foolish, dangerous, or illegal. If you use this rationalization in your parenting, please consider how unsound this thinking is.

Adults sometimes communicate this belief to kids. More often, it is communicated in a conversation between parents and friends. Most of the time, parents use this thinking when it's related to a risky activity. But this rationalization offers no useful information when you are assessing whether or not you should allow your child to engage in dangerous, foolish, or illegal behavior. While it may be true that you did *x*, *y*, or *z* when you were your child's age, that fact is irrelevant to your child's present situation. Sometimes parents have difficulty separating what they did growing up with what their child is currently dealing with. This can be at their child's peril.

Consider this logic: A dad grew up near a small lake where he had access to a fishing boat with an old outboard motor. On hot summer days, he and his friends would take the boat out on the lake, swim, and go tubing around the lake to cool off. Thinking back on those summer evenings, he recalls that he and his buddies never bothered wearing life jackets.

Fast-forward thirty years. This dad now has a seventeen-year-old son, and he discovers that his son just spent a weekend at a friend's lake cabin. All weekend they were tubing without life jackets. If the dad thinks, *Well, we did that stuff when we were kids*, he is falling victim to a phenomenon known as the *narrative fallacy*. In logic, the narrative fallacy is our need to attach a story or pattern to a series of connected or disconnected facts, which serves to distort the interpretation of the facts.

The narrative of this dad's personal tubing story is altering and interfering with the accuracy of the way he's interpreting his son's story. Most of us do this. If we hear a story or remember something that happened to us, even if it's as simple as how we got over a cold, it can alter data as we process current information.

For the son, tubing without a life jacket is exactly as dangerous (or as safe) as it is. Dad's experience tubing thirty years earlier without a life jacket (and not drowning) has nothing to do with the risk his son is taking now. We don't know what the probability factor is, but the son has the exact same probability of drowning in the lake, regardless of anything his dad did thirty years ago. Dad's experience tubing thirty years earlier is irrelevant to what he should decide to do about his son's weekend.

The narrative fallacy is most dangerous when the story involves danger. This would include anything a parent remembers fondly from his or her past that involved poor judgment—but where a high price was not paid. These memories serve to do nothing more than to distort thinking. This thinking can be distorted in either direction—it can make something dangerous seem safer than it is, such as parents who drove without incident while they were high as teenagers, or it can make something safe feel more dangerous than it is. If thirty years earlier a dad went skiing one time and broke his leg, this dad may perceive skiing as more dangerous than statistics or logic would support.

Allowing Smart Risks

The goal is not to keep our children totally safe. In fact, it is extremely dangerous to try to raise kids too safely, so we strongly endorse *smart risks*. The goal is to assess as accurately as possible the opportunity that is before your children.

Smoking weed (which increasingly may be laced with something to amp it up), drinking eighteen shots on your eighteenth birthday, driving after a drink or two, white-water rafting, sleeping around, getting a tattoo in Mexico, and yes—even skiing—are all things that are exactly as dangerous as they are.

These risks do not change because of your story. Your story can distort your judgment today with your own children. The fact that you may have engaged in some risky activities in your teen years without consequence should have no bearing on whether your child should engage in those activities. Remember, there is a better chance that your personal history is distorting your objectivity than that it is helping your thinking today.

It may be impossible to precisely weigh any risk, but we'll do a better job if we're aware that our stories are often not helping our assessment. Research, discussions, and an expert opinion can be useful, but someone's story is not.

Those Ineffective Threats, Reminders, and Warnings

There are exceptions, but a good rule to live by is to avoid threats, reminders, and warnings while raising your kids. When parents hear this concept, they sometimes respond,

"If I took away threats, reminders, and warnings I would have very little left. That's how I keep control as a parent." We think there are better options for influencing your kids.

Threats

Threats are simply ineffective. Their use is overrated. By using threats, you are teaching your son that he doesn't really have to listen to you until the threats start coming. Typically, a boy raised in a home that uses threats will tend to play a video game long after his bedtime because he doesn't even think about closing down the game until the threats start coming. Parents should not have to use threats at home to be taken seriously. For that matter, threats should not occur at school or work either. How would it feel for you as an adult to have an atmosphere of threats every day at your workplace?

Don't be fooled by the times that a threat produces the desired behavior. Threats may get your daughter to put her bike away. However, if we look at discipline from the perspective that it's meant to elevate a child's behavior across the board, are your threats working?

Here's a simple way to find out: If your daughter puts her bike away on the day she was threatened, we could conclude that threats didn't really work if she leaves her bike out again tomorrow. In this case, the threats did nothing to grow her up, despite the fact that her bike is now in the garage.

Also, many threats are unenforceable, vague, and poorly developed. Threats often teach your child that you don't know what to do or you don't mean what you say. In fact, you may actually feel a little out of control when you are expressing a threat. The classic ". . . or else!" reveals to your child with certainty that you have little or no idea what you are doing right then. Parents might as well say out loud, "I don't know what to do next," rather than the habitual ". . . or else."

Finally, threats usually reveal a parent's emotional investment in the outcome. The best learning environment for your child is when the parent has no emotional stake in the issue. This dynamic isn't always possible, but when it is present, it is powerful. This is when the child will most likely learn from an event. Parents who can stay emotionally detached improve the learning climate immensely.

Using this approach, a parent might say: "Clean the gutters and you can go out Friday night. Don't clean the gutters and I get to have you home with me. Either option is fine with me. I'd like hanging out with you this weekend anyway." This creates the best learning atmosphere at home. In the right setting, you could say something like: "You can mow the lawn Saturday and I will pay you twenty dollars. If the lawn isn't mowed by noon on Sunday, I will call your cousin and pay him the twenty dollars. We don't need to talk about it again and I am fine with either choice."

We are distinguishing between threats and data in this section. Repeatedly saying to your daughter, "You better keep that phone off at night or I'm going to give it to your brother," is only a threat if there is no follow-through and nothing changes as she sends texts throughout the night. However, if you calmly take the phone and give it to her brother, then that comment was data. Kids need to know the precise and accurate data or information pertaining to the consequences of their decisions. Too often statements that start with "You had better . . . " are threats because nothing significant ever changes in the child's world.

Reminders

Does reminding your child to do things make him a better "rememberer" or a better forgetter? We often hear parents say, "I remind him and remind him and my son still forgets." Of course he forgets. In a home full of parental reminders, the son knows that somebody needs to remember the dark blue jersey, and he knows Mom will do that. Reminders teach our children to be forgetters.

Parents may just think about the moment and forget their job is getting their kids ready for adulthood. They just want to make sure their child doesn't miss an event or forget to take her soccer spikes to practice. But they are missing the overall goal, which is raising a responsible, mindful, life-ready young adult. Solving the problem with constant reminders won't develop a child in this way.

Reminders also relieve the child of his or her personal responsibility and transfer it onto someone else. Often kids say something like this when they forget to take a makeup test or attend an appointment for the family photo: "It's not my fault; you didn't remind me."

Recently, a forty-six-year-old woman said that after twenty-three years of never once forgetting her husband's birthday, this year she forgot it. For years she had always remembered the day, but recently she had become accustomed to having her iPhone remind her about birthdays and had misplaced her phone the day before his birthday. It's fine to use a calendar to remember things. The point is simply that reminders make us forgetters. If we need reminders, they should be for some thing or event for which we take responsibility. We can hardly be angry with our child for forgetting a backpack if we have proven to him or her that it's our job to remember the backpack.

Warnings

There are limited situations where warnings are a good strategy. Warnings work at the airport or at a national park when we are cautioned about a situation we are unfamiliar with. For example, "Don't feed the bears," or "Please place all fluids in a plastic bag." Warnings work at home when the caution concerns a situation that may be new to our child.

For instance, telling a four-year-old that something is hot or telling a sixteen-year-old that the roads are slippery are examples of appropriate warnings. These give new and potentially important information. A warning that conveys new information is helpful and appropriate in the family. "Be careful; they're forecasting a storm for later this afternoon" is an informational warning and is helpful. Warning also works well when someone outside the family system makes the warning. The park ranger and airport announcements are not part of our personal family systems. Warning a neighbor kid or warning your niece may yield the precise and desired response because we are warning someone who is outside the family system.

These exceptions rarely take place in the family. This is why "don't warn" makes our list of parenting tips. The classic "I'm warning you" is meaningless, impotent, unclear, and self-sustaining. If your twelve-year-old boy is supposed to be off the computer by 9:00 p.m., warning him that it is 9:10 p.m. is not productive. Often warnings simply pollute the home atmosphere and fill it with tension and words that hurt relationships. When warnings are used repeatedly in the context of a family system, they become essentially worthless.

Kids learn at an early age what the *warning quota* is for certain offenses. They learn how many warnings usually accompany "Turn off your phone" and how many go with "You can't wear that top." It's almost like a softball player who knows how many balls he needs to take to get a walk. If there are five warnings to practice the violin, the child learns this and the first four warnings are meaningless.

It's far more effective, especially with a challenging child, to handle things in a way that doesn't involve warnings. For instance, in the family that adopts a practice where the TV is on a timer and shuts off at 9:00 p.m., there is be no need to warn, remind, or threaten concerning kids watching TV too late. The house is peaceful, and the kids just expect the TV to go off at that time. Granted, there may be some opposition the first two weeks this plan is implemented, but soon it will work smoothly.

Of course, periodic warnings are fine and can even serve a purpose in a family. The point is that in many homes, warnings have become meaningless background noise and are no longer an asset to the family system. If you listen to the dialogue in your home and hear more than one or two warnings in an entire day, they have probably lost their usefulness.

Unloading on Kids

Understandably, parenting can push some parents to the limit of their sanity like nothing else can. We have immense empathy for parents who are pacing the floor at 3:00 a.m. and wiping away tears while they repeatedly check the driveway, hoping their daughter or son will come home safely. We have both been these parents. We know many others who have gone through this as well, and it's terribly difficult.

In times when your relationship with your child is

maximally strained, it's important to remember that this child is also in pain and potentially in danger. It's also important to decide beforehand what messages you will never communicate, regardless of the situation. No matter how dark the blackness gets, don't ever tell your child that he or she is unwanted. Don't slip and say what you don't mean. Don't say it even if you do mean it. No one thing is as damaging to a child's psyche as being told he or she is or was unwanted.

Extreme comments sound like this:

- "I wish you were never born."
- "I regret that we adopted you."
- "I can't wait for you to leave home."
- "You were a huge mistake. We should have stopped at two children."
- "You have brought pain into my life since you were born."
- "Because you were born, my life was ruined."

Milder versions of the same comments are:

- "Next year you will be out of here and we won't have to deal with you."
- "You have always been more difficult than your brother, even when you were little."
- "Maybe you'll have a child like you someday, and then you'll know what it's like."

You may be mildly aghast to think that any conscientious parent would ever say those things. Yet they are said all the time. We hear about it in our practices. It may happen on a dark and scary night when your job is particularly difficult, when that youngest child is seventeen and you've been parenting for twenty-nine years and you're exhausted, or when you feel sorry for yourself. We can empathize with the situation, but you must work really hard to *not ever* say those words to your child, even if that's how you feel.

When things are derailing, parents need to remember the following:

- Don't take things personally.

- When a child's reaction far exceeds what seems reasonable, there's probably a lot more to the story than you know.

- If you had the missing information, a lot of what you're seeing in your kid would make sense.

- Words are like toothpaste. Remember, once they're out of the tube, it's hard to get them back in.

- Most confrontations are a result of months or years of history. These situations usually don't happen overnight.

If you've already said hurtful words to your child like those we listed on the last page, it's likely that you need to get more support. It may be appropriate for you to say to your child, "Last spring, when things were really rough between us, I said some things I never should have said. It would have been easy for you to think that you have only brought sadness to me. That's not true, and that was my fear speaking. That may even be part of why we're not getting along right now. You are very precious to me."

It's never too late to try to reconcile a wrong. Though it may take a while, both sides benefit from an apology.

There are numerous ways to express your feelings in a situation without a blatant rejection. You can say things such as:

- "I never thought we would be down this road together."

- "With your behavior, you are choosing to not live here anymore."

- "I love you, but I hate seeing you this way."

- "I wish you could know how much I love you. I know that it doesn't show when I get this angry at your lies."

We believe in honest and open parenting. Just be careful on this issue; it can be so damaging. Harsh rejection from a parent can wound a child's soul. Some parents reading this book may remember some hurtful things that were said to them. They will know firsthand what a hurdle that is to get over.

The GIST of It

- Avoid saying, "Just do your best." It usually works better to tell your son what you expect. More power to your daughter if she can do what you expect without it being her best.

- Be careful not to say anything so hurtful that you can never take it back.

- Threats, reminders, and warnings are not helpful.

- Your own childhood stories do not really help with current decisions and perspectives. Our stories are more about probability than they are about evidence.

- Be extra careful what you say to your child when you are hurt, scared, angry, or confused.

19

THE BLACK HOLE OF TECHNOLOGY

A dead thing can go with the stream,
but only a living thing can go against it.

G. K. CHESTERTON

HENDRICK WAS A TYPICAL eleven-year-old boy. He loved life and family and enjoyed a wide range of activities. He had always been a B student, but this year things had changed. He had become more irritable with family and seemed to be anxious most of the time. His grades had dropped, and the teacher said he didn't engage with learning. His family situation was stable; there had been no moves, divorces, illnesses, or deaths.

Two months earlier, Hendrick started playing Minecraft with his school buddies. Unfortunately, what began as an entertaining group activity became Hendrick's constant preoccupation. He thought about Minecraft all the time and spent hours on the video game console striving to build and create. This activity to enjoy with friends had become an isolating obsession. He had trouble sleeping, getting his chores finished, doing his homework, and just relaxing like he used to. His parents were concerned they were losing their son.

⟋⟍

"Why are the world's greatest public technocrats also its greatest private technophobes?"[1] This question, asked by author Adam Alter in his book *Irresistible*, speaks to what the creators of our tech-immersed world do in their own homes—they deliberately keep their children from the devices and apps they develop.

New York Times writer Nick Bilton interviewed several technology giants in late 2010 and found similarities. Steve Jobs seldom let his kids use an iPad. Chris Anderson, former *Wired* editor, instituted rigid limitations on all the devices at home, including forbidding screens in the kids' bedrooms. Twitter founder Evan Williams never allowed his kids to use iPads but made a large library of books available to them. Greg Hochmuth, one of the engineers who created Instagram, was quoted as saying, "There's always another hashtag to click on. Then it takes on its own life, like an organism, and people can become obsessive." Tristan Harris, former Google employee and design ethicist, stated, "There are a thousand people on the other side of the screen whose job it is to break down the self-regulation you have."[2]

Please, Not Another Technology Tirade!

For several reasons we're compelled to include a chapter on technology in this book.

First, all ages—from grandparents down to infants—now spend an increasing amount of time on screens, so a chapter on technology is important and essential. In fact, if you look around, you might notice that the effects of excessive technology aren't just a kid issue. Years ago, we consistently heard parents telling their kids to put their phones down. Now it's just as common to hear kids asking their parents to put their phones down. Because of this, it's hard for parents to confront their children about excessive screen time when their own use is out of control. Kids are increasingly viewing adults as merely hypocritical, and they have a point.

Next, we believe it's important for parents to recognize patterns and behaviors that suggest their child has an obsession, addiction, or just a distorted understanding of the relative importance of technology. Technology was created to be an asset in our lives, not an "everything." But for various reasons, including the way apps and programs are created to "hook" us, many people have lost a healthy view of where technology fits into the scheme of life.

Finally, there will be a time (and maybe we're already there) when technology will become so much a part of our lives, our interactions, and our identities that important parts of our humanity will be lost. Someday, our humanness could be replaced by a virtual identity, monitored and controlled by the next generations of Alexa, "Hi Google," and Siri.

This chapter is probably as hard to read as it was to write. Many of you will start reading it but not finish. It might hit too close to home, make you angry, or make you feel hopeless. You may see statistics you would just as soon not see. Push through it, though, because we may already be too close to the tipping point. We have included several practical tips at the end of this chapter.

Consequences of Screen Time for Kids:
What Research Is Revealing

The amount of time we're now spending on screens is shocking. The latest research on average screen time for American children ages eight to eighteen years is more than 53 hours per week.[3] This includes cell phones, laptops, video games, and TV. At more than seven hours per day, many kids do more screen time than sleep or school. Adults are not far behind. This amount of time has an effect on our ability to communicate, connect, and deal with adversity as we spend less and less time face-to-face. It also influences our emotions, our cognitive functioning, our sleep, and our attention spans.

At malls and in restaurants every day, it's easy to see babies under twelve months old with screens in front of their faces. Many times, the screens are placed there by their parents to keep them quiet, calm them down, or to free the parents to be on a screen. The problem with this strategy is that these little ones will not learn the ability to calm themselves and know that being upset is a normal part of life.

There are several concerning questions about current research:

"Are negative screen effects permanent or reversible?"
We don't know.
"How much time is too much time?" *We don't know.*

"Is the rapid rise in ADHD related to screen time?"
Maybe.
"Is the rising incidence of autism due to screen time?"
We don't know.
"What's the best way to treat screen addiction?" *We don't know.*
"Does screen time negatively affect learning?" *We don't know.*
"Do kids learn better or worse with technology?" *We don't know.*
"Is the uptick in teen depression linked to technology?"
Yes. This we know.

These are just a few questions that need answering. We hope that future research will help. The following categories of potential consequences of screen time reveal reasons for concern, including emotional effects, wasted time, changes in communication, cyberbullying, undesirable cognitive effects, sleep disruption, increasing addiction patterns, injury to overall health, contributions to ADD/ADHD, and neuro-anatomic and neurobiologic changes in children's brains.

Emotions
- Research has shown that excessive screen time creates kids who are irritable, moody, restless, oppositional, and easily angered.[4]

- Currently about 12.5 percent of teenagers in the United States are, or have recently been, depressed. This percent is drastically lower for teens who spend less than an hour a day on social media, and significantly higher for teens who are on social media more than four hours a day. (Social media includes texts, Instagram, Snapchat, etc.)[5]

- Excessive screen time in nine- to ten-year-old girls has been shown to lower self-esteem, and violent video games in preteen and teenage boys increase aggressiveness and disrespectful behaviors.[6]

- Screen time appears to be negatively affecting how kids understand their peers' emotional cues.[7]

- Most people who experiment with being off screens typically have the same positive response: relief.

Wasted Time

- Unbelievably, today's average gamer is thirty-four years old.[8]

- This average gamer has been playing video games for at least twelve years at eighteen hours per week.

- Twelve million monthly subscribers to the game *World of Warcraft* have spent 50 billion human hours of game time since its inception in 2004.[9] Half of the 2.1 billion worldwide Facebook users log in to spend an average of twenty-four to thirty-two minutes per day.[10]

- Candy Crush has thirty-two thousand new downloads per day, has been downloaded by more than three billion people, has 293 million monthly users, and generates an estimated $391 million per month in revenue.[11]

Communication Changes

- The art of conversation and sitting face-to-face with friends and family to dialogue about our daily experiences have been replaced with short, frequently misinterpreted tweets, snaps, emojis, and texts.

- In the business world, the cell-phone generation is reluctant to engage in direct communication with coworkers.[12]

- Google "millennial communication in the workplace" and you'll get millions of results.

- Millennials are averse to phone calls because that means they would have to have a conversation with a coworker, client, or boss.

- Seventy percent of millennials would prefer texting to any other form of communication, although emails are still okay since they don't have the same level of urgency that texts do.[13]

- Digital communications reduce interpersonal coping skills, which increases the likelihood of depression.[14]

American novelist Jonathan Safran Foer is credited with saying, "When we accept diminished substitutes, we become diminished substitutes."[15] This applies to the lost art of communication.

Cyberbullying

- It's easier to inflict pain on people when you don't see their pain. This is the reality of bullying with technology.

- Never before have we seen the level of bullying we see today. It's mean-spirited, vindictive, and destructive. With a little time and a few clicks on a screen, cyber-bullies can change their victims' lives. Cyberbullying is not a one-on-one thing; it's a mass distribution of gossip, slander, defamation, and backstabbing.[16]

- Victims are vulnerable to the dissemination of mis-representations about them, and their lives are destroyed, sometimes to the point of self-harm and suicide. News stories regularly report this tragedy.[17]

- Many times bullying happens with a repost or retweet that was never meant to be mean-spirited. Cyberbullying often happens without the bully being aware that he or she is a perpetrator or participant. But since bullying is worse the more widely it's shared on social media, these kids are violators too.

Cognitive Function

- Television viewing as well as one of the most popular child videos in the 1990s were ultimately shown to delay expressive speech development.[18]

- One study showed that television viewing before age three had a mild negative effect on later cognitive development.[19]

- Too much screen time reduces impulse control and negatively affects task performance.[20]

- Multiple studies have concluded that the more screen time a child is allowed, the poorer their academic performance will be.[21]

Sleep

- The natural circadian increase in levels of melatonin (the neurotransmitter that makes us feel sleepy before we go to bed) is suppressed by screen time, making it more difficult for us to efficiently fall asleep.

- Kids may spend hours trying to fall asleep because they are using screens in the evening.[22] In one study, just having a cell phone or computer on in their bedroom at night was associated with trouble sleeping.[23]

- The effects of chronic sleep deprivation cannot be underestimated. Avoiding depression, boosting immune function, and enhancing academic performance are all related to adequate sleep.

- Many child psychiatrists and sleep specialists now recommend turning off all screens two hours before bedtime—for kids and adults.

Multitasking

- Multitasking is one of the biggest myths in today's technology culture. We know that when we are interrupted, it takes a long time to fully return to the original task. (Research has determined it takes twenty-five minutes for someone to reengage with a task following an interruption.)[24]

- Multitasking is not a friend of mental health. While admired and encouraged in certain settings, it has no positive impact on mental well-being. Multitasking is also a huge contributor to stress and poor attention. We wonder whether it may be a contributor to symptoms of ADD.

- Studies repeatedly show that people have a significant drop in focus, productivity, and intelligence simply by having their smartphone nearby, even if no texts, calls, or alerts come in.[25]

- Clifford Nass, Stanford University professor of communications, said, "The research is almost unanimous, which is very rare in social science, and it says that people who chronically multitask show an enormous range of deficits. They're basically terrible at all sorts of cognitive tasks, including multitasking."[26]

Addiction Potential

- The potential for addiction is high for many forms of digital technology. Studies show that dopamine soars during video gaming and plummets when a person is not gaming, creating an intense craving to game again, get the fix you feel you need, and prevent feelings of anxiety.[27]

- Research has also shown a downregulation of dopamine receptors in the brains of excessive video gamers, requiring a higher level of stimulation to get the same intensity of feeling. This stimulation of the nucleus accumbens (our brain's pleasure center) makes us desire more of the same.[28]

- Video gaming decreases the oxygen levels in our dorso-lateral prefrontal cortex. This area of the brain puts experience into relevancy and context. Lower oxygen-ation of this area makes it more difficult to for us to fit the experience and rush of gaming into life's reality and discern the relevant importance of the experience.[29]

- These two neurobiological phenomena give the gamer a sense of accomplishment without his having accom-plished anything significant.

Overall Health

- General health is also affected by screen time.

- Obesity has been directly correlated to excessive screen time in children. Childhood obesity is epidemic, with studies showing that higher calorie intake is more likely after screen time.[30]

- Chemical markers for heart disease and cholesterol lev-els are elevated in fifteen-year-olds who spend an exces-sive amount of time on screens.[31]

- Bone demineralization and carpal tunnel syndrome have both been shown to be associated with excessive screen time in children.[32]

ADD/ADHD

- With attention deficit disorder (ADD) and attention deficit hyperactivity disorder (ADHD) diagnosed more than ever in the last twenty years—now at about 9.4 percent of all US school-age children[33]—the increase in children's screen time must be considered as possibly contributing to the epidemic.

- The United States' current incidence represents a 42 percent rise between 2003 and 2001, according to the Centers for Disease Control and Prevention.[34] In some areas of the country, 15 to 20 percent of students have been diagnosed with ADD or ADHD.

- Older studies concluded that the more television children watched, the more likely they were to be diagnosed with ADD or ADHD in school.[35] In fact, just nine minutes of a fast-paced television show decreased the tested attention span in young children.[36]

- Newer studies show that first-person shooter video games can improve focus and attention on certain activities but not others; the ability to control impulsive behavior decreases the more time an individual spends on the games.[37]

Changes in Brain Structure and Chemistry
Magnetic resonance imaging (MRI) studies of the brains of children who excessively use technology are concerning.

- Multiple Internet and gaming addiction studies have shown shrinkage and loss of tissue volume in the brain's gray matter, the place where processing occurs.[38] Processing includes planning, prioritizing, organizing, and impulse control.

- The area of the brain responsible for empathy, compassion, and integrating physical signs with emotions is the insula. The insula is damaged by excessive video gaming, affecting the skills necessary for developing the proper depth and quality of personal relationships.[39]

- The white matter layer of the brain is also affected, showing reduced thickness compared with nongaming teens. This means there's a loss of communication within the brain affecting cognitive, emotional, and survival abilities.

- Functional magnetic resonance imaging (fMRI) studies have shown an immediate and strong dopamine release during video gaming, affecting the brain's pleasure center.[40]

Exposure to Pornography

- According to a survey published in the *Journal of Adolescent Health*, adolescents exposed to pornographic sites are more likely to have multiple lifetime sexual partners, more likely to have had more than one sexual partner in the last three months, and more likely to have used alcohol or other substances at their last sexual encounter.[41]

- In a 2007 study, 66.5 percent of young men and 48.7 percent of young women from six US universities said that viewing pornography is an acceptable way to express one's sexuality.[42]

- According to sociologist Jill Manning, research indicates six detrimental marriage trends associated with porn: increased risk of separation or divorce, decreased marital intimacy, infidelity, increased appetite for abusive or unsafe sexual activity, devaluation of monogamy and child-rearing, and an increase in compulsive or addictive sexual behavior.[43]

What Are Parents to Do?

In our respective practices, we find parents are generally too permissive when it comes to technology. They are too permissive with their own technology patterns too. Many parents feel they've lost any semblance of technology control in their homes. There are no rules, and if there are, they're not enforced. But always remember, parents are the ones in charge. Parents pay for the Internet service, the electricity, and the phone. (Whether the parents or the adolescent buys the phone, it doesn't matter. Parents make the rules for their home.)

The US government has chosen to not be involved in regulating screen use for children or adults. However, certain child health organizations have policy statements and suggestions for parents. The American Academy of Pediatrics recommends no screen time for children under two years of age and limiting noneducational screen time to two hours per day for children over two years of age.

It's interesting that in other countries, governments are starting to become involved as they see the damage being done. In China, hundreds of addiction centers for video game and Internet addicts have opened. South Korea is following suit. South Korea enacted "Cinderella Laws" in 2011, which make it illegal for children to play online digital games between midnight and 6 a.m. The country eased some of the restrictions in September 2014, however, allowing parents to request that their children be exempted from the law.

To assess the degree of the problem in your home, see if everyone can put down their phone for a day or two without panic. Everyone in the household should be able to do that. The inability to go without phones for a couple of days of camping can indicate the degree of technology attachment your family members have developed. Here are some basic suggestions for parents regarding technology:

Step 1: Avoid Temptation
The first recommendation is this: Avoid temptation in the first place. In other words, don't get your kids violent video games, don't buy your children a smartphone when they're too young and not mature enough to handle the expectations, and don't allow them to have a TV, video game console, or smartphone in their bedrooms. As a parent, take a stand and stand for something. Many parents are inconsistent about what technology will be acceptable, and the kids know it. This mistake makes it a lot more difficult to reverse course down the road.

Step 2: Establish Rules and Expectations
Most households have no rules or expectations about technology. Each time a child is introduced to a technology, usage expectations should be clearly discussed, written down, and contracted, if necessary. Such a document states what the

technology is, when and where it will be allowed, how long it may be used during a given day, what consequences will happen if there's resistance to following the parents' rules, and current life expectations of the child such as grades, chores, etc.

Set expectations that are age appropriate and realistic. Here's an example contract:

Fourteen-year-old daughter gets her first smartphone.

Date: 10-10-19

Technology: iPhone 8

When and where she can use it: main living area, before and after school, not in bedroom

How long per day: two hours total on all screens, including the iPhone

Security: full disclosure to parents at any time of contacts, apps, and texting

Consequence for misuse, abuse, or defiance: first offense, three days; second offense, two weeks; third offense, indefinite confiscation.

Current life expectations: maintain a B average, be in bed by 10 p.m. on school days, complete chores without reminders, get up in the morning independently.

Contracts are meant to be regularly reevaluated and changed, depending on the child's compliance. All children are different, so contracts should reflect that. Consider your child's disposition and the level of trust that exists.

Step 3: Follow through with Consequences
(Be the Parent!)

Lack of follow-through is the single biggest factor that makes the problem of technology worse. Think about it. Follow-through is important, especially consistent follow-through. Kids thrive when they know what to expect from their parents. Sometimes moms and dads are distracted by life, work, technology, or exhaustion, but they must be consistent with consequences.

A parenting tool called scripting can be an effective way to follow through with your rules. It's a way parents can use as few words as possible, say what needs to be said without shaming their child, and then watch to see how their child responds.

Let's consider the fourteen-year-old who was given her first smartphone and contract. Let's say she took the phone in her bedroom for two nights. Instead of looking at this situation as a potential argument, the parents can use it as an opportunity for their daughter to learn about contracts and her parents' dedication to following through on the consequences for not respecting the agreement. An example script might read:

"Meghan, we agreed that you would not have your phone in your bedroom, but the last two nights you have. You will need to give up your phone for three days, and then we'll try again. I hope you can follow our agreement next time."

Now the parents can take the phone for three days, then give it back and see what happens next time. The script is simple, straightforward, and doesn't include shaming—just facts and truth.

Step 4: Foster Healthy Alternative Behavior and Activities

Many children have little to do when they're outside the classroom or home, and many do not have adults monitoring their activities during after-school hours. Three decades ago, mass-distributed electronic devices for every age were not an option. When kids had spare time, they went outside in their neighborhoods and built forts or played kick the can, jacks, or dodgeball. Today, it's hard for many kids to choose the better activity because if they're allowed to choose their option, many times it's a screen.

Alternatives to screen time could be a sport, a musical instrument, Scouts, Lego club, art classes—the list is endless. For families that are struggling financially, YMCA, Boys & Girls Clubs, and school-based athletic teams are options. Many privately funded organizations are open to all children, such as The First Tee, which teaches disadvantaged children the game of golf. It's the parents' responsibility to seek out different options for their children, options that don't include hours of individual, unmonitored screen time.

This is not to say that overscheduling your child is the right strategy either. Sometimes parents register their kids for *everything*, creating a child with no downtime who is stressed out by going here and there and everywhere. Balance is the goal, with a variety of outside and organized activities for each child that fits his or her interests, aptitudes, and passions. Parents need to discover the right balance for each child and be invested and dedicated to that goal.

A Final Word on Technology Addiction

If you're seeing addictive patterns in your child, seek help. For starters, there are questionnaires parents can complete about their child's screen patterns that will either suggest a problem or not. The IAT (Internet Addiction Test), the CTT (Childhood Technology Test), or the PCIAT (Parent-Child Internet Addiction Test) are easy twelve- to twenty-question surveys parents can use to assess their child's technology use.

The following resources may also be helpful for parents struggling with what to do for a child who is showing signs of technology addiction.

- *Net Negotiations: What Every Parent Should Know about Controlling a Child's Use of Technology,* by Kimberly S. Young

- "Understanding Online Gaming Addiction and Treatment Issues for Adolescents," by Kimberly S. Young in *The American Journal of Family Therapy* (http://netaddiction.com/articles/Online_Gaming _Addiction.pdf)

- "Parenting in the Digital Age: Strategies and Prevention," by Kimberly S. Young (http:// netaddiction.com/childrenonline/)

- PCIAT (Parent-Child Internet Addiction Test, https:// www.healthyplace.com/psychological-tests/parent -child-internet-addiction-test)

- The Center for Internet Addiction provides helpful articles and educational resources, including the IAT (www.netaddiction.com).

- reStart offers various services and programs for the digitally distracted (https://netaddictionrecovery.com).

- The Center for Internet and Technology Addiction offers several screening tools and other resources (www.virtual-addiction.com).

- *Internet Addiction: A Handbook and Guide to Evaluation and Treatment,* by Kimberly S. Young

The GIST of It

- Technology is part of life whether we like it or not.

- Parents should use technology to teach their children important concepts, including self-regulation, priorities, level of importance, and their digital footprint.

- Research is showing concerning results about how screen time not only changes the structure of a child's developing brain but also the neurochemistry.

- It is not yet known if these brain changes are permanent.

- The addiction pathways are the same for screen time, drugs, alcohol, and pornography.

- Make sure everyone in the family is as comfortable without their smartphone as they are with it.

20

OVERLOADED

He who sows hurry reaps indigestion.

ROBERT LOUIS STEVENSON

Jessie's Story

JESSIE WAS A CUTE NINE-YEAR-OLD GIRL who had a lot going for her. She seemed to excel at almost everything she tried. Her parents saw she had real potential in sports, music, and academics, and out of love, they wanted her to be exposed to every opportunity around her. The race was on to make sure she didn't miss any chance to experience or excel at all of her interests.

By the fourth grade, Jessie seemed to have the most passion for gymnastics and received coaching from top instructors while winning local and regional competitions. But she wasn't an elite athlete, and her parents' love for her made it hard for them to see that. So they maintained their pattern of racing around from workout to practice to meets without reflection.

The intensity of competition increased as Jessie grew older, and she had less time to spend with friends. Wanting the best for Jessie kept her parents focused on her ribbons and trophies, and they barely noticed her weight loss and depression. One day, while in her doctor's office, Jessie started to cry and blurted out the truth: "I hate gymnastics," she said. "I don't have any time to have any friends, watch TV, or be with my brother and sisters. Maybe I'm good at it, but I don't want to do it anymore."

ॐ

Commitments and Margin: Balance

Life for kids needs to be a balance of commitments with time for margin. Some kids just have too many commitments on their docket, while other kids are bored and need a push to become involved and active.

Too Much

Our Western culture offers kids too many choices. This is just a fact of parenting today. But the problem doesn't really lie in the number of choices our kid might have; it lies in how many opportunities we allow our kid to choose. This is a key point of parenting: It's the parents' job to decide what activities their child is to become involved in.

It's not uncommon to see a family living life on the edge and even wearing that hurried lifestyle as a badge of honor. These families allow multiple commitments for each child and are constantly going to this or that, while having only an occasional night free to enjoy a family dinner together. If your child is enthusiastic about being involved in many things, that's great. But remember, that same child will need to learn about balance and the importance of margin.

Now there's nothing wrong with being busy. Kids and adults who are busy tend to be productive, energized, and engaged with life and others. What we're talking about is being *too* busy. Being too busy has risks, including stress, exhaustion, and performing for the attention of others.

Busy kids tend to have too little margin in their lives, and from a parenting perspective, this question needs to be asked: "Is my child able to handle all the things in his or her life right now and still have downtime?" If not, a parent needs to intervene. Limiting commitments will be the strategy for parents of these kids. Also, it may be hard to discern whether your child can handle so many activities just by asking him or her. How many activities a child can handle differs from child to child. But the fact remains, everyone needs margin, as do the parents.

Too Little

On the other side of the coin are kids who seem to be under-involved. They have few interests, or the ones they do have they may not be very good at. Sometimes these kids become isolated and withdrawn and need a parent to push them to do something . . . anything.

It doesn't need to be a high-profile activity or one that gleans attention. It can be something subtle or focused on a passion. It could be a volunteer opportunity at an animal shelter, a part-time job at a consignment shop, or a neighbor-hood lawn-mowing business. Hanging out and screen time are not the kind of activities we're talking about.

Underinvolved kids tend to have too much margin in their lives, and when that margin isn't filled with something that is growth producing, they will start filling it with things that will not help them grow or become productive people. For kids who are underinvolved, parents need to be bold and require a commitment from them.

Margin: Why It's Important

Having margin, downtime, free time, or whatever you want to call it is important for everyone—adult and child. Margin allows us to recharge. Margin gives us space. Margin affords us the opportunity to be still, to listen, to relax, to disconnect, and to savor life. These are all reasons parents should remember when the next activity opportunity comes before your child.

Eric Hoffer, a philosopher who was awarded the Presidential Medal of Freedom, had this to say about margin: "The superficiality of the American is the result of his hustling. It needs leisure to think things out; it needs leisure to mature. People in a hurry cannot think, cannot grow, nor can they decay. They are preserved in a state of perpetual puerility."[1]

Having margin can also give kids the time to assess what they want to be doing and reflect on the current menu of options they have in front of them. One important skill for children to develop as they grow is the ability to make decisions about what they will become or stay involved in. A willingness to point out to their child when his or her life is too busy is part of being a parent, even when it creates tension or a moment of unhappiness for the child.

Is This My Agenda?

We encourage parents with overcommitted kids to ask, "Whose agenda is this coming from?" Is your child's love of baseball coming from him or you? If your daughter is really good at gymnastics like Jessie, are you using her accomplishments to bolster how you feel about yourself or your parenting?

Parents can fall into the trap of living through their child's accomplishments. This is a dangerous and slippery slope, as they may end up pushing their kids too hard and starting too early. Whether parents are escaping their own issues and relationships and replacing them with their kids' activities or just conforming to cultural expectations, the result is an out-of-balance child and an out-of-balance family.

Listen to what David Elkind, author of *The Hurried Child: Growing Up Too Fast Too Soon*, has to say about this: "Wrongheaded ideas have a nasty habit of catching on more quickly than correct ideas. The belief that earlier is better in relation to early childhood is one such wrong idea that seems to have caught on, and it is difficult to combat. With respect to sports, there is no reliable evidence that starting children early in an individual or team sport gives them a lasting advantage or edge."[2]

Perhaps parents are too overloaded themselves (with work, hobbies, training, or education) and their child has little opportunity to be involved in much at all. Sometimes margin is a luxury people can't afford during a certain season of their lives. A single mom with four kids under the age of twelve may not have the margin to allow each of her children opportunities. She may not have a chance to personally experience the benefit of margin. There is no reason to regret or feel shamed by such a situation. Although margin can be powerful, it may not always be available.

Other parents may become too enmeshed in their own lives and not have the margin to allow their child to have activities. Sometimes this is a subconscious thing or related to family events, finances, or other issues. Another adult will need to point out the reality between these parents' overloaded lives and their child's undercommitted life.

The bottom line is this: Be aware of what's your agenda and what's not.

Family Meetings That Don't Stink

For all the benefits that can come from a family meeting, it is surprising that they don't happen more often. Perhaps it's because too often they are a waste of time for all involved. Here are a few guidelines to increase the likelihood of a good outcome:

1. Keep it short. Two short meetings are better than one long one.

2. Use the discussion to include people, not to confront people.

3. Have the meeting with those who are willing to be there.

4. Don't force people to be at the meeting; weigh only the input of those present.

5. Remember and state that choices in a family affect everyone. Say, "That's why we meet."

6. Make sure everyone is listened to, but explain that not everyone's vote is equal. Parents still decide.

7. Know that meetings reduce manipulative communication in the family. Everyone there is hearing the same

information at the same time. This will decrease multiple dialogues that can happen behind people's backs.

8. Be open and honest about manipulation. Statements like "I think this is the summer we should all go to Glacier National Park, and I will try to convince you why" are good and transparent. Hidden agendas make people angry and suspicious.

The GIST of It

- Life needs to be a balance of commitments and margin. Too much of either has its consequences.

- Kids who are overcommitted need parents to teach them limits and narrow their activities.

- Kids who are undercommitted need parents to push them to some type of involvement that is growth producing.

- Living through your child is a slippery slope, so be aware of hidden agendas.

- A family meeting, when done correctly, can help family members stay connected, feel included, and have their opinions heard. If they haven't worked in the past, stay calm and don't give up. These meetings are worth the trouble.

21

LEARNED HELPLESSNESS

Depression is the inability to construct a future.

ROLLO MAY

FLORENCE CHADWICK WAS an American swimmer known for long-distance, open water swimming. She was the first woman to swim the English Channel in both directions, setting a time record each way. She was also the first woman to swim the Catalina Channel, the Strait of Gibraltar, the Bosporus (one-way), and the Dardanelles (round trip).

In 1952, young Florence Chadwick stepped into the waters of the Pacific Ocean off Catalina Island, determined to swim to mainland California, a challenge well within her reach. The weather was foggy and chilly; she could hardly see the boats accompanying her. Still, she swam for fifteen hours. When she begged to be taken out of the water along the way, her mother, in a boat alongside, told her she was close and that she could make it. Finally, physically and emotionally exhausted, she stopped swimming and was pulled out. It wasn't until she was on the boat that she discovered the shore was less than half a mile away.

At a news conference the next day she said, "All I could see was the fog. . . . If I could have seen the shore, I would have made it." It's hard to hang in there when you can't see the goal or know what's coming next. Eventually your only option seems to be quitting.

The American Psychological Association calls learned helplessness the "landmark theory of the century." If you have a happy, socially well-adjusted, achieving child, this chapter may not make sense to you. We still think it is important and may apply to a child you know. If you have a child who has quit on life, is withdrawn, or has shut down, this chapter may be the first words that help you understand him or her.

Kids who have learned to be helpless aren't bad kids or lazy kids. They are kids who have *lost the belief that it is within their capacity to positively affect their own lives.* Having lost hope, they have learned to be helpless. They have little or no motivation or incentive to achieve, and they're not interested in learning new ways to cope with life's struggles. Their natural joy of learning seems to be gone, and learning is thus dramatically delayed. They won't readily accept praise, gifts, or kindness, and they are unaffected by criticism. They seem apathetic, disinterested, and hopeless. Even the simplest solution to a problem seems outside the realm of their comprehension. This resembles depression but is different. Depression is more pervasive, but learned helplessness functions primarily within a system.

Learned helplessness has likely been around forever, but it wasn't until the last century that we began to understand it as different from depression or a circumstance where someone "quit on life." While many kids respond well to pressure and believe they can better their futures, our schools see numerous kids who don't. At home, a child struggling with learned helplessness is often found in his or her bedroom lying on the bed with earbuds on.

The Origin of the Concept

This concept resulted from a 1941 study, a 1967 study, and subsequent research by American psychologist Martin Seligman and his colleagues at the University of Pennsylvania. That research led Seligman to coin the term *learned helplessness.*

Quite by accident, Seligman discovered that the conditioning of dogs led to outcomes that opposed the predictions of behavioral psychologists at the time. In these studies, designed to explore depression, dogs were used to test certain effects of classical conditioning. Ivan Pavlov and his dog experiments made classical conditioning (Pavlovian conditioning) famous. First, Pavlov let the dogs hear the sound of a metronome before they were fed. At first, the dogs salivated when presented with the food. But after a few repetitions of the metronome sound followed by the food, the dogs salivated at the sound, even before they were given their food.

Both the 1941 and 1967 studies found that a certain pattern of conditioning created responses of high anxiety or depression in the animals. The findings of the 1941 study ("Experimental Neurosis," by O. D. Anderson and Richard Parmenter Anderson) concluded that the anxiety of the dogs and sheep peaked when they could not figure out the link between the warning sound and the reinforcement. In short, the animals were at times called upon to "solve" association problems—to distinguish between one stimulus and another. One stimulus would be reinforced with food and the other was not reinforced. It didn't matter if the reinforcement was positive or negative. When the dogs and sheep couldn't figure this out, their behavior would shift markedly.

The study concluded that the animals became considerably distressed and "showed a state of profound inhibition" when the problems facing them were beyond the animals' ability to achieve or decode. These dogs would eventually give up and start functioning in an avoidant, anxious, and distressed manner that was evident by measurements of their behavior, heart rates, breathing, and posture. These changes did not go away, even years later.

In Seligman's research, the behavior of three groups of dogs was evaluated. In the first group, dogs were strapped into harnesses for a certain period of time and then released. The dogs in the second group were placed in the same harnesses but were subjected to electrical shocks that could be avoided by pressing a panel with their noses. The third group received the same shocks as those in group two, except they were not able to control the shocks' duration. For the dogs in the third group, the shocks seemed to be completely random and outside of their control. Group three dogs learned they had no influence over whether they were shocked or not.

Seligman inadvertently discovered that dogs that had received unpredictable electric shocks failed to take action in subsequent situations—even those in which escape or avoidance was in fact possible. Surprising to most behavioralists at the time, this scenario resulted in the dogs simply lying down passively and whining. Even though they could have easily escaped the shocks, and the shocks were not too severe, the dogs didn't try because they didn't know when they were coming or to what they might be connected. But dogs that had not received the random shocks immediately took action in subsequent situations.

Why were these studies so monumental and significant? In both of these experiments, the animals that believed they had no ability to affect or predict the pain or the reward in their lives behaved in ways that suggested they were troubled, fatigued, and hopeless. The animals' response was to quit everything—the researchers had inadvertently taught animals to go against every instinct and quit on life. They had learned to be helpless. Seligman is credited with being the first to use the phrase *learned helplessness,* and it has been used and studied since this time.[1]

The impact of learned helplessness has been demonstrated in a number of different animal species, but its features and characteristics can also be seen in humans. Learned helplessness is the condition in a human or animal that has learned to behave helplessly. In this condition, subjects fail to respond to their environments, even though there are opportunities for the subject to avoid a painful situation. As a result, they have almost no ability to adapt to changes in their lives or environments.

How Does This Principle Relate to Kids?

Professionals who work with youth note that when some children adopt the view that they cannot understand or change a situation, they begin to truly believe there is nothing they can do to better their condition. These kids quickly become depressed, anxious, helpless, sad, or bored, and their learning slows to nearly a halt. Performance deteriorates as they become less likely to solve problems, even when the problems are identical to those solved before their helplessness set in. Essentially, they quit and "lie down," not caring when the next "shock" is coming.

We started writing this book when a troubling observation turned into a question: "Why are teenagers today acting in similar, predictable, and peculiar ways?" After years of working professionally with teens, we noticed a pattern where teens withdraw to their rooms with seemingly unwarranted fatigue and hopelessness. This pattern appeared to be more prevalent in adolescents than we had seen in previous decades. We then, like many others, noticed a sobering parallel.

Those earlier animal experiments (along with dozens of others not cited here) gave clues to what was going on in adults and children who experienced learned helplessness.

- When adults or children cannot predict the response to their behavior, or they are unable to decode what will bring punishment or reward, significant anxiety is created. This anxiety dramatically slows learning, and these people become indifferent to praise or criticism.

- When adults or children come to believe they have no real ability to control the outcomes of their situations, they quit trying. Achievements in their lives are replaced with boredom, helplessness, anxiety, withdrawal, and depression, which also all dramatically slow learning.

Logic is no longer a factor when learned helplessness sets in. We see this with kids who were once social and resourceful but are now paralyzed by the simplest tasks. An example is a boy who performs poorly on math tests and assignments, then studies hard and still fails a unit test. Over time, he begins to believe that *nothing* he does will have any effect on his math performance. When later faced with any type of math-related task, he may experience a sense of helplessness. He won't even attempt to do math problems he may have completed successfully two years earlier. Learned helplessness has set in, and a new problem, other than math, has been created.

This connection appears to be supported by the frequent number of teens who, in moments of unguarded honesty, say they feel they can never do anything "good enough."

It's Not Laziness

From these kids' perspective, effort seems futile so they give up trying. But it isn't out of laziness. This is important to remember. They procrastinate and only accomplish tasks that require little effort. They may meekly strive for unattainable goals, but they won't strive for any attainable goals. It's almost as if they are avoiding positively completing a task. They look depressed, and in this state, they are often angry. They feel that they are too stupid to learn, so *why try?* Or they may wonder why everything is so difficult for them compared with their peers.

Learned helplessness creates three basic deficits in the child—cognitive, emotional, and motivational—all of which destroy the child's desire to learn. In the motivational deficit, learning stops when the necessary hope and predictability of life are missing. Too often it's said that the child is not trying, but research shows that when these children have learned to be helpless, it's no longer an issue of effort. Children who have experienced learned helplessness believe they have no control over their world or the learning process, and it hurts too much to try.

There certainly was nothing lazy about the animals in the experiments, and this is not an issue of laziness in kids. Those experimental dogs must have felt as if they were locked in an emotional room with no door to the outside. With no escape in sight, there was no reason for them to try. Many teenagers find themselves in this same predicament, and though it may look as if they don't care, it's more accurate to say they have lost hope.

How This Occurs in Families

Something is happening in some families in our culture that's creating learned helplessness. We knew this was true from our own experience, and it can be powerfully validated by just a few Google searches on the topic. Hundreds, maybe thousands, of professionals and researchers have come to the same conclusions. We know it's true, but that doesn't mean we have totally figured out how it happens. Here are some theories.

In both of the experiments cited in this chapter, the source of pain that the study animal responded to was electrical shock. The shock for the teenagers can be anything painful. Life produces discomfort on a regular basis: homework, rejection, chores, failure, or scolding—basically anything. Pain or difficulty isn't the problem, nor is the quantity of pain and difficulty. The problem is when the subject feels helpless and hopeless to control or alter the pain that's present.

The Effect of Alcoholic Homes

Our first professional exposure to explicit learned helplessness was watching clients raised in alcoholic homes. We noticed right away that they did not believe they could influence or sway a good outcome out of even the most basic situations. They *did* believe they could medicate their pain, but not that they could avoid it or produce any type of victory out of their circumstances. It was clear that the lives of these individuals were missing the linear functioning needed for problem solving. While they needed to learn and believe they could piece solutions together, this ability eluded them.

Simply, the positive or negative reinforcement they received in their alcoholic homes had nothing to do with their performance and was outside their realm of predictability. As kids, these people had no confidence at all that putting a series of good choices together would actually pay off for them. They didn't believe cleaning the kitchen, mowing the lawn, or doing homework would be consistently noticed or appreciated. As kids, they might have been scolded for doing these things instead of being thanked.

Receiving love, affection, insults, and rejection depended more on where the alcoholic parent was in his or her addictive remorse cycle than on the child's performance or pleasantness. Likewise, these kids could break curfew, hit a sibling, or fail a unit in math. If this coincided with the alcoholic parent's guilt and contrition about excessive drinking, the child might have received praise and affection.

Too often, favorable and unfavorable outcomes in the child's world were tied to a variable that had nothing to do with the child's conduct. This is far too complicated and dubious for any child to decode. The dynamic creates a depression and helplessness that sometimes lasts a lifetime. These kids, like the dogs and sheep in the experiments, couldn't figure out what was coming next or how to decode the family system.

It's important to note here that even the rewards (food, praise, affection, presents, etc.) mean little to these kids because they don't know when or why a reward comes. The animals in the studies wouldn't even eat a treat because they didn't know when the shock was coming. Many kids in alcoholic homes won't accept the love from a gift or embrace because they don't understand why it's coming at that point in time or what might be coming next.

The main point: Randomness is often the rule in dysfunctional homes. Addictions, affairs, painful marriages, secrets, absence, media, and chaos can all contribute to an environment that is too irregular and unpredictable for a child to figure out and therefore feel secure.

It's All around Us

It's interesting that this pervasive pattern doesn't just exist in troubled homes; we are now seeing evidence of learned helplessness in higher-functioning homes and throughout society.

Let's look at the sources of pain in kids, the rewards they really want, and the systems they need to decode.

We believe kids don't want (the adverse stimuli or shock):

- confusing stress
- ambiguity in parents' moods and expectations
- to feel not capable

- never to feel done
- expectations that seem impossible or shifting
- to feel they are defective when they do anything short of excellent
- to be on guard or on call all the time

We believe kids really want (the reward):

- inner peace
- clarity of expectations
- to believe they are competent
- to know when they are done
- to believe that a task is achievable
- to believe good enough is good enough
- to learn tasks at a suitable age and developmental stage
- to understand that life isn't easy and life won't feel easy
- to know when they're not on track
- to know that they are loved
- to know what is expected of them
- to know that if they do what is expected, more won't be added
- to predict somewhat accurately when they are or aren't in trouble
- to know there is help for them when they are stuck (but not so much help that it makes them feel defective)

Overfunctioning Parents

Hovering or overfunctioning parents are often identified as major contributors to learned helplessness in kids. Parental overfunctioning usually leads to an underfunctioning child.

These are the parents who are overly helpful and do too much for their kids.

In the home, it can look like this: One of the parents wakes up an older child in the morning, makes his or her lunch, and gathers all the essentials for the teenager's backpack while watching the clock to make sure he or she is on time. This behavior undoubtedly contributes to learned helplessness. Kids want to feel at peace and competent in their lives. While they are grateful for Mom or Dad's help, all this help severely threatens their sense that they can sufficiently manage their lives on their own.

Hovering parents are certainly part of the problem, but there's much more to it than that. Stress is another contributor to learned helplessness.

The Vicious Cycle of Achievement Stress

Learned helplessness causes stress and anxiety—but stress and anxiety also cause learned helplessness. We feel stressed when we are ill prepared for something. The stress creates fear, and fear slows or stops learning so we can't get out in front of the challenge.

The stresses on today's children are too many to enumerate. At least half of them are unnecessary. For one, kids are hurried along in their growth. They are tested, ranked, pushed, and pressured—from admission tests to get into kindergarten all the way through to college-level Advanced Placement classes starting as early as the sophomore or even freshman year of high school. Everything from sex education to algebra is taught earlier and earlier. Schools and parents, trying to cram their children (students) into the top 5 percent of society, compete in one-upmanship.

Some kids respond well to pressure, and it brings out a wonderful side in them. But others don't handle pressure and stress well, and it stifles their learning and their creativity. When these kids are confronted with tasks they are not ready for, they blame themselves for their deficiencies.

This is an important distinction. There is a difference between *knowing how to achieve something* and *being ready to achieve something*. One sixteen-year-old may be ready to drive a car in city traffic, whereas another sixteen-year-old may know how to drive but not be ready to drive in city traffic. When a child knows he isn't ready to drive in traffic and life pressure tells him he should be ready, he feels defective. Some kids have the GPA and cognitive ability to handle college academics but are not ready for college. When parents, teachers, adults, or peers tell a teenager he should be ready to do something and he isn't, the teen may think, *There must be something wrong with me.*

Kids who don't rise to the challenge in pressure situations and who conclude they are defective because they are not ready for something when others say they should be are candidates for learned helplessness. The ages at which children are ready for sleepovers, contact sports, being home alone for a couple of days, college, babysitting, calculus, or studying abroad are all very different. Learned helplessness can result from pressure to enter into a world for which the child is not developmentally ready.

Social Stress

Unbeknownst to many, it's stressful for kids to hang out with peers who are holding back their growth.

Often teenagers will choose the short-term gain of

immediate acceptance over the long-term gain of growth. It's a subconscious decision to choose friends who will quickly and easily accept them rather than choosing a group of friends who have growth or accomplishment as a goal.

For all kids, the quickest bond is with other kids who are expecting little of themselves. Shoplifting or stealing test answers can result in immediate recognition or approval from a group that is not growing.

Even when kids fight feverishly for the right to choose their own friends, it's very stressful for them when they choose friends who are behind them on the maturity curve.

"Show me your friends and I'll show you your future" is a saying recited by professionals who work with youth. While this is not always true, it's true enough to make us pause and consider the effect problematic friends can have on our kids.

It's for this reason that parents need to intervene when kids make poor friend choices. Too often parents are tentative or reluctant to fight this battle. This is a battle worth fighting, however, since friends have a powerful impact on our children's choices and growth.

> For those who will not allow you to move forward
>> will eventually lead you backwards
>> for nothing that stands behind
>> will invite you to move ahead.[2]

Ultimately, it's the parents who must decide about which friends are healthy or unhealthy for their child, especially in younger years. This has more to do with how that friend is affecting their kid, not whether the parent likes the friend, the friend's parents, or some other factor.

We encourage parents to be very proactive in this, taking the time and effort to get to know their child's friends, inviting them over to see how their child interacts with them, communicating with the friend's parents, and so on. Sometimes first impressions are right on, and sometimes they're way off.

Taking the time to have a relationship with your kid's friends says two things to your child: *I care about the kids you hang out with* and *I'm willing to get to know them before passing any judgment.* Parents can and should be involved in managing their children's friend choices through the middle-school age. Once kids are in high school and beyond, the parent's voice in this matter is diminished.

The Moving Carrot

In many homes, especially conscientious homes, parents are eager for their child's ever-increasing achievements. Usually this approach is motivated by love, but it mimics the studies using dogs and shocks.

Here's how it looks: A teenage girl is given a limited list of expectations. She believes that this covers the scope of what's expected of her. In other words, she believes she knows how to avoid "the shock." It might sound like, "All we expect is that you turn in all your assignments, study for your tests, and help out a little around the house." The girl uses this to build a rough perception of what is expected of her. The reward she is looking for is to feel like she is *done* with what's expected of her. (One of the stressors for adults and children is that they never feel done.)

Then slowly, over the next several months, forty new expectations get added: Clean the kitchen, lose five pounds, watch your little brother, start violin lessons, go to church, unload the groceries, clean your room, etc. Over months and even years, this girl stops believing that she is ever going to be *done*. Being done is the reward she is subconsciously looking for.

There's nothing wrong with holding too many expectations for a child. However, there is something terribly wrong with a home life where a child lives perpetually on guard. Some teenagers may have heard four or five corrective comments just during the course of making a snack. You can see the parallels to the animal studies, assuming that peace or "being done" is the reward the child is looking for, and nagging or reminders are the shock. The teen cannot figure out what to do to stop the corrections.

Negative reinforcement is a form of communicating related to learned helplessness. This simply means that something unwanted (adverse) stops temporarily when the dog does the desired behavior. It seems like this should work, but it only works for a while. Then the dog quits, making no effort to relieve the pain even though it knows how.

We have often observed families where criticizing and nagging stop temporarily when a child does the right thing. The dictionary describes nagging as "persistently annoying or finding fault with someone."[3] Faultfinding can be very easy to do when we have a child who is falling short on so many fronts. A truly loving parent may easily convince himself that he is not faultfinding but just pointing out the numerous shortcomings in his thirteen-year-old's behavior. This is another reminder to *parent quietly*.

The Hole Is Too Deep

Imagine a boy taking part in an outdoor endurance event. His legs are well muscled, and he can step up to fifteen inches. If he were placed in a fourteen-inch-deep hole in the ground, stepping out would be easily accomplished even with his hands tied. In a hole four inches deeper, however, escaping would be very problematic.

Whether it is missed ACT tests, six English assignments due, no money, a messy room, lost friends, lost status, or a lost passion for life—kids with learned helplessness often have dug a hole too deep to get out of in one step. It drives parents crazy when a child they love more than life itself, who is wonderful and precious, repeatedly messes up eight things a day and does virtually nothing right. How do you help a child when too much help partially created the mess in the first place? Parents can feel like they're between a rock and a hard place.

This is a legitimate and real problem, and we want you to know that you are not alone. Thousands of parents feel the same way.

It's All about Perceptions

Learned helplessness is all about perceptions. We are all driven by our perceptions of expectations, and also by hope, opportunity, learning, and even hopelessness. We repeatedly take in information, pass it through our belief systems, and come out with perceptions. These can be accurate or inaccurate, but they drive our lives.

When a woman we meet tells us about an event in her life, she's telling us the information she took in, the belief she has about that information, and her experience or perceptions of the event. This usually happens beyond her awareness. She thinks she is just telling us what happened.

We all see events and then pass that data through a belief system, even before we actually know what happened. In the case of learned helplessness the belief is, "I don't believe I can figure out how this system works," or "I don't believe I can affect the outcome of the challenge before me." Once that belief sets in, it affects how we experience every challenge. Your child didn't suddenly *become* helpless—your child just suddenly *believed* he or she was. His or her perception became reality.

People stuck in dead-end jobs, those fighting a second or third battle with cancer, heavy smokers who have tried numerous times to quit, alcoholics, people with obesity, or people stuck in abusive relationships are all likely candidates for learned helplessness. This can happen to anyone who believes life will never get any better. Anyone who has been shocked too many times and can't decode how life works can surrender to this belief.

Help for the Helpless

To reduce or head off learned helplessness in your home, first consider your attitude toward teens in this situation. Have compassion on these kids—they aren't lazy or bad. Let good enough be good enough. A child with learned helplessness may be a great kid, but he is never going to be an overachiever or exceptional in any measurable way until his beliefs change. That is fine. Just enjoy him.

Next, if you overfunction as a parent, gradually cut back on your help, reminders, and doing things for your child. Part of your child's underfunctioning is you overfunctioning.

Offer to work with your daughter in the beginning, but *do not* do anything *for* her. Working *with* her is immensely healing. If she quits, you quit. Often a tutor with a contagious love of learning can help with this role. Make sure you don't nag your child. Use a sticky note on your son's door, send him a text, or place a note in his backpack. Just avoid nagging.

It's easier to avoid nagging if you let the little stuff go while holding the line on the minimal reasonable expectations you have agreed to. Hold your child accountable to those. (It won't help to give too much grace.) Focus on The Two Things concept discussed in chapter 12. If your child is developmentally behind, focusing on too many things will cause another setback.

Tell your child the following messages when appropriate:

- Clearly and briefly tell your child that he has or hasn't met your expectations, but that you are neither thrilled nor angry. Use minimal encouragement or criticism—just give the facts.

- When it is true, tell your child that she is doing fine. Tell her to relax. Tell her she is "done" for the day. Say it as often as you can when it's true.

- Tell your child that he is on his own timetable, and you aren't worried about racing other kids to the finish line.

- Repeatedly affirm that you aren't worried about how your child will turn out in the end. She might not go from high school to college, but if she does go to college, she'll be ready for the challenge. (If your child is using drugs, depressed, hanging with a dangerous crowd, cutting, or is exhibiting other concerning behavior, then certainly tell him or her you are worried.)

Finally, try to do the following:

- As a favor to your children, occasionally disconnect them from technology so they can find some peace. Don't let them take their smartphones to bed, to Grandma's, on a walk, out on the boat, or other places where the goal is to be doing something other than being on their phones. It may be more convincing if you are willing to shut yours off in these situations too.

- Do not allow excessive isolating.

- Allow your child to struggle and experience the cost of underachieving. Take away your son's car or Xbox privileges. Remember: The problem isn't that he can't handle life; the problem is that he believes he can't decode life. (This is why many kids will drop the helplessness and do well at deer hunting or white-water kayaking, or golf, or boarding. Those are arenas where they believe they have control and they know the rules.) Make your rules at home believable.

- Changing the rules or expectations based on the child's mood or level of being ovewhelmed adds to the problem. Remember, you are trying to create a system that is unambiguous and believable. Who would respect a system that changed every time someone's mood changed?

The GIST of It

- When children lose the belief that they can positively affect their own lives, they lose hope and learn to be helpless.

- Unpredictable households can be a contributor to learned helplessness.

- Learned helplessness results in the child's inability to adapt to changes in his life or environment.

- Kids can recover when they learn they can control the outcomes in their lives and experience success.

22

THE IMPACT OF STRESS

Reality is the leading cause of stress
amongst those in touch with it.

JANE WAGNER

Benjamin's Story

ON THE OUTSIDE, Benjamin looked like a high-functioning sixteen-year-old. He was popular at school, played varsity sports, achieved academically, and participated in a variety of extracurricular activities. To all appearances, he was a nice, well-rounded young man. Yet Benjamin was in turmoil, experiencing a combination of anxiety, fear, and anger. He lived an emotional roller coaster on the inside, while outwardly portraying a life of achievement and success.

Benjamin was an expert secret keeper. His father was present in the home but fighting his own demons. His mother suffered severe depression. Their marriage was falling apart, and the family's financial situation was difficult.

Benjamin knew all the details of his parents' reality. His entire identity was wrapped up in not letting the world know his home life was the opposite of what it appeared to be. He struggled to fall asleep, felt like his mind was always going a million miles an hour, and lived with an intense and constant fear that his friends might someday find out about what he had to deal with at home. He was anxious and frequently experienced panic attacks. He worked very hard at keeping everything looking good—anything to prevent the real truth from being known by the world.

Benjamin was experiencing stress.

Megan's Story

On the other end of the spectrum, Megan was a girl we might call a wallflower. She was average at almost everything: grades, number of friends, sports and music abilities, and life in general. Nothing was wrong with Megan. She was fine just the way she was—she was just average.

But influenced by the culture around her, Megan compared herself with every above-average girl in her class and always felt like a failure. She told herself, *You'll never be really good at anything.* She worried about not having a boyfriend, not being in the popular group at school, not being smart enough to go to college, and not having a nice complexion.

Every day she experienced life defeated, hopeless, and stressed, except for the days she made herself mindlessly busy. On those days, she experienced mostly nothing. Most days she just wanted to give up. She told herself that her life would always be meaningless and futile. Many times she thought of running away and starting new somewhere else where she might be able to be above average. She even thought about ending her life, yet she wasn't sure that she would succeed at that either.

Megan was experiencing stress.

The Stress Reaction

Parents need to know how much stress can influence their child. To help understand this, we'd like to address what happens in the child's body when he or she becomes stressed. This stress leads to predictable and sometimes bizarre behaviors. The hope is that parents will not only better recognize stress in their child but also respond in ways that foster their child's ability to deal with stress now and in the future.

When a child experiences an emergency, there is a release of stress hormones in his or her body. In turn, these hormones mobilize what is physiologically needed to deal with the situation. A frightening movie scene, being chased by a vicious dog, falling, or any traumatic experience can trigger this stress hormone release. This normal process helps kids protect themselves from danger or injury. Adults also experience a similar release of stress hormones to deal with emergencies in their lives, although adult emergencies tend to be different.

Two major systems produce stress hormones in our bodies. The sympathetic adrenomedullary system produces adrenaline from the adrenal glands that lie just above the kidneys. Adrenaline quickly gives us the "fight or flight" response that we need to protect ourselves when we are in danger. Our bodies can produce adrenaline in a split second. Adrenaline increases the heart rate and diverts blood away from the gut and skin (which are nonessential in an emergency), allowing more blood to be available to muscles and the brain. Our blood sugar increases due to adrenaline's effect on the liver, and this energy source allows us to react to stressful situations. Most people know when this "right now" hormone enters their bloodstream.

The second stress hormone is cortisol, and it's released through the hypothalamic-pituitary-adrenal system. Cortisol, which is also produced in the adrenal glands, takes longer to produce in our bodies (about twenty-five minutes), but it has a longer-lasting effect. Cortisol reacts with receptors inside of the cell, regulating gene transcription and modulating metabolism at the cellular level. Eventually, the body experiences physiological and behavioral changes.

How Children Are Affected

Scientists are just beginning to understand how stress affects the brains of young children. We know that newborns have low levels of cortisol in their bloodstreams and those levels increase during the first six months of life. Around three months of age, the infant's cortisol patterns start to look more like adult patterns, including a circadian peak of cortisol release in the early morning. We know that babies experience an increase in levels of cortisol during medical examinations, blood draws, and other traumatic events. Repeated exposures to stress will induce chronic increases of cortisol, leading to an increase in fear behaviors, increased caution, and symptoms similar to PTSD.

Stress also can have a detrimental effect on brain function, including cognition and memory. The presence of higher cortisol levels in infants and young children is associated with smaller electrical changes in the brain during memory

formation. New memory formation is impaired. Preschool-
or daycare-age children who have high cortisol levels have a
more difficult time maintaining attention. Attention span is
an important factor in a child's ability to self-regulate. These
children have more trouble maintaining self-control because
of their higher cortisol levels.

In summary, cortisol from stress plays an important role
in memory formation, attention span, and self-regulating
behaviors in children. One must wonder if there's a connection between increased stress in children and the epidemic of
ADD/ADHD, relative lack of self-regulating behaviors, and
academic underachievement.

Children who experience chronic and high levels of stress
appear to have even more significant consequences. As mentioned before, stress increases cortisol levels in our bodies.
Once the stress is relieved, cortisol levels return to normal.
But in children experiencing high and long-standing stress,
cortisol levels remain high, even after the stress has been
appropriately dealt with. Children with chronically elevated
levels of cortisol show problems with their motor development, physical health, social skills, and mental function.
They tend to function in a state of fear, and their coping
mechanisms become habitual.

Stress is encountered in four different stages of early
childhood. In the first stage, alarm sets in. The child experiences a surge of adrenaline and feels afraid and agitated. In
the second stage, the child appraises the situation and tries to
find meaning in what has happened. At stage three, the child
tries to figure out how to cope with the new reality. The child
may develop several possible ways to deal with the stress he or
she is experiencing, or may *not* figure out any way that helps

him or her through this difficulty. Stage four is when the child executes one or more of the coping strategies. A child with a low natural ability to deal with adversity may experience alarm in certain situations more quickly than average and may experience stress with milder and more varied stress opportunities. This child will often exist in a chronic state of stress and disruption.

Signs and Symptoms of Stress

Kids can be quite good at disguising their stress, but the signs and symptoms are many. Parents often don't want to think that their child is stressed out; they would rather find a medical reason for their child's symptoms. Parents and doctors may go down roads of evaluation that ultimately delay discovering what the child's real problem is.

Signs and symptoms of stress fall into four categories: physical, behavioral, emotional, and cognitive. Although the following lists are not exhaustive, it's clear that much of what brings patients to a psychologist or pediatrician can be attributed to stress in the child's life or family. A thorough medical and psychological evaluation may be needed to determine what is causing the child's symptoms.

Physical symptoms of severe stress might include any one or several of the following: chronic abdominal pain, headaches, diarrhea, constipation, dizziness, nausea and vomiting, chest pain, heart palpitations, frequent colds, and body or muscle aches.

Behavioral symptoms of stress include increased or decreased appetite, sleep problems, isolation, neglect of responsibilities, drug or alcohol abuse, annoying behavior, and nervous habits like nail-biting and picking.

Emotional symptoms include moodiness, depression, agitation, being short-tempered, and feeling overwhelmed.

Some children experience cognitive symptoms of stress such as poor memory, concentration difficulties, excessive worrying, negativity, and inappropriate judgment. Kids going through divorce in their families often struggle with cognitive difficulties in their academic performance and focus.

The Three Kinds of Stress

Not all stress is bad. In fact, stress can be an important part of a child learning resilience or responding appropriately to a threat. Many experts believe there are three kinds of stress: positive stress, tolerable stress, and toxic stress. As clinicians, we tend to see the children in the second or third categories.

Positive stress usually comes from a short-lived adverse situation. This might include a spelling test or a first sleepover. This stress may cause minor hormonal fluctuations and physiological adjustment. With appropriate support from the adults in their lives, children with positive stress learn the skill of overcoming both it and adversity.

Tolerable stress results from more significant events, which might include losing a close relative, moving away from long-term friends, experiencing a house fire, or having a significant illness. Tolerable stress causes a more significant physiological response in stress hormone levels, but with time and appropriate adult support, the children eventually recover and return to their normal physiologic state.

Toxic stress is a different animal. It activates both arms of the body's stress response to very high levels and for long periods. Examples of toxic stress include chronic neglect, emotional or physical abuse, exposure to family violence, homelessness, and severe economic hardship, to name a few.

Without the support of positive adults who are not contributing to their stress, kids experiencing toxic stress grow up with stress-induced diseases such as depression, substance abuse, and heart disease. The more a child is exposed to toxic stress, the more likely he or she is to develop later problems. The good news is that the effects of toxic stress can be prevented and reversed in children with early adult intervention and changes in the child's environment and caretakers.

Helping Children through Stressful Situations

Some kids are unable to cope with life's challenges and stresses in preschool, elementary school, middle school, and beyond. Too many children are growing up on medication to help them stay calm, react less, pay attention, be more pleasant, be happy, and not self-destruct. Some children's thinking is truly distorted from reality. Most of these children have experienced events that have changed them but have never been guided through these events to an appropriate resolution, closure, or a healthy perspective.

How to Radically Reduce Stress

Think back to a major event in your childhood and consider how poorly or how effectively the adults in your life handled it. How would you have turned out if your parents, coaches, or other adults had handled major events in your childhood differently?

We see many good and bad examples of this with our patients. Thankfully, many divorces today are handled in ways that are respectful to kids and minimize the stress they experience. However, divorce is sometimes handled in ways that leave scars in the children and families involved. Parents who have separated or divorced are experiencing pain themselves and can unintentionally manipulate their children to fit their reality. They may blame the divorce on their former spouse with little consideration of how this may negatively affect their children.

The divorce event can take on a life of its own, including lies, defamation, revenge, hate, spite, and hostage taking. Adults may not help the children to understand the separation in age-appropriate ways. The resulting experience for the children is stressful, confusing, and negative. It is no wonder so many adults recall such negative and hurtful memories about their parents' messy divorce decades earlier. (When it's handled in a kind and thoughtful way, kids can recover nicely from a divorce.)

Another example of a stress dynamic is the preteen girl who's cute but average looking, doesn't fit into skinny jeans, isn't in the popular group at school, and has little athletic ability. These combined factors could be considered an "event." Janis Ian's song "At Seventeen" is poetry set to music describing this scenario. How should parents handle this situation so the daughter has a chance of growing, maturing, and thriving through this time in her life?

Many parents respond by giving their daughter the false message that she is just as pretty as the other girls. But the daughter's idea of pretty or beautiful is based on Photoshopped faces on the covers of teen magazines. Her feeling of unattractiveness at school is the reality she lives in every day. No matter what her parents say about her being beautiful or pretty, she won't be convinced.

Do You Respond or Overreact?

Some parents overreact to their child's stress, while others underreact. The goal is to figure out how to appropriately respond. Parents appropriately responding to events in their child's life use positive stress and provide healthy coping skills, learning, and cross-application.

Remember, the goal is not to have your child be stress free. This is not to say that the parents' way of handling stressful events in their child's life affects the outcome 100 percent, but it's one of the most important factors.

Let's start with an event that induces stress in a child's life. It doesn't matter what it is, just that it elicits a child's stress response. The child's stress hormones then kick in. Cortisol and adrenaline run through his or her bloodstream. The parents can choose how to respond: overreaction or guidance. Each parental response has its own implications for the child and the family.

Overreactive parents fuel the stress hormones in the child by elevating their and their child's arousal states. Their response creates an environment where it's difficult for anyone to think logically. Everything becomes emotional for the child *and* the parent. This stress cycle builds and builds into a vicious dynamic for everyone involved.

The guiding parent sees stress in his or her child and responds to it in a way that helps define how much or how little stress the event really deserves. The primary form of guidance should be guiding the child *about* the problem, not necessarily guiding him *through* the problem.

Helping Kids View the Problem

A girl who completely loses her temper upon finding a rip in her pants needs help adjusting her reaction. This stress might be ranked a two out of ten, but she is reacting as if it were an eight out of ten. Comments like "This is really not a big deal; I can fix them," or "We have time to go home and get a different pair of pants," should be utilized rather than helping her process the situation as if it were an eight in importance.

The parent's goal is to reassure the child that this event is a little speed bump in life, not a sinkhole. Just because your child sees an event as a disaster does not mean that it *is* a disaster, and it should not be responded to as such. Do not let your child define the seriousness or importance of a stressful event. Parents need to do the defining.

Stress is a potential learning opportunity for the child. Many things affect the parents' ability to teach and guide: exhaustion, impatience, marital discord, work, family illness, etc. Yet the parents' discipline of teaching and guiding their children is a critical way their children eventually learn about life. As they say in Africa, "All young male elephants need a bull elephant."

Most importantly, remember many of the behaviors we see in our children are simply a manifestation of stress. Kids are bombarded with triggers that elicit a stress response: family turmoil, news reports, peer pressure, temptations, excess responsibilities, and a lack of margin, to name a few.

Your response to stress is pivotal in helping your child learn to positively handle stress. Unfortunately, many parents react to a child's stress in ways that increase the stress. Parents need to be a calm and stable influence for their child, calling out his or her competence. If you don't do this, your child may never learn to put stressful events and dynamics into the proper perspective.

The GIST of It

- Stress causes predictable physiologic changes in children that can lead to complaints and behaviors mimicking various diseases and maladies. Stress should be considered when medical causes have been eliminated.

- Kids who live in states of chronic stress can have permanent changes that may be difficult to normalize.

- Not all stress is bad. It can be helpful in teaching kids resilience and how to deal with adversity in their lives.

- A parent's overreaction to his child's stress makes the experienced stress worse. This makes it less likely the child will learn how to deal with stress in positive ways.

Final Words

WE'VE PRESENTED OUR THOUGHTS on parenting and believe the principles described here offer a better way to parent than what is usually practiced.

Remember, for you to "grow up" your children, *you* need to make the most changes. Consider how your parenting behavior affects your child before concluding that a particular issue is solely your child's problem.

Parenting can be the most difficult and tasking endeavor of your life. There is nothing in this book or any other that can assure a parent of an easy road. In truth, some kids are really difficult. Some kids are easy, but some kids will require patience, focus, talent, and foresight—and this will still be a long, sometimes tiring journey. This is a book about efficiency and the likelihood of outcomes. We believe these principles are a parent's best chance at making parenting fun, exciting, and rewarding. That is all. Looking at parenting differently will determine the amount of change that happens. We think you will be happier for it and live more peacefully.

The biggest benefit will be kids who grow up much more ready for life. The greatest fear of many parents centers around watching their kids reach adult age unable to manage their lives, themselves, or their relationships. That can be very painful for parents—and for their young adults.

It doesn't matter what your child has been diagnosed with. What matters is that you start to understand what you need to do, or not do, to help him or her be ready for the adult world. Whether your child has been labeled difficult, high-spirited, stubborn, or feisty, you can adjust your parenting to fit the child.

Think about it this way: If your child presents a degree of difficulty of eighty-five on a scale of one hundred, and your parenting ability is average (a fifty), you are going to have difficulty unless you learn ways of parenting that child at an eighty-five. Likewise, if you have an easy child who presents with a degree of difficulty of ten, you could be a below-average parent and the child would turn out just fine.

Joy in the Journey

Simplifying life will be an integral part of your success as a parent. Simplifying will create positive memories and build relationships that are based on the desire to be together as a family unit. This does not necessarily mean family time with the entire family. Some kids respond much better to one-on-one time with a parent. Also, this doesn't mean your family can't have a hundred things going. It is possible to simplify without cutting back. Simplifying means less urgency, less intensity, less shame, and less anger. Whatever issue your family is facing, it will likely go better with a simple solution.

We also want all parents to have fun. When we look at things differently, creativity and spontaneity can become part of the norm again. Instead of experiencing each day frantic, discouraged, or disillusioned, we can enjoy the ride as we watch our kids grow up. Parenting was meant to be a wonderful adventure, not an exhausting plod. We've met too many parents who can't wait for their kids to leave the house. We say, take back the joy of the journey!

We strongly encourage you to develop and grow in your other relationships too. This is such an important thing for your children to see. In the end, what parents pass on to their children will affect their children's generation as well as the generations beyond. Family dysfunction breeds more dysfunction.

But all of us have the ability to learn to see things differently. Whether you are a single parent or part of a couple, and whether your children are biological or adopted, challenged or gifted in any way, there is good news in the pages of this book. Parents who were not parented very well have the ability to change their family's trajectory now and in the future—and to do this with more peace and less effort.

If you would like to work through the ideas in this book with other parents, you can download a free study guide with additional Christian content at Tyndale.es/GIST.

Acknowledgments

This project started out in dialogue form ten years ago as an idea spawned from meetings with a dozen other couples struggling with the parenting endeavor. The manuscript got its beginnings on an island in Canada and became a reality in a cottage on the Northern Ireland coast, overlooking the Irish Sea.

This endeavor has taken us from our respective practices to places of intense reflection, and from the comfort and confidence of our own experiences as dads to humbling places of personal realization. It's the closest thing we can imagine to childbirth, knowing full well most women who have birthed a child would laugh at that claim.

With that said, we need to give some thanks and offer our deep gratitude to several very important people in our lives who have put up with us individually and as a writing team. Our wives, Carolyn Anderson (Mike) and Susan Johanson (Tim), have been a constant support over many years. They believe in what we do in our professional lives and what we have attempted to do with them for our own children and foster children. Both of our wives are extremely wise women, phenomenal moms, and wonderful companions with whom to travel the parenting journey. Our children—Kellan, Reid, and Brieg Anderson and Annika, Emily, and Luke Johanson—have been the greatest source of joy for us, as well as challenge. What part we have played in their amazing journeys we will never know.

Thousands of our clients, patients, and their parents have made our lives meaningful. It has been a privilege and honor to come alongside them to help them in some small way. Our respective staffs, coworkers, partners, nurses, and lab personnel all have made that process easier for us, and we are thankful for them all.

Although not a complete list by any means, the following individuals and entities deserve special mention: Tim Proue, Doug Berg, Bob Dykstra, Michele Tennesen, University of Arizona Pediatric Residency Program, and Metropolitan Pediatric Specialists.

Michael W. Anderson, LP
Timothy D. Johanson, MD

Notes

CHAPTER 3: THE NATURE OF LIFE

1. M. Scott Peck, *The Road Less Traveled* (New York: Touchstone, 1978), 15.
2. Wikipedia, s.v. "Grit (personality trait)," last modified April 14, 2019, https://en.wikipedia.org/wiki/Grit_(personality_trait).

CHAPTER 8: JUST SHUT UP!

1. Garrison Keillor, *Lake Wobegon Days* (New York: Viking Penguin, 1985), 274.

CHAPTER 15: THE ORIGINS OF SELF-ESTEEM

1. Merriam-Webster Online, 2019, s.v. "esteem," accessed May 28, 2019, https://www.merriam-webster.com/dictionary/esteem.

CHAPTER 19: THE BLACK HOLE OF TECHNOLOGY

1. Adam Alter, *Irresistible* (New York: Penguin Press, 2017), 2.
2. Alter, *Irresistible*, 2–3.
3. Henry J. Kaiser Family Foundation, *Generation M²: Media in the Lives of 8- to 18-Year-Olds*, January 20, 2010, 11, https://www.kff.org/wp-content/uploads/2013/04/8010.pdf.
4. Angie S. Page et al., "Children's Screen Viewing Is Related to Psychological Difficulties Irrespective of Physical Activity," *Pediatrics* 126, no. 5 (November 2010), http://pediatrics.aappublications.org/content/pediatrics/early/2010/10/11/peds.2010-1154.full.pdf.
5. Jean M. Twenge, Gabrielle N. Martin, and W. Keith Campbell, "Decreases in Psychological Well-Being among American Adolescents after 2012 and Links to Screen Time during the Rise of Smartphone Technology," *Emotion* 18, no. 6 (September 2018): 765–780, http://dx.doi.org/10.1037/emo0000403.
6. Stefanie Braig et al., "Screen Time, Physical Activity and Self-Esteem in Children: The Ulm Birth Cohort Study," *International Journal of Environmental Research and Public Health* 15, no. 6 (June 2018): 1275, https://doi.org/10.3390/ijerph15061275; Sandra L. Calvert et al., "The American Psychological Association Task Force Assessment of Violent Video Games: Science in the Service of Public Interest," *American Psychologist* 72, no. 2 (February–March 2017): 126–143, http://dx.doi.org/10.1037/a0040413.
7. Yalda T. Uhls et al., "Five Days at Outdoor Education Camp without Screens Improves Preteen Skills with Nonverbal Emotion Cues," *Computers in Human Behavior* 39 (October 2014): 387–392, https://www.sciencedirect.com/science/article/pii/S0747563214003227.
8. "Industry Facts," Entertainment Software Association website, accessed May 28, 2019, www.theesa.com/about-esa/industry-facts/.
9. Kate Cox, "Nearly 6 Million Years of *World of Warcraft* Healthy for Players'

Brains," March 7, 2012, Kotaku.com, https://kotaku.com/nearly-6-million
-years-of-world-of-warcraft-healthy-for-5891421.

10. Adam Levy, "People Spend As Much Time on Instagram As Snapchat," August
5, 2017, The Motley Fool, https://www.fool.com/investing/2017/08/05/people
-spend-as-much-time-on-instagram-as-snapchat.aspx.

11. "Twenty-Five Amazing Candy Crush Stats (2019)," updated May 3, 2019,
https://videogamesstats.com/candy-crush-facts-statistics/.

12. Larry Alton, "Phone Calls, Texts or Email? Here's How Millennials Prefer to
Communicate," *Forbes*, May 11, 2017, https://www.forbes.com/sites/larryalton
/2017/05/11/how-do-millennials-prefer-to-communicate/#4f6eb896d6fd.

13. Larry Alton, "Phone Calls, Texts or Email?"

14. Elizabeth Hoge, David Bickman, and Joanne Cantor, "Digital Media, Anxiety,
and Depression in Children," *Pediatrics* 140, suppl. 2 (November 2017):
S76–S80, https://www.ncbi.nlm.nih.gov/pubmed/29093037.

15. Cited in Helen Riess, "The Power of Empthy," TEDx Middlebury, December
12, 2013, https://www.youtube.com/watch?v=baHrcC8B4WM.

16. "What Is Cyberbullying?" Stopbullying.gov, accessed March 7, 2019, https://
www.stopbullying.gov/cyberbullying/what-is-it/index.html.

17. Jamiel Lynch, "Police Accuse Two Students, Age 12, of Cyberbullying in
Suicide," CNN, January 24, 2018, https://www.cnn.com/2018/01/23/us
/florida-cyberstalking-charges-girl-suicide/index.html.

18. Frederick J. Zimmerman, Dimitri A. Christakis, and Andrew N. Meltzoff,
"Associations between Media Viewing and Language Development in Children
under Age 2 Years," *The Journal of Pediatrics* 151, no. 4 (October 2007):
364–368, https://doi.org/10.1016/j.jpeds.2007.04.071; Mila Vulchanova et
al., "Editorial: Language Development in the Digital Age," *Frontiers in Human
Neuroscience* 11 (September 5, 2017), https://doi.org/10.3389/fnhum.2017.00447.

19. Frederick J. Zimmerman and Dimitri A. Christakis, "Children's Television
Viewing and Cognitive Outcomes: A Longitudinal Analysis of National Data,"
Archives of Pediatrics and Adolescent Medicine 159, no. 7 (July 2005): 619–625,
https://doi.org/10.1001/archpedi.159.7.619.

20. Margaret D. Weiss et al., "The Screens Culture: Impact on ADHD," *ADHD:
Attention Deficit and Hyperactivity Disorders* 3, no. 4 (December 2011):
327–334, https://link.springer.com/article/10.1007%2Fs12402-011-0065-z.

21. Hanyi Yan et al., "Associations among Screen Time and Unhealthy Behaviors,
Academic Performance, and Well-Being in Chinese Adolescents," *International
Journal of Environmental Research and Public Health* 14, no. 6 (2017):
596, https://doi.org/10.3390/ijerph14060596; Kate Kelland, "Extra Screen
Time Drags Down Teenagers' Exam Grades, Study Finds," Reuters, September
3, 2015, https://www.reuters.com/article/us-health-screens/extra-screen-time
-drags-down-teenagers-exam-grades-study-finds-idUSKCN0R32KC20150903.

22. Monique K. LeBourgeois et al., "Digital Media and Sleep in Childhood and
Adolescence," *Pediatrics* 140, supp. 2 (November 2017): S92–S96, https://doi
.org/10.1542/peds.2016-1758J.

23. Lisa Marshall, "Kids Uniquely Vulnerable to Sleep Disruption from Electronics," *CU Boulder Today*, November 1, 2017, https://www.colorado .edu/today/2017/11/01/kids-uniquely-vulnerable-sleep-disruption-electronics.

24. Gloria Mark, Daniela Gudith, and Ulrich Klocke, "The Cost of Interrupted Work: More Speed and Stress," in *CHI '08 Proceedings of the SIGCHI Conference on Human Factors in Computing Systems* (Florence, Italy, April 5-10, 2008): 107–110, https://doi.org/10.1145/1357054.1357072.

25. Martha C. White, "Your Cell Phone Is Killing Your Productivity, but Not for the Reason You Think," *Money*, July 20, 2015, http://money.com/money /3956968/cell-phone-alert-productivity.

26. Clifford Nass, as interviewed on "The Myth of Multitasking," *Talk of the Nation*, National Public Radio, May 10, 2013.

27. David J. Linden, "Video Games Can Activate the Brain's Pleasure Circuits," *Psychology Today*, October 25, 2011, https://www.psychologytoday.com/us/blog /the-compass-pleasure/201110/video-games-can-activate-the-brains-pleasure -circuits-0.

28. Doug Hyun Han et al., "Brain Activity and Desire for Internet Video Game Play," *Comprehensive Psychiatry* 52, no. 1 (January/February 2011): 88–95, https://doi.org/10.1016/j.comppsych.2010.04.004.

29. Daria J. Kuss and Mark D. Griffiths, "Internet and Gaming Addiction: A Systematic Literature Review of Neuroimaging Studies," *Brain Sciences* 2, no. 3 (September 2012): 347–374, https://doi.org/10.3390/brainsci2030347.

30. Thomas N. Robinson et al., "Screen Media Exposure and Obesity in Children and Adolescents," *Pediatrics* 140, suppl. 2 (November 2017): S97–S101, https://doi.org/10.1542/peds.2016-1758K.

31. Gadi Lissak, "Adverse Physiological and Psychological Effects of Screen Time on Children and Adolescents: Literature Review and Case Study," *Environmental Research* 164 (July 2018): 149–157, https://doi.org/10.1016/j.envres.2018 .01.015.

32. Janice Neumann, "Screen Time Linked to Weaker Bones in Teen Boys," *Scientific American*, accessed April 1, 2019, https://www.scientificamerican .com/article/screen-time-linked-to-weaker-bones-in-teen-boys/; Eugenia Hoi Chi Woo, Peter White, and Christopher Wai Keung, "Effects of Electronic Device Overuse by University Students in Relation to Clinical Status and Anatomical Variations of the Median Nerve and Transverse Carpal Ligament," *Muscle & Nerve* 56, no. 5 (November 2017): 873–880, https://doi.org/10.1002 /mus.25697.

33. "Data and Statistics about ADHD," ADHD Home, Centers for Disease Control and Prevention, accessed March 8, 2019, https://www.cdc.gov/ncbddd /adhd/data.html.

34. "Trends in the Parent-Report of Health Care Provider—Diagnosis and Medication Treatment for ADHD: United States, 2003–2011," ADHD Home, Centers for Disease Control and Prevention, accessed May 20, 2019, https:// www.cdc.gov/ncbddd/adhd/features/key-findings-adhd72013.html.

35. Carl Erik Landhuis et al., "Does Childhood Television Viewing Lead to Attention Problems in Adolescence? Results from a Prospective Longitudinal Study," *Pediatrics* 120, no. 3 (September 2007): 532–537, https://doi.org /10.1542/peds.2007-0978.

36. Angeline S. Lillard and Jennifer Peterson, "The Immediate Impact of Different Types of Television on Young Children's Executive Function," *Pediatrics* 128, no. 4 (October 2011): 644–650, https://pediatrics.aappublications.org/content /128/4/644.

37. "People Who Play Video Games Are Less Able to Control Impulsive Aggressive Behaviour, Reveals a New Study," *The Telegraph*, August 4, 2013, https://www .telegraph.co.uk/technology/video-games/10221432/People-who-play-video -games-are-less-able-to-control-impulsive-aggressive-behaviour-reveals-a-new -study.html.

38. Greg West et al., "Impact of Video Games on Plasticity of the Hippocampus," *Molecular Psychiatry* 23, no. 7 (August 8, 2017): 1566–1574, https://doi.org /10.1038/mp.2017.155.

39. Chuan-Bo Weng et al., "Gray Matter and White Matter Abnormalities in Online Game Addiction," *European Journal of Radiology* 82, no. 8 (August 2013): 1308–1312, https://doi.org/10.1016/j.ejrad.2013.01.031.

40. Linden, "Video Games."

41. D. K. Braun-Corville and M. Rojas, "Exposure to Sexually Explicit Web Sites and Adolescent Sexual Attitudes and Behaviors," *Journal of Adolescent Health* 45, no. 2 (August 2009): 156–162, https://www.ncbi.nlm.nih.gov/pubmed /19628142.

42. Jason S. Carroll et al., "Generation XXX: Pornography Acceptance and Use among Emerging Adults," *Journal of Adolescent Research* 23, no. 1 (2008): 6–30, https://doi.org/10.1177/0743558407306348.

43. Jill Manning, "Pornography's Impact on the Family," testimony before the Subcommittee on the Constitution, Civil Rights and Property Rights in the Committee on Judiciary, US Senate, November 9, 2005, https://www.heritage .org/testimony/pornographys-impact-marriage-and-the-family.

CHAPTER 20: OVERLOADED

1. Eric Hoffer, *The Passionate State of Mind* (New York: HarperCollins, 1954), 105.

2. David Elkind, *The Hurried Child: Growing Up Too Fast Too Soon* (Cambridge, MA: Da Capo Press, 2001), 31.

CHAPTER 21: LEARNED HELPLESSNESS

1. For more information about Seligman's work on this topic, see his book *Helplessness* (New York: W. H. Freeman, 1992).

2. Bethanne Stafford (contributor), *Words through Life* (Marana, AZ, GISTWorks, 2014).

3. Merriam-Webster Online, 2019, s.v. "nagging," accessed May 28, 2019, https:// www.merriam-webster.com/dictionary/nagging.

About the Authors

Michael Anderson is a licensed psychologist with a private counseling practice in Minneapolis, specializing in adolescents and their families. In addition to parenting his own three children, Michael and his wife have been short-term foster parents for thirteen adolescents. Michael is a frequent speaker on the topics of mental health, parenting, and raising life-ready kids and has consulted with school boards, teachers, coaching staffs, and youth leaders in implementing many of the principles in this book. He has also been a supervisor of foster homes.

    Dr. Tim Johanson is an associate professor of pediatrics at the University of Arizona, where he is privileged to teach the next generation of pediatricians. He enjoys training his pediatric residents in the art of coaching parents about behavior problems in their children. His clinical research involves the impact of adverse childhood experiences on parenting. He and his wife have three grown children. He enjoys cooking, golfing, and spending time with his wife, as well as speaking around the country on the principles of GIST parenting.